Word Play Place

Essays on the Poetry of John Matthias

WORD ~ PLAY PLACE

ESSAYS ON THE POETRY of JOHN MATTHIAS

EDITED BY

Robert Archambeau

Swallow Press • OHIO UNIVERSITY PRESS • Athens

Swallow Press/Ohio University Press, Athens, Ohio 45701

© 1998 by Robert Archambeau

Printed in the United States of America

All rights reserved. Published 1998

Swallow Press/Ohio University Press books are printed on acid-free paper
♾™

05 04 03 02 01 00 99 98   5 4 3 2 1

Library of Congress Cataloging-in-Publication Data

Word play place : essays on the poetry of John Matthias / edited by
    Robert Archambeau.
            p.   cm.
        Includes bibliographical references (p.   ).
        ISBN 0-8040-1008-0 (cloth : acid-free paper)
        I. Matthias, John, 1941–   —Criticism and interpretation.
    I. Archambeau, Robert Thomas, 1968–
    811 '.54—dc21   98-19478
                                                            CIP

a book about a poet
for a teacher and a friend

Contents

Preface   ix

Acknowledgments   xi

Abbreviations   xiii

Introducing John Matthias   1
ROBERT ARCHAMBEAU

John Matthias's *Bucyrus*   20
MICHAEL ANANIA

The Poetry of John Matthias: "My Treason and My Tongue"   26
VINCENT SHERRY

Two Poems and the Aesthetics of Play   35
JERE ODELL

The Herald and the Void: A Tribute to John Matthias   50
IGOR WEBB

The Shorter Poems of John Matthias   61
MICHAEL BARRETT

You Keep the Cart before the Horse, See,
So They See It Moving but They Don't Know How   84
PETER MICHELSON

John Matthias's England   104
JEREMY HOOKER

Between Revolutions,
or Turns: John Matthias and $\dfrac{\text{the American Avant-Garde}}{\text{British Experimentalism}}$ 115
ROMANA HUK

viii   A Gathering of Proper Names: The Onomastic Poetics
of John Matthias   133
BROOKE BERGAN

"To Find the Song"—John Matthias and the Legacy of David Jones   154
KATHLEEN HENDERSON STAUDT

A Poem Is a Place Is a Walk: A Reading of Two of
John Matthias's Sequences   168
LARS-HÅKAN SVENSSON

Petitio, Repetitio, Agensay, Agengrownde, Matthias   201
JOHN PECK

Bibliography 1971–1997   237

Notes on Contributors   247

Preface

In the diversity of the American poetry scene there are poets and there are poet's poets, and there are even poet's poet's poets. John Matthias, whose always-polished work can be both refreshingly lucid and fascinatingly arcane, falls into all three categories. It is, I hope, excusable that Matthias's more arcane poems—the longer works that draw their energy from a poetics of place—receive more attention here than his more accessible poems: it was, and remains, my conviction that they simply require more extensive exegesis and commentary. Nevertheless, it should be noted that the Matthias we see in these pages looks a bit more like a poet's poet's poet than the Matthias we come to know from reading his work as a whole.

The essays in this book do, collectively, cover the major works and themes of John Matthias's career, but the volume should by no means be considered exhaustive. The influence of Ezra Pound, the epistolary poems, the place of Matthias among his contemporaries, and the poetics of Matthias's lyrical poems are all important topics for future critics and merit serious consideration. Let this book be not the final word on Matthias's poetry, then, but the beginning of a long and rich conversation.

Acknowledgments

The seeds of this book were sown in April of 1996, during informal discussions following an American Comparative Literature Association panel on John Matthias's poetry, and thanks are due to Jere Odell for organizing that seminal panel. Thanks are also due to the many people who supported this project along the way: John and Diana Matthias, Marjorie Perloff, Stephen Fredman, Chris Fox, Jennifer L. Warlick of the Institute for Scholarship in the Liberal Arts, College of Arts and Letters, at the University of Notre Dame (which helped make this book possible), David Sanders of Ohio University Press, and Scott Richardson, for valuable assistance with the manuscript. I would also like to thank Lake Forest College for generously supporting my research, and my colleagues in the English department for making a new colleague welcome. Among this last group let me single out Benjamin Goluboff, a fellow nocturnal haunter of Carnegie Hall, and thank him for wise counsel and compassion. Above all, let me thank my wife Valerie, now and always.

Abbreviations

The following abbreviations are used for books by John Matthias:

B	*Bucyrus*
BA	*Beltane at Aphelion*
C	*Crossing*
GW	*A Gathering of Ways*
SM	*Swimming at Midnight*
T	*Turns*

Word Play Place

Essays on the Poetry of John Matthias

❧ Introducing John Matthias

ROBERT ARCHAMBEAU

John Matthias is a difficult poet to place on any of the conventional maps of the literary terrain. Not only does his career seem nearly as deeply grounded in British institutions and frames of reference as it is in American ones—the Dutch poet and critic Peter Nijmeijer has called Matthias a "mid-Atlantic" poet—but his poetry embodies extremes of form and concern rarely united in a single body of work. His is a poetry both cosmopolitan and rooted in the particulars of known places; it is both intimate and arcanely historical; it is capable of both lucid lyricism and of pushing to the farthest boundaries of linguistic innovation. In fact, one of the best ways to characterize Matthias's work is to quote the words of Alan Shapiro, who, in introducing the poetry of James McMichael, Matthias's contemporary and Stanford classmate, praises McMichael for creating a poetry that is likewise difficult to locate in our usual taxonomies of poetry:

> the recent debate if not the recent practice of American poetry does seem to divide itself roughly into two opposing aesthetic camps: one based in the lyric of subjective life, the other in the skepticism of the intellect . . . if this dichotomy simplifies too much, it's useful nonetheless in helping us distinguish those poets, who do in fact conform too neatly to one camp or another, from those who resist identification with either extreme, whose ambition and achievement are precisely to bring together and integrate what in the work of their contemporaries is found mostly in isolation. (vii)

Matthias is just such an integrative poet, and if the lyric and epistolary side of his work receives less treatment in the present volume than the arcane and experimental side, it is not because the more intimate and accessible poems are less important to Matthias's achievement—"Poem for Cynouai" and

1

2   "Clarifications for Robert Jacoby" are among the most lucid and also the most profound examples of Matthias's work—it is simply that the more abstruse poems require (and reward) a more extensive critical scrutiny.

Another way to characterize Matthias's achievement is to note that, for all the dense intellectualism of the poetry, it is never abstract or unrooted—Matthias's poetry is never that of Wallace Stevens's "palm at the end of the mind." The poetry is always deeply immersed in the world of political and historical processes, and Matthias's imagination has from the first been drawn to the radiance of "precise historical dates, / not to mention exact geographical places" (*SM* 79). Even a cursory glance at the contents of a volume of Matthias's poems reveals a concern with the embeddedness of thought, action, and speech in particular historical and geographic contexts: titles like "Bakunin in Italy," "Alexander Kerensky at Stanford," "Spokesman to Bailiff, 1349: Plague" reveal a temperament and a poetic far from that of the poet who could write "Of Mere Being."

That the titles I've just listed, even when invoking so American a place as Stanford University, all refer to European places, events, or historical figures, hints at a third way in which to characterize the poetry of John Matthias. Like his early model Ezra Pound (and like the model of his juvenile prose, Henry James) Matthias belongs squarely in the Europhile wing of American letters. While England is the only country other than the United States where Matthias has made his home, the nature of his residence there is, in one respect, like that of Pound, of whom Donald Davie has written: "an American like Pound came to *Europe;* and if he came to England, it was to one of the provinces of that larger cultural entity" (17). There is a profound sense of the continuity of Europe, particularly of Catholic Europe, in Matthias's poetry, a sense perhaps more readily available to an American than to an Englishman or a Spaniard or a Swede, who will be inclined to approach Europe in terms of its parts, its differences and contrasts, rather than as a whole. And, while Matthias takes history from the earliest times to the present day as his frame of reference, his storehouse of images draws disproportionately from the European middle ages—it is no accident that "The Fair Maid of Ribblesdale," the only poem in the whole of Michael Anania's work to draw its energies from medieval imagery, is dedicated to John Matthias.

To understand the genesis of these three characteristic qualities of Matthias's work—its historical and political concerns, its Europhilia, and its drawing upon diverse stylistic schools—one needs to begin at the beginning, and in as unlikely a place as Columbus, Ohio, where, in 1941, John Matthias was born. Matthias was born into a politically connected family of Ohio

Republicans, and his father served for many years on the Ohio Supreme Court; so in one sense political concerns came to Matthias as naturally as they had come to Robert Lowell: politics was simply the family business, and the value of things, in the Matthias household, had everything to do with their relation to political influence. Although Matthias was to rebel against the particular brand of politics represented by his family, his sense of thought, art, and action being deeply rooted in the world of power, politics, and historical processes is very much the legacy of his family background, a permanent part of his character despite the occasional attempt to cast aside his paternal inheritance, "this heavy and judicial German / in me called Matthias" (*BA* 66).

When, in "Clarifications for Robert Jacoby," Matthias records his childhood play with Jacoby, his cousin, he gives a picture of the family environment and its very pragmatic concerns:

> You wanted then, you said,
> To be an actor, and your father—a very practical
>   lawyer—said he found that funny, though
> I think we both intuited
>   that he was secretly alarmed.
>
> With little cause. You were destined—how obvious
>   it should have been!—to be professional,
> Respectable, and eminent. Still, you put in time
>   and played your child's part
> With skill and grace.
>
> There is a photograph of us taken, I believe,
>   in 1950. Your plumed hat (a little
> Tight) sits sprightly on your head, your cape
>   (cut from someone's bathrobe) hangs
> Absurdly down your back, and in your hand you
>   brandish the sword of the patriarch
> Himself, grandfather M., Commander in Chief
>   Of the United Spanish War Vets.
>   *My*
> Plumed hat is slightly better fitting, if less
>   elegant, my sword a fencing foil with
> A rubber tip, my cape the prize: something from
>   the almost legitimate theatre, from

My father's role in a Masonic play where he spoke,
  once each year before initiations
On some secret, adult stage, lines he practiced
  in the kitchen all the week before:
Let the jewelled box of records be opened
  and the plans for the wall by the
South west gate be examined! (*SM* 79)

But the poem shows us more than just the Republican Ohio of the 1950s: it takes us into the imaginative life of Matthias's childhood, and in that imaginative life, in which the accouterments of the Free Masons and the United Spanish War Veterans become emblems of a courtly world, we see the seeds of Matthias's Europhilia. The luminous world of play into which the mundane is transmuted here is, whatever else it may be, profoundly European rather than American in its imagery. This is not to say that, had Matthias played at cowboys and Indians rather than at knights in armor, he would have written a poem like Dorn's *Gunslinger* rather than "East Anglian Poem" or "A Compostela Diptych," but the spontaneous enthusiasm with which Matthias was to react to the visible presence of the past in the English countryside later in life had a great deal to do with its resonance with the imaginative world of his childhood.

It is tempting, too, to find in Matthias's early life the source of his stylistic eclecticism, the sense of the breadth of poetry's possibilities that has underwritten the range of his achievement. While a student at the progressive Deweyeite University School in his late teens Matthias came to study under Donald Bateman, an enthusiastic young teacher who had recently arrived from Kenyon College, then a hotbed of the New Criticism being practiced by John Crowe Ransom and Allen Tate. During the school day Bateman versed Matthias in the rigors of close reading and the poetry of T. S. Eliot, but on weekends Matthias and his friend Joel Barkan were avid followers of the San Francisco Renaissance, as interpreted for the rest of the country by Time-Life. While Bateman introduced Matthias to the academic tradition, Matthias introduced himself to the alternative tradition, reading his early Beat-influenced poetry over jazz in the local coffeehouses.

It was with a mixed portfolio of prose and of poetry juvenilia based on both Beat and Eliotic models that Matthias was precociously admitted to the University of Utah Summer Writer's Workshop. It was 1959, Matthias had just graduated from high school, and the workshop teachers he was about to meet were two poets who were to have enormous influence on his later life:

Stephen Spender and John Berryman. The workshop, as Matthias records in "An Afterword for Paul Mariani," did not begin auspiciously:

> I arrived at the University of Utah straight from my high school graduation ceremony in June of 1959. I was seventeen years old and utterly unprepared to meet a man like Berryman. On the first day of the fiction workshop—the course he taught during the first week of the conference, taking over poetry from Stephen Spender in the second week—he passed out copies of three brief stories which I had submitted a few weeks before arriving. Having always been praised by my indulgent high school teachers for whatever writing I produced, I of course assumed that my genius was about to be proclaimed by this strange, intense man who placed the accents of words on unusual syllables. . . . I can remember my folly of leaning over to my right and proudly identifying myself to a fellow member as the author of the pages that were, alas, about to be annihilated. The job done on the stories was as unremitting and detailed as it was devastating. I don't think a single sentence escaped censure or ridicule. . . . In spite of the shock of the opening day's workshop, I found myself warming to the man tremendously. On the whole, he let me off the hook after that first blast, although, from time to time, he would remark that the only person who had learned anything from him so far was "young Mr. Matt-i-as" (as he insisted on pronouncing my name then and when we met again later on). (*Reading Old Friends* 175–76)

Despite this unpromising initial meeting, Matthias and Berryman were to become closer over the next decade, as Matthias progressed from student to graduate student to professor and from neophyte to promising young poet, and as Berryman's fame grew and grew. *Herman's Poems,* a series of lyrics published as a chapbook by Sceptre Press in the United Kingdom in 1973, are perhaps the most Berrymanesque of Matthias's poems, and the fact that they were never collected into any of his subsequent volumes shows the relatively peripheral influence of Berryman's poetics in Matthias's career. It was in other, subtler ways that Berryman was to influence Matthias: it was Berryman's reading of *Homage to Mistress Bradstreet* at the Utah workshop that convinced Matthias of the painstaking labor and craftsmanship necessary for great poetry, and Berryman became an early model of what a poet's work could be.

6   Spender, "tall and enormously ungainly" (177), was more aloof, not really believing in the idea of a writer's workshop and not taking the proceedings as seriously as Berryman, and he seemed, even at the age of fifty, less a practicing poet who might be emulated than the relic of another era. What Spender did provide, though, was the idea of a poet intimately involved with the political, with concerns beyond the individual psyche, and it was the poetry of Spender and his generation of English poets that Matthias was to pursue with the most concentration during his student years, first at Ohio State, where he studied from 1959 to 1963, and later at Stanford.

At Ohio State Matthias studied English and continued to write poems, including "After a Lecture on John Donne," which appeared as his first published poem in the magazine *American Weave*. He remained in contact with Spender, who came to campus on a lecture tour, and met the writer Peter Taylor, a friend of Robert Lowell's then teaching at OSU, who introduced Lowell's work to Matthias, but by and large Matthias kept his writing to himself and did not seek the company of other students writing poetry. His pursuit of the poetry of the Auden-Spender generation took the form of a senior thesis on the political poetry of the 1930s, in which agitprop appears as a disease that destroys all but the strongest poetic talents. This study (and the encounter with Spender that inspired it) may well have saved Matthias's own talent, serving as a kind of inoculation against the agitprop impulse in the protest poetry of the 1960s. When, years later, Michael Anania, then a young editor with Swallow Press in Chicago, was to read the poems that went into *Bucyrus,* his first impulse was to react to their craft, to "precisions [which] seemed to me at the time to offer a forceful alternative to the dominant poetics of the moment" (see "John Matthias's *Bucyrus,*" included in this volume), precisions particularly rare in a poetry as politically aware as that of Matthias.

Two other events from the Ohio State years take on special significance in light of the shape of Matthias's later career. His 1963 attempt to write a novel based on his voyage to Turkey in pursuit of his first serious girlfriend two years earlier is the first. The novel, or novella, *By Way of the Ruins,* never appeared as a book, and the author himself dismisses it as being of little importance, a neo-Jamesian effusion about Americans abroad—although Christopher Isherwood, to whom Matthias sent the manuscript, didn't share this judgment. Isherwood saw not just promise but the fulfillment of promise in the work, and sent it to an equally enthusiastic Spender, who was then editing *Encounter.* Had the piece been shorter, it would have appeared in that magazine, but despite his desire to print it Spender found it impossible to include due to length, and, except for an excerpt entitled "Alto Luogo Ayasuluk" in *TriQuarterly* in 1976, it has never appeared in a national publication. That excerpt is significant, though, in that it shows one of Matthias's characteristic structures—the opposition of the player and the man of responsibility—already fully developed. Such later pairings as Prospero/Lenin and the child-as-player/the-child-as-worker come directly out of this early opposition of the acrobat and the officer:

> The Turk goes through his routine of stands, balances, twists. He's a very good acrobat. A talented acrobat, and he stares. He can juggle peaches, bananas, and apples. He can do it both with his hands and his feet, and an assistant can perch on his head while he does it. Champagne glasses are nothing, by dozens, balanced on elbows, and after a somersault, none of them breaks. A chair on each shoulder is stable, standing on only one leg, and at the same time, on one leg, a table rests on each knee. And after all this, with tables and chairs firm and secure, he bounces beach balls with his feet and juggles six grapefruit. Through all of the acts, he keeps staring, and the Major wants me to talk. Major wants me to talk about Turkey. I should tell him about the things that he'll see, things that he'll like and won't like. I should talk to my major and not stare at the acrobat. But have you ever seen such an acrobat, Major? He could spin you by the toe on his nose and you would still want to talk to me about Turkey. It's going to be law and a family, you said. How fine it must be to enjoy your work. Honest to God, you're such a good major, a marvelous major, an American major. But look at the Turk, how he stares. (91)

The acrobat who distracts us from what we should be doing and the conversations we should be having; the major, enjoying his work, oblivious to the strangest and most magnificent spectacles: these characters, and the impulses they represent, appear again and again in Matthias's poetry. The tension is never entirely dispelled, but like his narrator, Matthias cannot get over the Turk's stare, cannot speak in the way the world of responsibilities requires.

The second event of significance from this period even more graphically foreshadows later concerns. In the summer of his senior year Matthias found himself mired in the tedium of the Ohio State Auditor's Office, typing up audit report after audit report in painstakingly precise format, until one day he decided to insert a line of Wallace Stevens into one of the reports. No one

8 noticed, and he began to insert larger and larger passages of Stevens, eventually whole poems, wedged into the precisely delineated tabs and margins of a State of Ohio auditor's report. None of this was uncovered until his reports had consisted of nothing but Stevens for some time. (Incidentally, it is a testament either to the tolerance of the Ohio auditor's office or to the political influence of Matthias's family that he wasn't fired for this—he was fired for wearing a "Congress on Racial Equality" button at an official public function, such being the wisdom of the Ohio State Auditor's Office). Read such early important poems as "Bucyrus" or "Statement" with the Ohio State Auditor's Office in mind, and the manipulation and modification of discourses of power by those subjected to them takes on a new frame of reference—in some sense the more Kafkaesque elements of those poems are the products of an experience lived out in a hot, stuffy office in Columbus, by a young man waiting to leave for another city and another life. The other city was Palo Alto, seat of Stanford University, and the other life was to be an adult's life, of marriage, divorce, and both new responsibilities and new freedoms.

Nineteen sixty-three was a good year for poets at Stanford University. James McMichael and Kenneth Fields, both graduate students there at the time, were about to be joined not only by Matthias but by John Peck and two future poets laureate, Robert Hass and Robert Pinsky. The story of this remarkable gathering of poets, and of their varied reactions to what Matthias has called the "stern eye" (*Reading Old Friends* 39) of Stanford's resident poet Yvor Winters has yet to be told, though their varied responses to the ambivalence toward modernism held first by Winters and then by his replacement Donald Davie is central not only to an understanding of the stylistic eclecticism of poets like Matthias and McMichael, but to the history of modernism and postmodernism in American poetry in the late twentieth century. Matthias, like Hass but unlike most aspiring poets at Stanford, never attended Winters's writing classes, but he did attend Winters's literature classes of the mid-sixties, the atmosphere of which is best captured by Robert Pinsky's account in "Essay on Psychiatrists" in a passage anthologized by Matthias in the 1979 *Five American Poets*. Here Winters appears simply as "the Old Man":

> it is all bosh, the false
> Link between genius and sickness,
>
> Except perhaps as they were linked
> By the Old Man, addressing his class
> On the first day: '*I know why you are here.*

You are here to laugh. You have heard of a crazy
Old man who believes that Robert Bridges
Was a good poet; who believes that Fulke

Greville was a great poet, greater than Philip
Sidney; who believes that Shakespeare's Sonnets
Are not all they are cracked up to be . . . . Well,

I will tell you something: I will tell you
What this course is about. Sometime in the middle
Of the Eighteenth Century, along with the rise

Of capitalism and scientific method, the logical
Foundations of Western thought decayed and fell apart.
When they fell apart, poets were left

With emotions and experiences, and with no way
To examine them. At this time, poets and men
Of genius began to go mad. Gray went mad. Collins

Went mad. Kit Smart was mad. William Blake surely
Was a madman. Coleridge was a drug addict, with severe
Depression. My friend Hart Crane died mad. My friend

Ezra Pound is mad. But you will not go mad; you will grow up
To become happy, sentimental old college professors,
Because they were men of genius, and you

Are not; and the ideas that were vital
To them are mere amusements to you. I will not
Go mad, because I have understood those ideas . . . .' (147)

This stern and cautious way of Yvor Winters, this world of definite moral values, close critical scrutiny, and an almost puritan watchfulness against the possibility of error and madness was only half of the world of his students in the mid-sixties, though, and another way of experiencing life and art that was coming to life in the hills around Palo Alto and in San Francisco was equally real. This was the world of Ken Kesey and Allen Ginsberg, of the Hell's Angels, of acid-taking and protest, and in the opposition of the Wintersian world to the nascent counterculture we see the old opposition in Matthias's life—between Donald Bateman of Kenyon College and the Beat-influenced jazz-and-poetry scene—writ large and purged of innocence. A number of the poems from *Bucyrus* were written in the interstices between the world of Kesey and the world of Winters, and even when the subject is an Ohio boyhood one feels the tension between liberation and order, between the social id and the social superego, as one certainly feels it in these lines from "Swimming at Midnight," the best and most enduring short poem of Matthias's Stanford years:

> naked as fish, a boy and a girl.
> (Nobody comes here: nobody looks:
> nobody watches us watching us
> watch.) Except the police.
> Thighs slide into the moon.
> Humbly, into the stars: Mirrored,
> flashes a father's red eye, a
> blue-bitten mother's red lip: No
> Swimming Allowed In The Quarry
> At Night. (Anyway, nevertheless
> and moreover: feel how warm!) here,
> among the reflections. (Feel the
> water's mouth and its hands, feel
> them imitate mine: can there truly
> be any danger?) (*SM* 3)

It would be going too far to say that the flashing red eye of the father and the law is also the "stern eye" of Winters, but the palpable tension between Winters's white-knuckled grip on sanity and order, on the one hand, and the political/social/sexual/chemical anarchy on the other ("can there truly be any danger?"), finds its way into "Swimming at Midnight," which under different circumstances of composition would have been a very different poem.

The Bay Area tension between anarchy and Wintersian order informs other poems from *Bucyrus,* including the title poem, which juxtaposes authoritarian mental discipline with liberation, and the important and difficult "Poem in Three Parts" (written in Indiana in 1968), whose witch-trial scenes play out in another context all the social and political disarray of the Bay Area in the mid-sixties. Robert Duncan, who rightly saw that the poet's sympathies lay more on the side of the social id than the social superego, caught the ethos of this anarchic environment exactly, complete with all its melodrama, when he described this new poet and his work:

> Matthias is a goliard—one of those wandering souls out of a Dark Age in our own time . . . carrying with him as he goes in his pack of cards certain key cards that come ever into his hand when he plays: the juggler (as he was to be portrayed later in the Tarot), the scholar whose head is filled with the fame of learning and of amorous women and the heretic remembering witch-hunts yet to come. (undated letter)

The most palpable manifestation of Matthias's sympathy for the countercultural world outside the Wintersian classroom lay in his involvement in the antiwar movement, an involvement that included direct action and that found its way into the poetry as well. But the English generation of the thirties, the subject of Matthias's thesis at Ohio State and his never-finished Stanford dissertation, remained a cautionary example, and the political poems of this period have a rare self-consciousness regarding the relation of art and anger. "Independence between Christmas and New Year's Day," which was written at Stanford and was to appear in *Bucyrus,* is very much an antiwar poem, but an antiwar poem that goes beyond the registering of anger to a questioning of the relation of art to the historical situations that give rise to it:

> . . . Sixty-six in the year
> of our war and on earth peace
> bad winter weather . . . .
> This, among dishes seen:
> Daily news. Also, a faustian fox
> of a fellow, fed:
>> Below the eye
>> A time of adjustments.
>> In broken Asia, blood.
> "In a cosy room
> I'll paint my
> beard a regal
> blue for the sake
> of delight . . . no hand
> of mine will end, my
> love, my warrior brother,
> War . . . ."

"Is the weather wrong?
Am I scribbled out?
Season of hibernation forced,
A time for the painting of beards!" (*B* 9)

The weather was certainly wrong, but what to make of this painting of beards? He must do something, in the face of the historical wrong, but "no hand of mine will end . . . War." The awareness of powerlessness and complicity, as well as of the wrongness of the weather and the strangeness it drives us to raises this poem above the agitprop of both the thirties and sixties.

Many of the other poems in *Bucyrus* were to come out of Matthias's first marriage, to Ann Evans in the summer of 1964, and the bad emotional weather that was to follow. "Fragments for an Epithalamion" commemorates their wedding, but the title proved prophetic of their divorce two years later, and "Moving to London from San Francisco U.S.A.," "On My Birthday Near Divorce," "Who Walked with Her," "Homicidal" and "Suicidal" (later retitled "Diptych"), and "Above These Seas" chronicle that divorce in a series of poems that shows Matthias working, uncharacteristically, in something like a confessional mode.

The move to London came in 1966, when, on the recommendation of Christopher Isherwood and Stephen Spender, Matthias received a Fulbright fellowship to pursue his unfinished thesis on the Auden generation, "Poetry in Public: A Study of the Backgrounds, Theory and Practice of English Political Poetry in the 1930s." The impetus for the move came not only from scholarly reasons but also from personal and political entanglements that had become difficult to bear. There was also the draw of a city that was both a grand storehouse of the visible past to which Matthias had always been drawn and the idea of a literary city inculcated by Wilfred Stone, the director of Matthias's dissertation and early academic advocate of the Bloomsbury group. The world of Bloomsbury was, of course, a long lost one when Matthias arrived in London to share a rambling house in Islington with his friend and fellow activist Igor Webb, but the city proved congenial to Matthias. It was here that he met Diana Adams, his second wife, through whom he would later be introduced to the Suffolk that nourished his poetry. It was during Matthias's Islington sojourn, too, that the majority of the poems in *Bucyrus* were written, and it was here that he began to associate with a number of English poets.

London offered Matthias a view of English poetry unavailable on the other side of the Atlantic. Matthias arrived in London just in time for the

publication of the Fulcrum edition of Basil Bunting's *Briggflatts* and for the
new excitement about David Jones and other British modernists in the pages
of *Agenda*. Having been told by Donald Davie that there was no indigenous
British modernism, Matthias delved deeply into the very tradition Davie had
denied existed, editing *23 Modern British Poets* as a wake-up call to those who
felt that, in poetry, "'British' means *old* or *tired* . . . Philip Larkin rather than
Tom Raworth" (ix).

When Matthias returned to America late in 1967 for what he then
thought would be a single year of teaching at the University of Notre Dame
(an appointment that actually became permanent), the protest culture he was
still very much a part of was about to be shaken to pieces in the violence,
fear, and confusion of the 1968 Chicago Democratic Convention and its
aftermath. Along with Peter Michelson, then the great radical figure on the
Notre Dame campus (who also happened to be writing *Pacific Plainsong*
down the street from the house where Matthias was finishing "Poem in
Three Parts"), Matthias was gassed by the rioting Chicago police, and he and
Michelson saw a number of their students beaten up badly. In the months
that followed, he, like many others, fell into a mood of general despair and
disillusion:

> I was not, I suppose, untypical of my generation in the 1960s by
> becoming sufficiently caught up in the machinery of protest and the
> language of neo-Marxist analysis to feel in the end both confused
> and inauthentic, "dragging passions, notions, shapes of faith / Like
> culprits to the bar," and subjecting everything, including the plea-
> sures I took in a new marriage, in the birth of my first child, in soli-
> tude, and in the arts to a rigorous inquisition with respect to means
> and ends considered in the context of political activism. I remember
> telling [Peter Michelson] in late 1968 that I felt oddly off balance.
> (*Reading Old Friends* 41)

Just as his lack of balance had to do with a kind of relentless self-interroga-
tion like that of Wordsworth calling his passions to the bar amid the wreck-
age of his revolutionary enthusiasm, Matthias's way back to balance had to
do with a Wordsworthian search for the comforts of known places. "At a particular point in the 1960s," Matthias wrote, "I went as intentionally to
Wordsworth as one might reach for the right medicine in the medicine
chest" (41). The place was not Ohio, which has never figured largely in
Matthias's work, nor California, which he found "melodramatically impressive"

but which "clearly wasn't mine" (43)—rather, it was a particular English place, one that seemed to be ineradicably his. As he put it, "When I married my [second] wife, I also married East Anglia, Suffolk, the Aldeburgh and Orford coasts, the river Deben, the town of Woodbridge and the village of Hatcheson" (46). This countryside was to be his home every summer for thirteen years, and for several full-year stays as well.

When in 1973 Matthias went to spend his first full year in the English countryside, in the village of Little Shelford, he was going to a place he had already learned to love, and as a poet who had begun to establish himself, having published *Bucyrus* with Michael Anania's Swallow Press in 1970. Despite the Wordsworthian impulse that helped Matthias adapt to English village life, it was not the nurturing fosterage of Nature that he found to comfort him there, so much as it was the sense of the weight and permanence of the past, and one finds him almost drunk on the tactile presentness of the past in "Epilogue from a New Home," one of the many poems in *Turns* written during this year at Little Shelford:

> There's a plague pit
>   just to the edge of the village.
> Above it, now mostly covered with grass,
>   a runway for B-17s: (American
> Pilots back from industrial targets). Tribes
>   gathered under my window;
> They'd sack an imperial town: I'll wave
>   to my wife at the end of the Roman road. (*T* 104)

This intoxication, though, was of a calming rather than a disorienting kind, and history in its tactile, bodied manifestation (Matthias's childhood imaginations made real) became the steady keel for the "oddly off-balance" Matthias.

Many of the poems of this period, though, particularly those collected in the first of the three sections in *Turns,* continue to reflect very contemporary and very American anxieties. "Halfdream after Mandelstam: Who Spoke of the Language Itself," dedicated to his former students Rory Holscher and John Hessler, is one such poem, and its opening stanzas capture the off-balance tensions and deep social divisions from which Matthias sought refuge:

> I see America closing in on my friends.
> Once I was angry, once I protested in poems.
> Mandelstam: May 13, 1934: I see
> The Kremlin's mountaineer in America.

Words, words: the poem an execution.
They are gunning for Roy and John.
I can see them come in the night.

There is no place to hide.
Their aim is single and passionate.
I see America closing in on my friends. (*T* 28)

These anxieties aren't confined to the American section of *Turns,* however: even when Matthias's poetry seems to be at its most English, it often reflects very American concerns. "The Administration of Justice," an unpublished light poem written around the same time as "Halfdream after Mandelstam" draws its imagery from the English world of the tactile past, but the poem's dark comedy and paranoia were certainly forged by the aftermath of the 1968 Democratic Convention. While written as a private joke to be shared with the poet Ernest Sandeen, his colleague at Notre Dame, it is worth quoting here for the way its very English appearance expresses exactly those American anxieties present in "Halfdream after Mandelstam":

"Well who will bring the instruments
And who will bring the block?"
"The surgeon and the sergeant of the woodyard, dear."
"And will the master cook appear
With mallet, knife and lock?"
"With the surgeon and the sergeant of the woodyard, dear."

"And will they bring the searing irons
And bring a pan of fire
With the surgeon and the sergeant of the woodyard, dear?"
"The farrier and yeoman bring
The searing irons and fire
With the surgeon and the sergeant of the woodyard, dear."

"And do they serve up wine and ale
And are there kegs of beer
Coming with the sergeant of the woodyard, dear?"
"The custom is for all to drink
The surgeon's health, I fear,
Who is toasted by the sergeant of the woodyard, dear."

"And will they cut your heart right out
And will it then be clear
To everybody thinking you a good bard, dear,
That any man who loves me true
Will hold his tongue in fear
Of the surgeon and the sergeant of the woodyard, dear."
(Letter to Ernest Sandeen, June 26, 1974)

The period leading up to Matthias's first full year in East Anglia produced not only some of Matthias's best work in his more lucid idiom, but some of his best work in his more arcane idiom as well, including the title poem of *Turns,* which, taking Thomas Hardy's Jude the Obscure as its title figure, becomes an inquiry both historical and personal, a meditation on the obscurity of modernism and on the charge that "Poem in Three Parts" and similar poems were simply too obscure to be appreciated. It is L=A=N=G=U=A=G=E poetry *avant la lettre,* and justifiably one of the most praised poems in the Matthias canon.

By the time *Turns* appeared in the United States in 1976 (a year after its publication in the United Kingdom), Matthias had spent two more summers in Suffolk and was just returning to England, this time to spend a year writing poetry at Cambridge as the first poetry fellow of Clare Hall. Here he was in close contact with Göran Printz-Påhlson, whom he had befriended earlier in Suffolk, and the two began to collaborate on the translations that were eventually to appear in the book *Contemporary Swedish Poetry.* Matthias was also in almost daily contact with his old Stanford friend Robert Hass, now living in the house where Matthias had lived in Little Shelford, and beginning to write *Twentieth Century Pleasures.* It was in Cambridge that many of the poems of the 1979 volume *Crossing* were written, including the comic Batory and Lermontov poems, in which Matthias,

who has children
and a wife
who is middle class for life (*BA* 87)

bids farewell to his earlier self and his "postactivist consternation" (*Reading Old Friends* 42).

What follows this farewell, for Matthias, is a continuation and development of his interest in the long poem, both in translation—Matthias and Vladeta Vukovic, with constant input from Charles Simic, spent the decade from 1977 to 1987 translating the Serbian epic *Battle of Kosovo*—and in his original work. The most significant new work in 1983's *Northern Summer,* the title poem and "A Wind in Roussillon," is on a large scale, and is a forecast of Matthias's greatest achievement, seven years in the making, the 1991 poem in three parts, *A Gathering of Ways.*

The concern of *A Gathering of Ways* is ground (both physical and metaphysical) lost and found. The first ground of the poem is the first ground where Matthias had truly felt at home, the English ground of "An East Anglian Diptych." If the poem, with its lists of lovingly named places, seems at times elegiac, this has everything to do with the circumstances of its composition. When Matthias sat down to write the poem in the summer of 1983, it was in the full knowledge that he had lost the place he was writing about, having had to abandon the house in Suffolk. The loss was devastating, as it was the loss of the dreamworld of the visible past, the very world of childhood play that he had woken, one day, to find real. Writing in 1988 of his predicament a year after the composition of "An East Anglian Diptych," Matthias described his way forward:

> If my own place had been lost except in memory—one attempt to visit it found the house itself converted into a "Bed and Breakfast"— what was there to do? Making a virtue of necessity . . . I decided to stay in Indiana for a while and read a little history. I thought I could *try* to feel "at home on the earth," even in South Bend. Moreover, as an act of will, although still believing firmly with David Jones that the poet must "work within the limits of his love," I began to write a long poem called "Facts from an Apocryphal Midwest" . . . I could only hope that an act of will might, in the curious processes of composition, become an act of love. (*Reading Old Friends* 55)

Having lost the place where he had found refuge from an unmanageable country in unmanageable times, he willed himself to be another kind of poet, at home on another kind of ground.

The citing of David Jones here is of particular importance, as it is during the 1980s and early 1990s that Matthias is most deeply involved with Jones, involved even on a day-to-day basis for extended periods of time as he edits first *Introducing David Jones* (1980), then *David Jones: Man and Poet* (1989) and the *Selected Works of David Jones* (1993). And Jones is very much the presiding spirit of the longest and most thoroughly successful part of *A*

18   *Gathering of Ways,* "A Compostela Diptych." What we find in this poem is
Matthias's third and truest ground—neither England nor America but
Europe, Spain and France in particular but Spain and France as a synecdoche
for *Europa,* for the Catholic West, an entity as numinous and powerfully felt
here as is the Mediterranean Europe in Pound's *Cantos.* This is a place in
which Matthias's powerful sense of the rootedness of things in historical
processes finds scope, a place resonant with the visible past, a place both
expressively lyric and richly arcane, a place (literal and otherwise) that nourished like no other could this mature flowering of Matthias's work, a place,
as he says at the end of the poem, "that invited and received my song" (*BA*
192).

A quiet period followed the publication of *A Gathering of Ways,* as is to
be expected after the completion of a project of that size and significance, but
was soon followed by the publication of Matthias's collected longer poems,
Beltane at Aphelion, and his selected shorter poems, *Swimming at Midnight.*
This second volume included a number of new poems, many of which
develop the Yugoslavian material that had interested Matthias since his co-
translation of *The Battle of Kosovo* (one, "The Silence of the Stones," is dedicated to Charles Simic, who provided such invaluable assistance with the
Kosovo translation). Matthias has since continued to work in both longer and
shorter forms, and the recent completion of two important sequences, "Pages
from a Book of Years" and "Cuttings," shows Matthias writing with undi-
minished strength, indicating that we may expect the gathering of new energies and the exploration of new ways.

Works Cited

Anania, Michael. "John Matthias's *Bucyrus.*" In *Word Play Place: Essays on the Poetry of John
    Matthias.* Ed. Robert Archambeau. Athens, Ohio: Swallow, 1998.
Davie, Donald. *Ezra Pound: Poet as Sculptor.* New York: Oxford University Press, 1964.
Duncan, Robert. Letter to John Matthias. Undated.
Matthias, John. "Alto Luogo Ayasuluk." *TriQuarterly* 36 (spring 1976), 88–93.
———. *Beltane at Aphelion: Longer Poems.* Athens, Ohio: Swallow, 1995.
———. *Bucyrus.* Chicago: Swallow, 1970.
———. Letter to Ernest Sandeen. August 4, 1974.
———. *Reading Old Friends: Essays, Reviews, and Poems on Poetics, 1975–1990.* The Margins of
    Literature Series. Albany: State University of New York Press, 1992.
———. *Swimming at Midnight: Selected Shorter Poems.* Athens, Ohio: Swallow, 1995.

————. *Turns*. Chicago: Swallow, 1975.

————, ed. *23 Modern British Poets*. Chicago: Swallow, 1971.

Pinsky, Robert. "Essay on Psychiatrists." In *Five American Poets*. Ed. John Matthias, 146–49. Manchester: Carcanet, 1979.

Shapiro, Alan. Foreword to *The World at Large: New and Selected Poems 1971–1996,* by James McMichael, vii–xiii. Chicago: University of Chicago Press (Phoenix Poets), 1996.

John Matthias's *Bucyrus*

MICHAEL ANANIA

"The change *is* the emotion on thought"
—John Matthias, "Statement," *Bucyrus*

The final section of John Matthias's first book, *Bucyrus*, opens with "Statement," a prose poem about the sculptor Gaudier-Brzeska. It is a parable concerning craft. Gaudier, in search of artistic freedom, trains himself perfectly in the craft of stone, and when he is imprisoned in a cage of stone by the state, in a matter of minutes he takes the stone walls apart with his perfectly trained hands and goes home:

> So then Gaudier. Gaudier choosing craft and consciousness, choosing freedom. So then Gaudier—Gaudier refusing to be enslaved by refusing to know, Gaudier refusing imprisonment. But they tried, the governments and their jailors, they tried, the governments and their jailors unconscious and therefore unfree, to jail, in the war, this conscious spirit, this Gaudier. But Gaudier loved freedom, and because he loved freedom learned craft. Because he loved freedom learned craft so perfectly that he became a craftsman of genius. And his medium was stone. Stone were the jails of the governments and the jailors. Stone was his medium—a genius with exquisite perfectly trained controlled and controlling hands. Free hands. Free because they knew craft. Jails, Penetentiaries, Sanatoriums, all made out of stone. Stone walls, many feet thick. Stone jails, Jail-thick stone walls where they put him, craftsman and free, they—the governments making their wars.

> Minutes after they threw him there in his cell, minutes after they locked him in that cage of stone, Gaudier, Pound's friend the vorticist, took, with his bare hands, an eight-foot-thick wall apart and went home. (*B* 60)

The identity drawn between literal freedom and artistic freedom turns, in the parable, on the two uses of stone, but Matthias means Gaudier's "statement" to be understood as his, as well. Language is the poet's medium, as obdurately textured and compacted as granite. Like stone, also, it is confining, the basic material of the confinements of family, culture, and state, and like the stone, it becomes elastic through craft. Gaudier's argument in the poem is that instinctual behaviors change in the application of consciousness and emotion—"necessities become conscious, become emotion and thought. The change *is* the emotion on thought" (*B* 59). The change, however, is limited by the weight of culture, figured here by the repressive state, whose bonds are only broken when the combination of emotion and thought toward a goal is executed with a perfectly trained sense of craft.

One of the first things you are conscious of in John Matthias's early poems is the extraordinary delight they take in the application of craft. There is a sense, even when the materials of the poems are entirely strange, of the poet's absolute certainty over the placement of each syllable, that the precisely laid out alchemical formula in Part Two of "Poem in Three Parts," the incantations that surround it, the curiously broached fragments later in the same piece, and the rhyming tirade all have the same exactitude. In shorter Matthias poems of the period the same sense of speech as a crafted occasion is achieved by abbreviation. The poems strain, almost to the breaking point, their own lyricism with a sharp, abrupt sense of phrase:

> As I say,
> I work. I
> live alone.
>
> But if you
> really want
> to, then ok.
>   ("Letter," *B* 5)

or by warps and collapses in ordinary syntax for which the musical momentum of the poems must compensate:

> Zero on ice.
> Tire spun: smoke
> to three a.m. Hail
> and also headlight
> dimming. Oddly out.
>   ("Homicidal," *B* 29)

22   It is a self-imposed, strange virtuosity that places such stress on a throwaway word here like "also" and makes a phrase like "Oddly out" and its abrupt period bear the weight of a strophe.

These short, curiously authoritative lyrics were among the first Matthias poems I read. John was just back from England and submitted the poems for what was to have been volume two of the *New Poetry Anthology*. The book never appeared, but my response to the submission began our long friendship and was the first step in the publication of *Bucyrus* and the remarkable series of Matthias books with Swallow, including *Turns*, *Crossing*, and *Northern Summer*, and, most recently, the two volumes of new and selected poems, *Swimming at Midnight* and *Beltane at Aphelion*. The late 1960s were as strange for poetry as they were for the rest of American society. There was an enormous amount of activity. Magazines sprouted everywhere. Poets from every conceivable school were allied in readings against the war in Vietnam, and there was an earnest effort on all sides to reinstate poetry's political credentials. The extremes were topical polemics about injustices of all sorts and the familiar neo-Georgian minute encounter with nature grown virtuous by its obvious, but unstated, aversion to modern society and the military-industrial complex. An enormous range of personal, social, and chemical experimentation, some of it daring but much of it merely self-indulgent, was being called "the Revolution." In that peculiar context Matthias's shorter poems were particularly forceful. They treat always a disjunctive breech between affection and the exigent world, and in poems like "Homicidal" and "Suicidal" (later published together as "Diptych") take an early seismic reading of the anxieties incipient in a society that has been liberated without having been changed.

> Carpet flames.
> Chain grip: incense
> in a cup. Violins
> and mandolins re-
> corded. Oddly off.
> Stumble dancer,
> rafter slanting down.
> (What is now beyond
> you now my dear?)
> Hold it (having
> hardened) with a kiss.
> He had lied
> for years.
>   ("Suicidal," *B* 30)

They insist, as well, that disorder requires a special clarity of language and form. Their abrupt, often arbitrary precisions seemed to me at the time to offer a forceful alternative to the dominant poetics of the moment.

Matthias soon presented me with two longer pieces whose pertinence to the political situation and its poetic corollaries was much more acute. There are a number of different ways to approach "Bucyrus" and "Poem in Three Parts." Both texts are extremely rich. But rereading them now with a conscious effort to bring to mind that first, nearly thirty-year-old reading, they are united in my mind by their cultural politics. Both poems are about language in the same sense that the "Statement," the Gaudier-Brzeska poem, is about stone.

"Bucyrus" is an intricately reflexive allegory that deals with cultural and linguistic tyranny as they are transmitted and amplified by family. The three sadistic aunts control Ada and Aben through their control of several levels of language. They are the keepers of the stories, that is of history. In periods of stress, of disobedience, the stories of Bucyrus and Becky, his waitress seductress, and of the aunts' and Ada's and Aben's origins have to be recounted exactly, after the fashion of a ritual renewal of relics. Ada's effort to alter the story and create a revised Becky (who, in the aunt's version of events, broke into Bucyrus's house by force) is a form of treason against the household and is punished:

> "Becky got into the house because Bucyrus loved her," Ada said. "Bucyrus let her in."
> "Recite your text!" said Oam.
> "Becky got into the house because Ada says Bucyrus loved her," Aben said. "Please don't hit me. Please don't punish her."
> "Recite your text!" said Ooney and Olley. (*B* 45)

Like Clove and Malone in Beckett, Ada senses that if she can change the story, she can in some liberating measure control it. The aunts are also in charge of the sacred texts, the books of Bucyrus's discipline—Richard Baxter's theology and L. Ron Hubbard's *Dianetics*. They are also the beadles of the discipline Bucyrus left behind for Ada and Aben, Anglo-Saxon grammar. The grammar, recited like a catechism, is just one of the incantatory elements in the poem. In application the discipline it provides is both arbitrary and mysterious, so it is exactly suited to tyrannical authority. Reflexively, it surfaces into the story an oblique source of the craft out of which some freedom might be crafted. It allows Matthias to introduce directly into the text an instance of language study removed from both emotion and thought by

24   its inaccessible terminologies and the requirement of rote learning. The equation offered between rote learning and ritual pertains to every level of discourse in the household, and the resulting control is celebrated by the aunts through sadism and perversion, which the final incantation, "Come rub my thighs," elevates to sacrament.

"Poem in Three Parts" is much more ambitious and complex, but it can, to some extent, be read as both an extension of "Bucyrus" and a response to it. If Ada and Aben illustrate the confining aspects of language, "Poem in Three Parts" is an effort to manipulate and eventually pass through some of language's most difficult barriers through craft. The initial incantations in "Poem in Three Parts" are *found*. Significantly, they come from areas of belief, alchemy and witchcraft, from archeological strata of language and politics in which the elements are very tightly bound. Rehearsing them has several purposes. They set, as I suggested earlier, a standard of precision for the poem's later inventions and impress into the poem the ritual sense that precise ordering is efficacious and ontological. The found elements from the witch trials, which Matthias "spells" through fragmented incantation, have their own inherent politics, a historical form of social and political suppression which used the language of witchcraft both as accusation and exorcism. Learning these veins and stress lines in language is, in Matthias's view, similar to the sculptor's practical sense of geology. The stone, as it is worked, yields along the lines of its history, and Matthias uses repetition toward incantation as an analytic device, reversing, freeing the bonds within a text. The recurrences become an examination of obsession. This is particularly true of the witch trial materials and of the efforts to absolve music of its connection with alchemy and prohibited ritual in Part Two.

The poem also has a contemporary area of reference. In Part One the "spelling" of materials found in congressional testimony concerning nuclear and chemical weapons stockpiling associates present-day policy with alchemy and witchcraft. The Bogue Banks story in Part Three involves an intricate array of incompatible, ritualized language systems. The legal version of property, which has its own tightly bonded incantation, is opposed to the personal, hereditary view, and the calamity at the center of the story has to be unraveled and judged within the language of the courts, which chants within its own closed circle.

In his writings on sorcery and magic, Lévi-Strauss distinguishes two kinds of thought, one normal, the other pathological (167–85). Normal thought is always at work on things that tend to withhold their meanings, ordinary objects and occurrences that require deliberate, even methodological understanding. Pathological thought exists in a world surfeited with meaning, where the problem is the attribution of excess emotional significance to particular occasion. These attributions and the efficacious application of charms and incantations are the sorcerer's work and can achieve a temporary balance between the two modes of thought.

> In a universe which it strives to understand but whose dynamics it cannot fully control, normal thought continually seeks the meaning of things which refuse to reveal their significance. So-called pathological thought, on the other hand, overflows with emotional interpretations and overtones, in order to supplement an otherwise deficient reality. . . . We might borrow from linguistics and say that so-called normal thought always suffers from a deficit of meaning, whereas so-called pathological thought (in at least some of its manifestations) disposes of a plethora of meaning. Through collective participation in shamanistic curing, a balance is established between these two complementary situations. (181)

So the sorcerer's cure of the individual is also a social curative. When these moments result in socially authorized translations of phenomena into stable fabulations, a language is created that is equally impenetrable on all sides. "Poem in Three Parts" attempts to deal with a variety of these impenetrable occurrences in language and politics by recirculating earlier, manifest instances of pathological language through them. Much of the play with magic and shamanism in recent poetry has been an exercise in the accrual of provocative significance, one more patchwork of sentimentality to add to the motley. Matthias's use of magic and incantation in "Poem in Three Parts" is political not just because of its various topical applications in the poem but because of its effort to employ the craft of language to penetrate the bonds between language and socially and politically authorized pathology.

Works Cited

Lévi-Strauss, Claude. *Structural Anthropology.* Trans. Claire Jacobson and Brooke Grundfest Schoepf. New York: Basic Books, 1963.
Matthias, John. *Bucyrus.* Chicago: Swallow, 1970.

❧ The Poetry of John Matthias
"My Treason and My Tongue"

VINCENT SHERRY

Your tired evasions, euphemism-lies.
Civilized man and his word-hoard.
Will you be relinquant
Or relinquished.

Name and title. Religion and rank.
Put a check in the column.
Put a check in the bank.

If you'd be only a little bit clever.
If you'd be occasionally.
If you'd be forever.

If you'd be my government.
If you'd be my gal.
If you'd be my treason and my tongue. (*SM* 14)

My title comes from a poem John Matthias wrote in the early seventies, "If Not a Technical Song American: Statement, Harangue, and Narrative." His title adds to mine another word, a cardinal value and binding agent: technique. Now, if Pound was right, and technique is the test of a man's sincerity, then the modernist's phrasing must be varied to catch the conceit of this poet, the concept of this essay: "Treason is test of Matthias's sincerity." This adage points through his poetry back to the source of an energy that is direct and clearly forceful in its release and yet extremely complex in its productions, an energy that quickens in the act of rebellion and yet quickly defers to the very institutions it has seemed to challenge; an energy that is crossed by the appeasements to which it runs, seemingly, as a matter of course. Here I want to track that course. Ultimately, I want to ask whether it runs the usual *ricurso* of revolution—turning on a reverse curve back to what was left behind or betrayed, a kind of treasoner's Moebius strip—or if that apparent retrograde is an unlikely *gradus ad Parnassum,* a movement *forward* into new zones of awareness, a breaking open of new poetic possibilities.

But against whom—or what—is treason perpetrated? The usual suspects are rounded up in another early poem, "Three around a Revolution," a short sequence that turns around the 1917 Revolution and positions poetry, at least for the sake of argument, in alliance with that political energy:

> There must be horses, there must be women,
> There must be lawsuits. There must, moreover
>
> And eventually, be justice. There must be words.
> I write down words. (*SM* 28)

Language, conscripted here in the service of justice and law, moves the poet in the direction of progressive egalitarianism, and so, in the fiction of this poem, takes him before its political constituency, a mass audience, where, however, he makes a mess of it, treasonously, elegantly:

> Yesterday I spoke for hours and nobody stirred.
> Rapt. They cheered. I am a hero.
>
> I said words like *action, money, love, rights*
> And was moved to elegance, alliteration,
>
> Saying, apropos of what I did not know,
> *Palfrey, palindrome, pailing, palinode, palisade.* (*SM* 28)

If poetic art begins this passage as a language of the new social compact, of conventional reference and collective demand, as the words of praxis uttered in expectation of what they mean and require, that compact is subverted in the last line: words as weapons in class warfare have been sold out for the emblems and implements of an antique martial aristocracy, a foregone order invoked by a language out of key with our time but rhyming with itself and with the poet's own delight in the repeated sound, in sheer sound. And the two words not representative of this counterrevolutionary order, *palindrome* and *palinode,* only mean counterrevolution in a way more essential and relevant to the poem. There is the lexical sense of *palindrome,* as in "Able was I ere I saw Elba," which moves forward, letter by letter, by going back, and simply spells out the reversal of the current on which the revolutionary has been borne up, as in his *palinode,* a formal retraction.

To put this treason in terms of conflicts broadly historical and political is not to scant those dimensions of personal history and private fury from which this force acquires its true depth and drive. Behind the word of law and justice stands the lawyer, the judge, the justice of the Ohio Supreme Court, John Matthias's father, who casts the son's pleasure in words *qua* words, in the eroticized body of language, in that more starkly romantic light of Oedipal sedition. The title poem in the new selection of shorter work, "Swimming at Midnight," tells of an adolescent eros stolen from the forbidding gaze of the father, a "red eye" cast in anger at the boy's primal delight in the sensuous medium of water and on the older poet's pleasure in the very texture and corporeality of these words:

> Thighs slide into the moon.
> Humbly, into the stars: Mirrored,
> flashes a father's red eye (*SM* 3)

The scene of primary conflict is revisited years later in a recent poem, "After Years Away," where the older son sleeps in the deceased father's bed and recovers that place as a site of first erotic delights:

> First my bed, then his, now mine again—
> just for a week.
>
> He died in it, my father, where for years
> I'd lie beside my pretty love,
>
> alive and indiscreet. (*SM* 150)

And the poet reclaims that triumph over the father, as the narrative of the poem unfolds, in a language as peculiar as it is potent:

> While he lay dying & while I sat reading books,
> she swept his mortal breath away,
>
> I think.
> When she heard the ringing here . . .
>
> And then swept circles round & round the bier
> as I said *Gnostic, Bogomil.* (*SM* 152)

To most readers *Bogomil* sounds like an unfortunately named shopping mall **29** in northeastern Ohio. But the word is uttered in the narrative and rhetorical fictions of this poem as a magical counter known only to the poet, that Gnostic. It hums like a tuning fork for the poetic career that began on that bed: a sound whispered in defiance of observance at the father's obsequies, a word of treason against the paternal law and the *logos* of law. It is a word that glories in the very otherness it sounds and refuses to give away. It rhymes with the cultivated unknown, with the dark spaces that define the shapes of light on Matthias's canvasses, with the negative but essential energy of obscurity.

The poetics of obscurity—and something of their complex, indeed contradictory, economy—are caught in the title poem of the 1975 volume "Turns: Towards a Provisional Aesthetic and a Discipline." This poem opens with a translation of the opening scene of *Jude the Obscure* into a regional dialect of Middle English. Where Hardy's "schoolmaster was leaving the village, and everybody seemed sorry," we hear "The scolemayster levande was the toun / and sary of hit semed everuch one" (*SM* 48). This passage initiates a deliberation through the poem on the uses of obscurity like this, and on obscurantism, but our attention is centered best in the figure of the schoolmaster, who focuses the fully antithetical energies of this poetic. On one hand, the pedagogue offers from his word-hoard and reference-trove the splendid alterity of unfamiliar speech; on the other, this is our familial tongue, our own language in its deeper memory and resonance. It is strange only in the ways of the uncanny or, more suitably, the "unheimlich," in the double implication of the German word's literal and Freudian meanings: not homey or not familiar but only because too intimate and well known, and strange only because repressed or, here, forgotten.

This is the paradox that defines the enlivening conflict of Matthias's verse. Here is a poet who must work, as it were, way out in the center. He is an idiosyncratic radical who is only trying to get back to a common root; a poet-magus whose extravagant novelty and apparent strangeness are really aiming to reclaim and consolidate a language that is already there, the true depth of our civil speech. If this is the second turning of Matthias's Moebius strip, a turning back upon the first turning, I imagine it thus not to dissolve this project into its own oppositions but to identify the terms of a complex synthesis that sets a standard of achievement unique to this poet, that sets him a charge. It is to speak the dialect of the tribe as though it were a foreign language, or, in a mildly Freudian parlance, to keep a filial eros nervously and treasonously alive within the father's language. It is this rebellious and estranging energy, after all, that tends and preserves paternal inheritance, indeed uncovers the legacy, for it is the paradox of our culture, where backgrounds are not shared, where the collective inheritance that matters is a matter of apparently esoteric cultivation, that poetry must find a source in these alien and forbidden powers.

The register in which this project is pitched might best be described by a phrase from a recent poem, "The Silence of Stones," which invokes a rite stumbled upon in a walking trip in Bosnia, in Herzegovina:

> enigmatic
> standing stones proclaim
> some mode of life that lost its way
>
> . . . .
>
> Hieratic, fetishistic. (*SM* 148)

Magisterial and obsessive, the persona of Matthias's poetry of archaeology is at once august and secure in the materials he is surfacing and yet neurotically obsessed because these objects of attention are not part of a whole culture actually lived in; they are recovered and hoarded and magnified one by one. This voice finds a natural balancing point—and something like its intrinsic subject—in witchcraft or "black" magic, which represents the received rituals of a religious culture in a sexualized form, animating these with the energy of the repressed. How close this power lies to the source of Matthias's energy may be measured by its early prominence in his first major poem of length, "Poem in Three Parts," a sequence that returns elliptically to the opening prospect of male witchery and phallic rites.

The energy I am describing here, however, defines primarily a young man's poetic. It is the energy I knew in John Matthias in the years of my own first acquaintance with him in the late 1960s and early 1970s. What happens to it as the poet ages and it is used to recover progressively more of the obscured past? The risk at the center of this enterprise lies in its very success: the unknown past, raised majestically and numinously like the walls of Troy to the poet's lyre, becomes a set of city streets, mapped and named. Or, to put the problem in terms closer to Matthias's own originating energy: does one turn and testify against the witches, treasonously conscripting their treason into the priesthood of the established church? Or punish them as heretics, as in "Words for Sir Thomas Browne," a poem positioned at a moment of intellectual history remarkably similar to the crisis point of Matthias's poetry, a crisis point it helps to identify? This is the moment when the old magic is becoming the new science, when alchemy is becoming chemistry, and when

the numina of ancient pagan rites have become names in a taxonomer's catalog. And here, out of a grief that is synonymous with nothing more or less
than old age, at the death of a son, Thomas Browne turns against the extreme
and eccentric and heresiarchial creeds of his youth, the early alchemy that
formed the basis of the later chemistry. This is a turn recorded in the terrible
beauty of the poem's final section, which opens with a quote from the dead
son's last letter, tracing yet another image of backward-moving revolution:

> *As though the soul of one man passed into another,*
> *opinions, after certain revolutions, do find men & minds*
>
> *like those that first begat them.*
>
> Staring fixedly at Tom's
> last letter in your hand, thinking of that trial where
>
> one alleged his chimney had been cursed & yet another that
> his cart had been bewitched and also all his geese,
>
> you well might suddenly embrace that sweet & generous heresy
> that tempted you when you were young: that all are saved—
>
> yourself & Tom, those witches in the court of Matthew Hale,
> Epicurus, Lucan & Pythagoras, cruel doctors who revolve
>
> ephemerides, husbands who attend to husbandry, sons and
> daughters, brothers aunts & sisters, wives.
>
> And yet you said: *God saves whom he will . . .*
> and thought the wretched women damned at Edmund's bury.
>
> And thought you heard Tom's ship explode at sea. (*SM* 61–62)

How to keep the heresy sweet and generous even as its energy recovers
and builds a tradition like an orthodoxy? That is the problem and paradox I
seek to define, if not to develop and resolve. It may at least be said that there
is in the later poetry an effort to turn this energy into a prosody of the pro-
founder kind, a measure or pace of consciousness in the sounding of the
deposits. Listen to the movement as he approaches the final moment in the
Spain section of the "Compostela Diptych," the combination of evocation

32 and explanation here. This is the raising of the poetic unknown by the
inspired *vates*—he deploys the repetitions of rapture, taps the strength of the
strange from foreign words—and the laying out of context and background
by the patient *clericus,* whose anecdotes of the ordinary and daily make those
icons of the *magus* seem creaturely and real. These several tones are swept
into a single idiom, a measure and a voice as poised, seamless, and integral
as the historical imagination:

> Long before *it is*
> *and ever shall be* under overhanging
> rocks at San Juan de la Peña . . . where they say, they *say*
>
> the Grail came to rest and made a fortress
> of the monastery there carved beneath a cliff-face roof
> where dowsers conjured water out of rock
>
> in Mithra's Visigothic cave & his tauroctonous priest
> drove the killing sword, like Manolete,
> in the shoulder of the bellowing great beast
>
> to burst its heart & bleed the plants & herbs across
> the mountainside that monks would one day
> gather there, bleed the wheat they'd make into their bread.
>
> Everything, everything was still. As it was in the beginning
> long before the silence of the abbeys,
> the silence of the abbots in their solitary prayer,
>
> the silence of the brothers cutting hay & tending sheep
> at San Millán of the Cowl,
> the silent sacristan measuring and pouring oils—
>
> the weavers and the tailors and the copyists at work,
> Cellarius among his stores of wool and flax,
> Hortulanus in his garden tending bees—silence broken only
>
> as Hebdomadarius, finished with the cooking, rings a bell
> and even old Gonzalo de Berceo looks up happily
> from silent pages where his saint has walked the mountains

in the language of Castillian *juglares* which is not,
God knows, the language of the Latin clerks. *Andaba por*
  los montes
por los fuertes lugares, por las cuestas enhiestas,

but silently, and all around him it was very still.
As it was in the beginning before silence,
in the silence that preceded silence, in the stillness

before anything was still, when nothing
made a single sound and singularity was only nothing's
song unsinging . . . aphonia

before a whisper or a breath, aphasia
before injury,
aphelion of outcry without sun . . .

　　　　　　　　　　　Long before *it is*
and ever shall be under overhanging
rocks at San Juan de la Peña, at San Millán of the Cowl,

at Loyola's Casa-Torre and the shepherds' huts
of Bertsulari in the Pyrenees
when no one spoke of *fueros* or *tristitia* or *spes,*

and there were neither rights nor hopes nor
sadnesses to speak of.
Then in the high and highest places everything was still.

As it was in the beginning. As it will be in the end. (*GW* 113–15)

"To elliptically gloss," goes the injunction at the end of "Turns," that locus classicus of obscurity, and this phrase catches the fine and strong double rhythm of concealing and revealing that times the disclosures in these later poems. This is not a technique so much as a sincerity, and it works—or not—as a function of attitude—call it wonder—at these materials. Once in a while wonder is staged, as when a stylistic mannerism of David Jones is used to feign discovery of the already known, when questioning is rhetorical:

34   "Were days measured once again by Kalends, Nones, and Ides? Was Solstice equinox and equinox the solstice? Did lunar phases intersect the solar year?" (*GW* 83). My question is not rhetorical, however: it goes to the issue of the longevity of discovery. And it has been answered, again and again in this poetry, by the turns that surprise and the poetry that bears out the delight of that surprise.

Works Cited

Matthias, John. *A Gathering of Ways*. Athens, Ohio: Swallow, 1991.
————. *Swimming at Midnight: Selected Shorter Poems*. Athens, Ohio: Swallow, 1995.

❧ Two Poems and the Aesthetics of Play

JERE ODELL

John Matthias's poem "Double Derivation, Association, and Cliché: From *The Great Tournament Roll of Westminster*" begins with a list and a refrain:

> (I)
> The heralds wear their tabards correctly.
> Each, in his left hand, carries a wand.
> Before and after the Master of Armour
> Enter his men: three of them carry the staves.
> The mace bearer wears a yellow robe.
> In right & goodly devysis of apparyl
> The gentlemen ride.
> The double-curving trumpets shine.
>
> Who breaks a spear is worth the prize. (*SM* 72)

These words come from another list, the tournament roll cited in the poem's title. The tournament was staged in 1511 to celebrate the birth of a son to Henry VIII and Katharine of Aragon. The tournament was part masquerade, part liturgy, part sport, part arts festival, part international diplomacy, and part military combat. These lines may have been occasioned by an early crisis in Matthias's life as a poet. He writes in his essay "Places and Poems: A Self-Reading and a Reading of the Self in the Romantic Context from Wordsworth to Parkman":

> I was not, I suppose, untypical of my generation in the 1960s by becoming sufficiently caught up in the machinery of protest and the language of neo-Marxist analysis to feel in the end both confused

and inauthentic, "dragging passions, notions, shapes of faith / Like culprits to the bar," and subjecting everything, including the pleasures I took in a new marriage, in the birth of my first child, in solitude, and in the arts to a rigorous inquisition with respect to means and ends considered in the context of political activism. (*Reading Old Friends* 41)

In part, his response to this crisis was to begin reading Wordsworth. In retrospect, Matthias saw his need for Wordsworth as similar to John Stuart Mill's. Mill found that in the midst of his intellectual and emotional life "all feeling was dead within [him]" and that he was more "a stock or a stone" than a human. Mill wrote in his autobiography:

> What made Wordsworth's poems a medicine for my state of mind, was that they expressed, not mere outward beauty, but states of feeling, and thought coloured by feeling, under the excitement of beauty. They seemed to be the very culture of the feelings, which I was in quest of. (89)

Matthias's decision to read Wordsworth (or any of the Romantics) is a moment of great interest, one Matthias himself partly examines in his essay. What he expected to find there and cultivate for the sake of his own poetry, even for the sake of his own mental health, was a way to heal the split between drudgery and life, work and play. As he writes in "Places and Poems," he was looking for a world that didn't keep the place for the artistic soul "separated from the place in which we earn our living" (*Reading Old Friends* 52). Accordingly, in Matthias's perspective, Wordsworth escaped the urge always to be working by finding the particular place, the lake country, in which he could, as Whitman said, "loaf and invite the soul" (45).

Though place is central to Matthias's own thinking about his work, and is perhaps essential (in his view) for a healthy imaginative spirit, and though Suffolk temporarily became Matthias's place, the location in which he could invite the soul to loaf, for my purpose, and in my reading of Matthias's poetry, the urgency of place is usurped by that of play. In fact, whatever the place—South Bend, Indiana; Suffolk, England; Columbus, Ohio; the Wessex of Hardy's *Jude the Obscure;* or sixteenth-century Westminster—the poet must situate himself in relation to the act of writing, both the play and the work at hand. Matthias grounds his poetry not in location but in action; while the place changes, the poetry must go on.

It is no coincidence that many of the poems that Matthias wrote after his disciplined turning to Wordsworth and to Suffolk, though rich in the lore of local history and culture, focus on the centrality of play to the human experience. Included in this turn are poems he wrote for his daughters, celebrating their playful childhood, especially "Poem for Cynouai" from *Crossing*. This new focus was not so much to emulate Wordsworth's fascination with childhood, its supposed natural status or its supposed innocence, but rather to use childhood as a means of recovering the idea of play. Matthias writes in "Places and Poems":

> If my own route to the responsibilities of being an adult was through my children, it was also through my children that I found the route to childhood. And one thing I wanted to learn on my way to childhood and back again had something to do with the meaning play. (50–51)

Arguably, what he found by returning (in poetry) to childhood, his own by way of his daughters', was an aesthetic of play (albeit "provisional," as he calls it in the allied poem, "Turns") by which the writing and reading of his poetry can be not so much judged as enhanced.[1]

This provisional aesthetic enters the poet's work not by precept but by example, by play itself. The beginning of "Double Derivation" does not announce the subject but exhibits it. The list catalogs the accouterments of courtly tournaments: tabards, wands, servants, staves, a band leader in a yellow robe, all the trappings of late chivalry. This train of particulars identifies play as artifice. And yet, avoiding the kind of abstraction that waylaid Mill, the words themselves exhibit the poem's playfulness. Reading the chronicle of play, one can also read the poetry as play—the humorous tone, the exuberant detail, even the archaic English: "In right and goodly devysis of apparyl / The gentlemen ride" (*SM* 72).

Part II turns the poem in a slightly new direction, making its search for an aesthetic not only more explicit but also comparative. It begins: "Or makes a forest in the halls of Blackfriars / at Ludgate whych is garneychyd wyth trees & bowes" (*SM* 72). Here, "or" works like a double hinge upon which the poem swings to other subjects. It is not just a poem about Westminster but (as in other sections) a poem about Ludgate, shipyards, Bosworth, Flodden, Empress Wu, Henry VII, Shakespeare, the Globe, and two old men playing chess in a garden. "Or" tells us that to pretend in this way is as much as to pretend in that way; these too are worth the prize.

Though many have considered poetry in terms of play, among them Johan Huizinga (alluded to in part IV) Matthias makes play the vehicle as well as the subject of the poem. He uses the festivities and tournaments of the sixteenth-century court to create his own world of play. The tournaments like the one that sponsored the production of *The Great Tournament Roll of Westminster* were often raucous affairs, even if their ostensible purpose was to serve as a means of "eschewing . . . Idleness the ground of all vice, and to exercise the thing that shal be honorable and to the bodye healthfull and profitable" (Anglo 21). Politically these events demonstrated the wealth, sophistication, and magnificence of the court. This specific event was meant to demonstrate Henry's political, military, and sexual prowess. In Westminster the king used the tournament in a way not unlike a military parade; it demonstrated his financial strength, intimidated his foreign and domestic rivals, and encouraged his allies. As the roll was the record of this event, it also allowed Henry the opportunity to give the future an elaborate self-portrait. In fact, after René d'Anjou's and Philip the Good's tournaments, upon which Henry's were modeled, the party had become much more than the armed encounter of chivalry. Combat (or sport) was often preceded and concluded by poetry, dance, and extravagant charades. "Eschewing Idleness," the contestants would often enter the tournament field in fantastical costumes—dressed as nuns, friars, monsters, or (in one case) piloting a large fake ship across rolling fields and through the shield-hung trees (Anglo 39). This supplies some of the material for Matthias's lines:

> Who will decorate the golden tree,
> Employ properly the captive giant
> And the dwarf? Who will plead
> His rights despite decrepitude . . . ? (*SM* 76)

The knights (including Henry) assumed stage names (some of which Matthias evokes): Joyeulx Penser, Bon Vauloir, Valliant Desyr, or (for the king) Noble Couer Loyal. The roll itself was a part of the artistic festivity, which often (as in the case of *Westminster*) concluded with a poem. Even when the tournament event became violent, when knights were unhorsed and unhinged, the seemingly incongruous arts festival kept pace. In the same way, the phrasing Matthias adopts from *The Great Tournament Roll* mixes the language of the jousting score sheet with the tone of celebration. Even when the words themselves chronicle violence, war, and death, they are full of play, stuck on play, as in part V,

> Who breaks a schylld on shields
>   a saylle on sails
> a sclev upon his lady's sleeves . . .
> And in the north, & for the nearer rival.
> Who meteth Coronall to Coronall, who beareth
> a man down:—down the distance to Westminster,
> down the distance in time. (*SM* 74)

and part VI,

> Slaughter out of ceremony, famine
> out of feasting, out of power
> parsimony, out of revels
> revelation . . .
>   As an axe in the spine can reveal
>   As an arrow in the eye.
>
> Who breaks a spear is worth the prize. (*SM* 75)

In addition to the play world and text of the sixteenth century, Matthias discretely uses other much more personal moments of play; for example, though we do not recognize it until later, all of this sixteenth-century theatricality could actually be read as the poet's recollection of his own childhood play. This play becomes most obvious in part IV; here we are introduced to the poet's childhood, his cousins, and their world of (sometimes interrupted) play:[2]

> & like the Burgkmairs
> *these* illuminations:—
> where, o years ago, say twenty-two or
> say about five hundred,
> cousins in the summertime would
> ritualize their rivalries
> in sumptuous tableaux.
> Someone holds a camera. Snap.
> In proper costume, Homo Ludens wears
> Imagination on his sleeve.
>
> . . . .
>   I remember that. (*SM* 74)

My attention to Matthias's use of childhood in this poem is not merely to show the adult poet reading Wordsworth and recalling the past, but to show him reimagining its play world. This poem begins with a playful reenactment of the tournament, but I believe the reader is asked to enter that play in a new form, to rejoin it twenty-two years later with the poet, in poetry. As the courtly ceremony is reincarnated in Matthias's childhood play, his childhood is simultaneously replayed under the pen, appearing ultimately on the page we read. Matthias writes, "& like the Burgkmairs / *these* illuminations." The Burgkmairs illustrated tournament rolls and other courtly records with woodcuts for the emperor Maximillian. Their illuminations became the model for Henry's own illustrators, in the same way that the emperor was also Henry's model. Thus one can read, "like the Burgkmairs / these illuminations" as well as "like the Burgkmairs / *these* illuminations." One must not forget, however, that these illuminations do not represent the poet's exact childhood, though they are inspired by memories, they are fed by books. Even yet, that he should have found them not in a trunk of costumes but in a collotype reproduction of a tournament roll is nevertheless another act of play.

I am not the first to write of Matthias's focus on play; Jeremy Hooker did so in his essay "Crossings and Turns: The Poetry of John Matthias." Hooker, an accomplished reader of Matthias's poetry, correctly claims one of the poet's subjects to be "man the actor, or player" (102). Hooker attends to play, its "theatrical rhetoric" and its "carnival atmosphere," insofar as that it illuminates the subject—human nature (101). In this regard, I think Hooker follows one of Matthias's sources, Johan Huizinga's *Homo Ludens: A Study of the Play Element in Culture*. Matthias's use of this book, however, extends beyond Huizinga's focus on human nature, even beyond Huizinga's own attempts at an aesthetics of play. In fact, *Homo Ludens* could be added to *The Great Tournament Roll* as one of the books found in the metaphorical trunk whereby Matthias constructs "Double Derivation." Matthias's poem uses many of Huizinga's subjects—war play, the guild system, the poet as *vates,* and (most obviously) the poet and child. Matthias even attends to some of Huizinga's terms, such as *jongleur,* which links poets and feudal regalia—heralds, boasters, braggarts, jesters, minstrels, and other court performers (Huizinga 39–42).

Huizinga, however, identifies poetry with play, perhaps even confines it to play. He writes:

All poetry is born of play: the sacred play of worship, the festive play of courtship, the martial play of the contest, the disputatious play of braggadocio, mocking and invective, the nimble play of wit and readiness. (129)

Though associating play and poetry liberates and reclaims a world of material for poetic festivities and tournaments, it also has its costs. These become evident when one looks closely at Huizinga's definition of *play*:

> It is an activity which proceeds within certain limits of time and space, in a visible order, according to rules freely accepted, and outside the sphere of necessity or material utility. The play-mood is one of rapture and enthusiasm and is sacred or festive in accordance with the occasion. A feeling of exaltation and tension accompanies the action, mirth and relaxation follow. (132)

Whereas this view of play (and by association, poetry) could revive Mill's stagnant sensibilities, freeing art from narrow pragmatism, it could also, when taken dogmatically, banish the poem from the realm of the efficacious to the world of mere "mirth and relaxation." The same emphasis seems evident in Jeremy Hooker's convincing affirmation of Matthias as the poet of play. Hooker writes:

> Matthias the poet knows himself to belong to the species Homo Ludens. Not surprisingly, therefore, there is more of Johan Huizinga's philosophy of play, which distinguishes man from the animals and inspires the creativity which shapes the human world, in John Matthias' poetry than there is Marxism. (103)

The terms of Hooker's dichotomy are unbalanced, stressing the playful aesthetic of Matthias's poetry at the expense of its utility, that is, if Marxism in this context is meant to suggest the concerns of work. Pushed to an extreme, such reasoning might raise questions about whether a poetics of play can produce "serious" poetry—in Matthias's case, elegies, poems about illness and war, poems for his uncle Edward, or poems for aging friends, such as "Everything to be endured" or his poem "26 June 1381 / 1977" on the beheading of Geoffrey Lidster (*SM* 12, 132, 44).

Huizinga anticipates (but doesn't manage to avoid) the inconsequence of this aesthetic when he misreads Friedrich Schiller's concept of *Spieltrieb* from *On the Aesthetic Education of Man*. Schiller postulated two contrasting motives for human action: *Strofftrieb* and *Formtrieb*. The object of the *Strofftrieb* (in Schiller's construct) is often material, or of concern to the body; the object of the Formtrieb is often ideal or conceptual, of the mind. The *Spieltrieb* was Schiller's solution to a perceived tension between these two drives, the dialectic of sense and form. About the human, Schiller writes:

> Should there be cases in which he were to have this twofold experi-
> ence simultaneously, . . . to feel himself matter and to come to know
> himself as mind, then he would in such cases, and in such cases only,
> have a complete intuition of his human nature. (95)

Poetry in Schiller's view deserves special recognition because it is "that kind of free activity which is at once its own end and its own means," because it is simultaneously ideal and material, knowledge and feeling, mind and body (209). Therefore, it is not merely a momentary beauty, but a way for human-ity to free itself from dualism. It is not this, however, that Huizinga criticizes, but rather the idea of *Spieltrieb* as "play-instinct." Huizinga writes:

> It seems preposterous to ascribe the cave paintings at Altamira, for
> instance, to mere doodling—which is what it amounts to if they are
> ascribed to the "play-instinct" . . . though the primary importance
> of play as a cultural factor is the main thesis of this book, we still
> maintain that the origin of art is not explained by a reference to a
> play-"instinct," however innate. (160)

Perhaps it is Huizinga's idea of humanity that is offended here; "instinct" suggests too much of the animal. When Schiller writes, "Man only plays when he is in the fullest sense of the word a human being, and he is only fully a human being when he plays," what bothers Huizinga is not that poetry might be "mere doodling," but that humans might be mere doodlers (Schiller 107). Anthropologist to the end, he sacrifices his aesthetics for his idea of human nature. Schiller, however, cannot and does not ignore the doodle objection; Huizinga merely misses the full course of the argument. Schiller interrogates himself, asking: "Is beauty not degraded by being made to consist of mere play and reduced to the level of those frivolous things which have always borne this name?" (105). Soon after, he writes: "With beauty man shall only play, and it is with beauty only that he shall play" (107). Perhaps the price that Schiller pays to keep play as an aesthetic prior-ity is to be obliged to regard the sort of play which is pragmatic and ugly as not really play at all. *Spieltrieb* is reserved only for the craftsman, the artist, and the philosopher—the real players in Schiller's world—only play as such deserves its name.

Matthias figures into all this not merely because of the affinities between his work and Schiller's, nor because of Huizinga's influence, but because Matthias also is testing play as an aesthetic—trying to see if it is ultimately useless. I think he survives or eludes both Huizinga's anthropology and Schiller's idealism. Matthias survives, in part, on poetry. Discursive prose "on the aesthetic" or "on the play-element" must eventually come to a point, say something, either by or about abstractions. Matthias's poetry, however, while it has the liberty of coming to a point, has the advantage often of serving as its own justification. It is not that Hooker's prose, or Huizinga's, or Schiller's, can't make the same claim, but that discursive prose is more likely to be designed for communication and utility than for purely aesthetic pleasure.

Hooker is right to call Matthias "both scribe and magician" (Hooker 105). "Double Derivation" comes very close to blurring the distinctions between subject and object, idea and poem, work and play. The poetry assumes a world-encompassing function; it works to play and plays to work, revels and reveals, illustrates and illumines. With poetic play, Matthias represents the human as player—"imagination on his sleeve"—and poetry as play. Thus while he writes as a chronicler, a constructor of fashion, a historian of war and death, of truth, of memory, the words play through the poem against even their own histories, making time, context, and culture a part of the carnival. From Max to Harry to James, the poem is at play.

The depth of Matthias's provisional aesthetic and the efficacy of play in a world of work becomes more apparent in the companion poem, "Clarifications for Robert Jacoby: 'Double Derivation . . .', Part IV, ll. 1–10; Part VII, ll. 1–15, 22–28." It begins:

> A moment ago, Robert, I thought I was watching
>   a wren, the one which nests
> By my window here, fly, dipping & rising,
>   across this field in Suffolk
> So like the one we used to play in, in Ohio,
>   when we were boys. But it was
> Really something that you, Dr Jacoby, would
>   be able to explain by pointing out
> To me in some expensive, opthalmological text
>   the proper Latin words.
>
> It was no wren (still less the mythological bird
>   I might have tried to make it)—
> But just defective vision: one of those spots
>   or floating motes before the eyes

That send one finally to a specialist. Not
    a feathered or a golden bird,
Nothing coming toward me in the early evening
    mist, just a flaw, as they say,
In the eye of the beholder.

Like? in a way?
    the flaw in the printer's eye
(the typesetter's, the proof-
    reader's) that produced and then
Let stand that famous line
    in Thomas Nashe's poem about the plague,
"Brightness falls from the air",
    when what he wrote was, thinking
Of old age and death, "Brightness,
    falls from the *hair*". (*SM* 78)

These stanzas focus on a pair of errors, one personal and the other historical. The first, a poet's misperception of a wren, is no wren, nor even an image of a wren, but rather a defect of vision, a speck in the poet's eye. This flaw is both recognized and (possibly) remedied by an adult, the poet's cousin and former playmate, Robert Jacoby. Jacoby "grew-up" to become a professional, an ophthalmologist, a worker rather than a player. The second error arrives in the third stanza and seems more akin in function to the second part of "Double Derivation"; it expands the subject beyond autobiography in the same way that part II of "Double Derivation" expands the subject beyond *The Great Tournament Roll*. Matthias introduces this error with some hesitation, "Like? in a way?" as if his metaphor might itself be mistaken, or perhaps fearing or hoping that the same might happen to one of his own poems as happened to Thomas Nashe's "A Litany in Time of Plague"—a printing error having turned an indifferent line into a great one. Though outside of the scope of the poet's childhood play, this act of misperception (like? the other) has achieved the same result as wit, imagination, and vision. Reader and poet are made to ask how this can be a great line when it was intended to describe brightness falling, like dandruff from the *hair*.

"Clarifications" begins with mistakes to challenge the aesthetics of play, the "carnival atmosphere" of "Double Derivation." If it does not doubt the act of imaginative play, it does relegate such play entirely to the world of the child, suggesting that it is lost after the child becomes an adult, a worker. At the outset, then, this poem is less a poem of *play* and more a poem of *work*. Here the adult doubts the legitimacy of the child's world, with its imaginary jousts and friends. Matthias, in self-critique, avoids shallow conclusions and (as I have suggested in regard to "Double Derivation") the dead ends of Huizinga's anthropological assumptions and Schiller's ideals.

Yet, before grappling with the function of work as self-critique in Matthias's "Clarifications," it is best to turn briefly to the autobiography, the story of a particular adulthood, and of past childishness, that makes this companion poem a "clarification." The poem claims to be written in Suffolk, though it remembers a childhood in Ohio. The poet used to play dress-up with his cousin Robert Jacoby. Both the boys had "professional" fathers. In addition, the poet's father was a Freemason, and in that role wore a cape and recited initiation chants in the kitchen. As the poem confesses, many of these details are preserved in a photograph of Matthias and Jacoby. The boys were unhappy; perhaps James had arrived, another cousin. James liked baseball and had a paper route at home in Columbus. The poet didn't like him. Jacoby, however, joined James and the fathers, the workers; he grew up and became a professional.

In "Clarifications" the ludic chant that drove "Double Derivation" gives way to the autobiographical, if flawed, eye of the poet looking back to his youth, not to Henry's court. What "Clarifications" clarifies is that "Double Derivation," though it seems to usurp the material of Henry's court, is actually as much an autobiographical poem as a historical one. In this poem we meet the cousins of part IV; we discover the actual photograph and the actual costumes that support the simile in part VII: "I reach for words as in a photograph / I reach for costumes in a trunk" (*SM* 76). In this poem we discover the source for:

> All the sticks & staves, the whole complicated
> paraphernalia accumulated to suggest
> Authentic weaponry and precise historical dates,
> not to mention exact geographical places. (*SM* 78–79)

Here we find the real artifacts, the real "ancient books" of "Double Derivation."

One should not, however, conclude too quickly, forcing a simple dichotomy on these poems. Though "Clarifications" *works*, recounting the past, correcting misperceptions, explaining the real facts that are often obscured in play, while "Double Derivation" *plays*, racing off into imaginary worlds, "Clarifications" is not merely a poem of work. It does not betray the play spirit that informs its parent poem by assuming adulthood—growing up while the world is watching. In fact, the poem concludes with a bold triumph of the ludic quality of poetry. The last image of the poem is an intricately layered product of the poet's continual reimagining. There is little in these lines that explicitly points to autobiography or history:

> A child plays with a stick. And jumps on both feet
>> imitating, since she sees it in the field
> (With a stick in its beak), a wren. She enters
>> the poem as she enters the field. I will
> Not see her again. She goes to her world of stick
>> and field and wren; I go to my world
> Of poem. She does not know it, and yet she is here:
>> here in the poem as surely as there
> In the field, in the dull evening light, in the world
>> of her imagining, where, as the mist descends,
> She is a wren.
>
> As I write that down she is leaving the field.
>> She goes to her house where her
> Father and mother argue incessantly, where
>> her brother is sick. In the house
> They are phoning a doctor. In the poem—
>> because I say so,
>>>> because I say once more
> That she enters the world of her imagining
>> where, as the mist descends,
> She is a wren—
>> She remains in the field. (*SM* 80–81)

In these lines all the optical distortions and poetic anxieties of preceding lines (and even by association the prior poem) are condensed in the imagined child at play, who herself pretends she is a wren, thereby both returning to and escaping from the poet's mote in the eye. The tournaments and dress-up games of "Double Derivation" are rescued from adult critique, the world of work, with these lines. Even the poet's own aging does not exile the poet from the world of play. Like Nashe's graying hair transformed, the poet's failing eyesight contributes to the poem's playfulness.

I do not want, however, to overgeneralize the predominance of play—especially by showing how the obviously less ludic poem succumbs to the child's world. This misemphasis is the same misemphasis that Hooker makes by opposing Marxism (a version of work) to play in Matthias's poetry. As much as Hooker is useful in allowing us to detect this unsteady antithesis, he also provides us with means by which to correct it. He writes about "26 June 1381 / 1977," another poem focusing (in part) on mistakes and accidents and playing upon historical detail—the peasant's revolt in Norfolk, Henry Despenser, Geoffrey Lidster (the executed leader), and some (mistakenly) damaged then (accidentally) recovered reredos: "While the sketch of the main connections is bound to sound clumsy, the poem lives in its imaginative recreation of key events and its meditation upon them" (100).[3] It is important, in fact, that Matthias "meditates" upon these "connections"; meditation, rather than evaluation (or even elaboration), allows Matthias, as Hooker contends, to write in paradox. In this, Hooker escapes his own oversimplified dichotomy, Marx to Huizinga. He writes:

> Matthias] is far from forgetting the claims of a reality that refuses transformation. In fact there is often a duality in his poems which prevents play from becoming merely indulgent when in terms of "Clarifications for Robert Jacoby," "reality itself" disturbs the "elaborate rituals." A fair summary of this important dimension of his work might be that the poet at his creative play makes poems that are themselves worlds, but makes them out of the stuff of reality, which exists independently of him, makes its own claims, questions the poet, and calls him to witness all that is not himself. (103)

Though Hooker gives us more than a "fair summary," I am more interested in the viability of Matthias's provisional aesthetic of play than in the problems of selfhood in his poetry. The two, however, as Hooker's remark implies, may be inseparable. For example, when in "Clarifications" Matthias writes of his cousin James, "He was reality / itself. I hated him" (80), is the adult poet reflecting (without ironic distance) upon "the real world" as such, thereby writing today as an uncomplicated poet of play? Or (as I believe) is the adult poet "reading" and accepting the playful world of his youth, though distanced and matured, strengthened by experience and work? In "Clarifications" Matthias's comments on "reality" follow his perusal of his own image in an old photograph. It is the expression on the boy Matthias's face to which the poet gives words: "Reality itself—I hat*ed* [it]." I emphasize the past tense of this hatred; Matthias has not escaped to imaginary worlds, nor has he embraced a "reality" called "work" or "Marxism." Instead, Matthias's

48   aesthetic aims to transcend both the adult work—"dragging passions . . . /
. . . to the bar"—and the child's indulgent play, what Huizinga calls "mere
doodling."

    As a way of concluding what one cannot conclude, I return to the last
lines of Matthias's "Clarifications." To set up his own conclusion Matthias
writes:

> [J]ust outside my window
> A child plays with a stick. And jumps on both feet
>   imitating, since she sees it in the field
> (With a stick in its beak), a wren. She enters
>   the poem as she enters the field. I will
> Not see her again. She goes to her world of stick
>   and field and wren; I go to my world
> Of poem. (*SM* 80–81)

Jacoby has gone to his world of work—Matthias writes, "[H]ow obvious / it
should have been!—to be professional, / Respectable, and eminent" (*SM* 79).
The girl who plays in the field "goes to her world of stick / and field and
wren." Matthias goes to his world of poem—not the world of work, not the
world of play. Though he says he will "not see her again," it is questionable
if he ever saw her in the first place. After all, she is as much a wren in the
field or a mote in the poet's eye as she is an actual girl. She is both inside and
outside the poet's adult self-consciousness in the same way that she is both
inside and outside the poet's troubled eyesight and the poet's poem. The
poet's world of poem is not exactly the child's world of the imagination—the
child is free to forget that her "Father and mother argue incessantly, [that] /
her brother is sick. [That] in the house / They are phoning a doctor" (*SM*
81). The adult poet does not forget; his poem reminds him of his mortality
even while it provides the child a reentry to the world of imagination. The
poem, unlike the works of adulthood and the carelessness of childhood, fully
embodies play without forgetting the responsibilities of mortality. Matthias
writes:

> In the poem—
>   because I say so,
>   because I say once more
> That she enters the world of her imagining
>   where, as the mist descends,
> She is a wren—
>   She remains in the field. (*SM* 81)

Notes

1. "Double Derivation" follows "Turns: Toward a Provisional Aesthetic and a Discipline" as one of "Three Poems on Poetics" in *Reading Old Friends*; the third is "Clarifications for Robert Jacoby." These poems first appeared in this sequence in *Turns* and again in *Northern Summer*.

2. One of these cousins, Robert Jacoby, appears in other poems, including this poem's companion piece and in "Edward," a poem focused on their war-shocked uncle.

3. In fact, this poem exhibits a technique familiar to Matthias, one poem commenting on another, exploring the subject across space and time, imagining the imagination, memorizing memory. "Double Derivation" and "Clarifications" fall into this category, as do "Turns," most of *Crossing*, and more recent poems, such as "Public Poem/Private Poem."

Works Cited

Anglo, Sidney. *The Great Tournament Roll of Westminster: A Collotype Reproduction of the Manuscript.* Oxford: Oxford University Press, 1968.

Hooker, Jeremy. "Crossings and Turns: The Poetry of John Matthias." In *The Presence of the Past: Essays on Modern British and American Poetry,* 97–105. Bridgend, Mid Glamorgan: Poetry Wales Press, 1987.

Huizinga, Johan. *Homo Ludens: A Study of the Play Element in Culture.* Boston: Beacon Press, 1950.

Matthias, John. *Crossing.* Chicago: Swallow, 1979.

———. *Northern Summer: New and Selected Poems.* Athens, Ohio: Swallow, 1984.

———. "Places and Poems: A Self-Reading and a Reading of the Self in the Romantic Context from Wordsworth to Parkman." In *Reading Old Friends: Essays, Reviews, and Poems on Poetics 1975–1990,* 39–63. Albany: State University of New York Press, 1992.

———. *Swimming at Midnight: Selected Shorter Poems.* Athens, Ohio: Swallow, 1995.

—*Turns.* Chicago: Swallow, 1975.

Mill, John Stuart. *Autobiography and Other Writings.* Ed. Jack Stillinger. Boston: Houghton Mifflin, 1969.

Schiller, Friedrich. *On the Aesthetic Education of Man.* Ed. and trans. Elizabeth M. Wilkinson and L. A. Willoughby. Oxford: Oxford University Press, 1967.

The Herald and the Void
A Tribute to John Matthias

IGOR WEBB

As a young man, John Matthias studied for a time with John Berryman. Matthias comes from Ohio; he was an undergraduate at Ohio State. The traces of Ohio that occasionally appear in Matthias's poems suggest to me a place rather like Sinclair Lewis's *Main Street*, if not altogether an emotional desert then a place of surface correctness and banality within which are repressed the rages of every emotional life.

But Berryman, in the late 1950s, must have seemed an amazing possibility for a young man dreaming of Poetry. Berryman, and Robert Lowell, and the others of his generation who were then seen as the main line, the magnetic main lode of American poetry insofar as a young writer was most likely to have perceived it—Berryman must have opened up for Matthias a vision of how he could get on paper his gifts, qualities that by their very nature his environment would have wished to deny.

Naturally, they were all a little crazy. They were all a little crazy, and the insistent, nervous connection between the gift for language and madness that "confessional" poetry pushed hard must have made an impression. In particular, the clichéd result of forcing emotion underground, that is, that it is likely to rush back out in unlikely ways, maybe as scream or nightmare, this apparent law of emotional life often asserts itself in Matthias's poetry.

Or let's say that this seems to me one clue, anyway, to the desire in many of Matthias's poems for tranquil, aimless, empty dreams, dreams he identifies with a redemptive language, a place in the soul that maybe he doesn't believe in but, insofar as he can believe in it, believes it is to be had not in our waking but in our dreaming.

One more point about Berryman. W. H. Auden's advice to the young man with an ambition to be a poet—that he should love not what he has to say, but words—captures nicely the obvious thrill of Matthias's poems from

the very start with the play and vocability of words. Here too I think Berryman must have had his effect, giving Matthias's natural bent a legitimizing
stylistic propulsion as he began to shape a style and to discover his voice.

> He doesn't sleep. He sits.
> He looks around.
> Afraid of quiet, bits
> Of dust and sound.
> He doesn't sleep. He sits
> And looks around.
> He was in love, he thinks.
> He cannot smile.
> He reads his early poems
> To learn his style.
> He doesn't write. He was
> In love. He thinks.
> He scribbles at a pad
> With colored inks.
>
> ("Portrait, Room and Dream," *B* 1)

Maybe there is something of the Cavalier poet too in Matthias, in the
special fondness for a grace that comes from elegance of phrasing. Who
knows exactly what this stanza means? The meaning is in the atmosphere,
which is created by the extreme simplicity of the language, the neatness of
phrasing, and the way that the distraction of the entranced protagonist is
transferred to writing for the certification of experience. The mesmerizing
power of words achieves in the poem a kind of dream-truth, an aesthetic formulation that serves in the stead of, or as the equivalent of, any other form
of meaning, since—at least for the poem's protagonist and its reader—the
obscurity of the poem's "subject" and the absence of rational thought or logical rhetoric render nil the possibility of any statement, or better of any construct, except an aesthetic one.

If it is important to Matthias, therefore, that art should triumph over
life, he is left with the vexing obstacle to this triumph, which is that the life
of art is at once our common life and also a chosen marginal vantage point
or (dis)location.

In the work of David Jones, Matthias discovered a way to get at the—
for want of something better, let's call them historical—facts of being. I don't
know when Matthias first came across Jones's grand, epic poems, but it was
certainly by the mid-1960s.

52   Jones's solution to a number of typical modernist problems, as well as his identification of those problems, are neatly spelled out in his prefaces to *In Parenthesis* and *The Anathemata*.

In Parenthesis is about the First World War. Of his experience as a soldier, Jones writes: "I suppose at no time did one so much live with a consciousness of the past, the very remote, and the more immediate and trivial past, both superficially and more subtly"(xi). This states with admirable economy the consequence for the imagination of the accident of finding oneself in the middle of a world-historical event. Although you could say that any moment in any life that somehow gets jostled into self-consciousness might have the same consequences for the individual's imagination, it turns out to matter whether the disruption is actually of enormous human resonance—for example, having fought in the First World War—or not. I will say more about this later.

The Anathemata, harder going for the reader, can be said to be about the very problem of composition it seeks to overcome.

> [M]ost now [1952] see that in the nineteenth century, Western Man moved across a rubicon . . . . something which was affecting the entire world of sacrament and sign. (15–16)

> [O]ne of [the poet's] main problems . . . concerns the validity and availability of his images. It is precisely this validity and availability that constitutes his greatest problem in the present culture-situation. (23)

> If the poet writes "wood" what are the chances that the Wood of the Cross will be evoked? (23)

> The mental associations, liaisons, meanderings to and fro, "ambivalences," asides, sprawl of pattern [of *The Anathemata*] . . . these thought trains . . . have been as often as not initially set in motion . . . by some action or word, something seen or heard, during the liturgy. (134)

Here Jones expands his focus from considerations of the consequence for the imagination of personal involvement in a huge event to consideration of the complex implications for the imagination of a cultural, albeit historically specific, *condition*. He is, again, admirably economical in describing that condition, as well as the dilemma it creates for a poet. His poem is at once an extremely ambitious attempt to reflect on, and to redeem, the condition that is the poem's subject, and to provide in its writing a solution to the difficulties that the condition raises for a poet as a writer.

And so, choosing a passage from *The Anathemata* at random, here is a glimpse of Jones's reflections and of his method:

> When on a leafy morning
>   late in June
> against the white wattles
>   he numbers his own.
>
> As do they
>   taught of the herdsman's *Ordinale*
> and following the immemorial *numeri*
> who say:
>   Yan, tyan, tethera, methera, pimp
> sethera, lethera, hovera, dovera, dick. (71)

This way of doing things, as much as Berryman's, clearly had a terrific impact on Matthias's own way of doing things. I am not a great fan of this kind of poetry, and maybe for that reason I find *In Parenthesis,* with its more easily graspable subject, its obvious rootedness and more readily identifiable allusions, a poem of greater power. Whatever else there is to say about *In Parenthesis,* everything in the poem depends on the fact that the poet was a soldier on the fields of Flanders. The poem may roam from the trivial immediate past to the canonical and historically momentous past, and may blend the personal and the impersonal, but everything, as I have said, depends on the rootedness of the poem in the soil, the real soil, of the battlefields of the First World War. The modernist's self-conscious and even ideological insistence on "the objective" is not a distraction in *Parenthesis.* The same cannot be said of *The Anathemata.* And no doubt for this reason I wish Matthias had not ventured as much as he has along the route of *The Anathemata.*

For my purposes here I will make two observations. First, the self-consciousness about problems of composition, the knowing effort to reconstitute a sacral aura around words, images, concepts admittedly "problematic," seems an archaic concern of the modernist generation. From the vantage point of the latter half of the twentieth century, after the Holocaust and the camps, the solution that Jones articulates and enacts appears as tending too much to the arcane, too much to the resource of sacred texts, and so perhaps in this context, simply mistaken. A better aesthetic for our century, for my money, is that of the "Polish poets"—Milosz, Rozewicz, Herbert, Szymborska, a group that could be extended to Holub from Bohemia, Primo Levi from Italy, and most recently Virginia Hamilton Adair from the United States. This is a poetry in the plain style, a poetry whose voluminous extirpated personal experience is universal, not as a result of some solution in composition of aesthetic program or rerouting of obscure sources—although this is also a poetry that has had to figure out how anything could be said in the face of the unspeakable—but because each of these poets has had to sort out in an especially unforgiving fashion what the dead might forgive the living for rendering gracefully. Only under such dispensation have these poets tried to say anything at all. And then, it has turned out, in the work of these writers, that the past—trivial and immediate, monumental and canonical— is a seed germinating in the present and quite capable of flowering.

Second, Jones, another Anglo-Catholic, points out that for him the crossed rubicon demarcates a very long period of cultural coherence and density on one side, and a modernity of incoherence and rapid change, indeed of desacralization, on the other. What is lost, so it is argued, is the permeating totality of faith. For the person stranded as a believer in an age when the word *wood* is unlikely to evoke anything more than nostalgia for "antique" French country furniture, the *aesthetic* problem is precisely how to reinfuse the sacred into language and form. But from the point of view of this person, a *religious* point of view, the task is more or less impossible, just as the cause is a lost cause. At best the poem may accelerate the everyday into the spiritual, but there is no way any longer to transubstitute the spiritual into the religious.

Now Matthias is not an Anglo-Catholic but a secular guy like most of us. His religion is poetry.[1] But the lost magnetism of religion itself, that old-style religion, is a kind of weak field within which his poems are constructed. He is acutely sensitive to the disturbance and dislocation, that is to say the lack of points of reference, of contemporary life. It is as if we carry with us on our way through the thickets of experience a rather beautiful compass inherited from a great-grandfather—except that out there the north pole has lost its magnetic pull. Who can be surprised, therefore, by the disoriented quality of so many of Matthias's poems? The poems register that something has happened or is happening, but the poet seems to have no way of understanding that happening. Still, the longing for meaning drives and troubles him. If rendered just as it is in its cultural moment, experience in Matthias's poems often as not resembles that banal Ohio of his childhood. The energy of the poem's reconstruction of experience comes therefore from a shift in context—whether that means to bring into the present the distant or immediate past, or one or another liturgy, or an acceleration of viewpoint something like the opening shots of the film *Blue Velvet.*

But none of this works very well, except poem by poem, and no construct stays whole very long. Little wonder that the poet desires a repose that is aimless, vacant, timeless:

> . . . all I want to do is drift on lang
> uage into dream. . . .
>   ("Northern Summer," *BA* 100)

But since lang/uage is broken (if for no other reasons than those David Jones gives)—its ability to name with authority, to register terror and the void and to overcome them by its means; that is, through an art so magical that it transforms the poet's fictions into belief (however evanescent)—none of this can be relied on.

In one of his early poems, Matthias writes,

> Verbum dictum factum, god in
> the vowels of the earth
>   ("Poem in Three Parts," *B* 86)

and he would like to assume this as a bardic axiom, which it may be, so long as one is not tempted to deny that poetry makes nothing happen, a temptation that is hard for any poet to withstand.

Let me now retrace the route of my remarks by returning to another early poem, set in Ohio, "Swimming at Midnight," which is a good place to begin reading Matthias. The poem is about loss of innocence. The poet is skinny-dipping at midnight with a girl in a forbidden place, an old quarry. This water is an archetype, Conrad's destructive element, with its fascinations, joys, and dangers. The poem's question is the innocent, awed question of the young:

> can there truly
> be any danger? (*B* 21)

In Matthias's poems there are many dangers. In "Swimming at Midnight" the entry into experience occurs under the eyes of the cops, parents, moon and stars, and of the watchful young couple eyeing each other. Close to sex is disgust, rage, anxiety, myth, and death. In any event, the principle at work here, and in all of Matthias's writing, is Conrad's "in the destructive element

56 immerse." Later the dangers are more subtle, oblique, and deadly than the danger of drowning that poses its threat in this early poem. The joys are harder won. In Matthias's work it is unusual for everyday pleasure to trigger reflection. Experience is always dangerous. This is the "Berryman" motif in Matthias's work, in the sense that if the banal Ohio-surface of things is non-experience, the real life is the repressed life. Many of Matthias's poems depict the immersion into this other, real life, which can be a dangerous business either because what's encountered is something loose and raging, or because the encounter itself is profoundly disorienting, or because the language or form aren't adequate to handle the danger. These poems enact the struggle for sanity in the face of various extremities: a recurrent but unspecified and only suggested danger, then, is madness. As in Berryman, this madness is an inventive (if dangerous) energy; but for this mad energy also to yield knowledge requires the shaman's redemptive magic in the form of an ordered poetic language. It is to the method of David Jones that Matthias turns for a restorative discipline against the disorientation and dislocation of dangerous experience.

I think this trajectory is well exemplified in the sequence "Northern Summer." The poem's epigraph is the last stanza of a poem by the Swedish poet Göran Sonnevi that Matthias and Göran Printz-Påhlson have translated. The whole of Sonnevi's poem, however, needs to be quoted:

a
Void which falls out of void, transparent,
cones, hemispheres,
fall through empty space.
Thoughtform, crescent, trajectory.

b
However relevant!
In the infinite freedom I can
keep back, give my notes resilience, in relation
to each other, to my whole body, which also
falls in infinity through empty space:
e.g.
Charlie Parker's solo in *Night in Tunisia* on May 15th 1953.

c
The flight of sentimentality through empty space.
Through its elliptical hole

an heraldic blackbird's
black wings, yellow beak, round eyes, with the yellow
ring, which defines its inner empty
space.
　　　("Void which falls out of void . . . ," *Contemporary Swedish Poetry* 67)

The nine sections of "Northern Summer" each depart from something in Sonnevi's poem and then, as Matthias's poem circles or immerses itself in its subjects, take in a complex present and past history. Matthias makes allusion to some of that history in a not-too-helpful footnote, but a full reading of the poem would require a venture into texts that I have not attempted. My intention is less to explicate "Northern Summer" than to show how it illustrates my reading of Matthias's work as a whole.

One theme in Sonnevi's poem is the relation between the void and the willful void-filling act of writing. But where Sonnevi insists on his location in an infinite emptiness, Matthias opens his sequence in a space he chooses to crowd with words and events. (Incidentally, these words and events are of the sort that Matthias has resorted to right from the start as the true signifiers of our historical, imaginative, and psychological experience—castles, kings, queens, princes, ladies, peasants, traitors, executioners, murderers, and bards.)

Language
moving upon consequence
Consequence
upon a language: Flight
of an heraldic bird
through space that is inhabited. (*BA* 94)

The location is Scotland, and Matthias settles into the poem a whole host of Scotsmen past and present, across the terrain of classes (there is a castle and a mine), including Stevenson, Scott, Macpherson, Robert Adam, John Knox, Hume, et al.—and also, Matthias. The latter seeks his place among these others.

I live between the castle and the coal mine
in a folly.

. . . .

. . . I am guest
of both the present and the past. (*BA* 94–95)

58   In the sixth section of the poem, a personal recollection intrudes:

> I hear my mother's voice reading Stevenson—
> or is it Scott? Someone's wandering lost
> among the heather. I must be eight or nine.
> I know I should be reading this myself,
> but when I read the words the voice I hear
> ceases to be hers. . . .
>   There is a space
> I have not learned to fill
> somewhere between printed marks and sounds
> and I am lost in some way too
> among the heather, frightened of the distances
> when all I want to do is drift on lang
> uage into dream. . . . (*BA* 100)

The appearance in Matthias's poems of those closest to him tends to fol-low the pattern above, whether he is writing of his mother, his father, his children. The rendering is of loss or failure to keep hold; what ought to have been known and intimate in life is sought instead in art. The real people, as the poems portray them, seem not quite to touch, and in art they slip from each other. In the painful and often wrenching poem for his daughter Cynouai, the tactfulness, indirectness, and heuristic inventiveness of play at once binds and holds apart the poem's family: the poet's father, the poet, and his daughter.

> [W]e don't say: "I'm here in Shelford"
> or: "You're riding"
> but: "I pretend to be in Shelford"
> and "You play at
> going riding." Nor does one say:
> "I hear your father's dead",
> but this instead:
> "I understand your father
> has played dying." (*C* 22)

Knowing what poetry cannot do, as Matthias beautifully recounts in "Epi-logue from a New Home," he nevertheless tries again and again to do it:

> Ah, Toby, what a thing to ask me.
>   To write a poem about your husband,

> Dead from cancer, whom I never really knew.
>   And you were perfectly serious . . .
>
>   .   .   .   .
>
>   . . . That ancient charge: to
>   read whatever evidence in lives or lies appears,
> In stones or bells—transform, transfigure then whatever
>   comedy, catastrophe or crime, and thus
>   Return the earth, thus redeem the time. (*T* 107, 108)

An enormous burden for the bard who was more priest than poet, how can a secular contemporary achieve it, for whom

>   Void . . . falls out of void;

for whom the round globe of his flesh, his whole body, also
    falls in infinity through empty space?

For whom every age, not only Macpherson's, is

>   . . . an age
>   of forgeries & fakes: Pretenders
>   old and young, gothic ruins in the garden (*BA* 104)

for whom enemies are friends, treason loyalty, and the words of our congress, our memorials, our bliss and epiphany slippery as fish and no more or less reliable than our enemy-friends and loyal treason.

    Herein may lie the use of David Jones's method. And yet for all the "opening up [of] 'unshared backgrounds'" Matthias finds himself, in the concluding section of "Northern Summer," staring "quizzically" at what he has written,

>   at language that has used me one more time (*BA* 107)

with a kind of robust attention at the difference between him and those many others whose lives, and writings, and visions have informed his own route without yielding a conclusion. All he has learned from David Jones leaves him short of belief. For Jones the void *was* redeemed: his meanderings and reconstructions began and ended in liturgy. For Matthias and Sonnevi, the heraldic is at best an instrument of irony, noting what place and time have vouchsafed with significance through a human activity and imaginative assertion that is nonetheless finally absurd. The poet's persistence is brave and lovely; his graceful achievements, like those heraldic

black wings, yellow beak,
round eyes . . .

appear a moment, pause

& disappear. (*BA* 109)

Note

1. In a letter to the editor of January 10, 1997, Matthias says that in fact at one point while working on *David Jones: Man and Poet* and beginning "A Compostela Diptych" he came very near to converting to Catholicism. [Ed.]

Works Cited

Jones, David. *The Anethemata.* London: Faber, 1952.
———. *In Parentheses.* New York: Viking, 1961.
Matthias, John. *Bucyrus.* Chicago: Swallow, 1970.
Matthias, John, and Göran Printz-Påhlson, eds. *Contemporary Swedish Poetry.* Chicago: Swallow, 1980.
Walton, James, ed. *The Space Between: Poets from Notre Dame, 1950–1990.* Notre Dame: University of Notre Dame Press, 1991.

The Shorter Poems of John Matthias

MICHAEL BARRETT

"This one fetches more light."
—DAVID JONES, "The Old Quarry"

I. The Stone Quarry
Near my grandparents' home at the outskirts of town,
a stone quarry was established, then abandoned,
nearly a hundred and fifty years ago.
—JOHN MATTHIAS, "Swimming at Midnight"

These are the opening words of one of John Matthias's first-published poems: his career opens at an excavation site.[1]

The poem grows out of the italicized information, a text that grounds it in a particular place. The poem writes that place in relation to law:

(Nobody comes here: nobody looks:
nobody watches us watching us
watch.) Except the police.

The poem opens that place in relation to sex and death—the body:

(Feel the
water's mouth and its hands, feel
them imitate mine

. . . .
can people
really have drowned?

. . . .

> well, dust to dust,
> a curious notion

The poem uses that place as field for invention:
> What
> young forms of vegetation emerge.
> What new colors of light. (*SM* 3)

In this essay I will attempt an anatomy of the work which evolves at this site. I read Matthias first along a vertical axis—as a transologist of place. The poet's psyche and soma are included in the excavation. I then read the character of his career along a horizontal axis—a traverse across stiles, a path struck by a pilgrim.

II. Transology

Matthias writes in relation to two strategies that may be called "archeological": the modernist and the postmodern. I'll use David Jones and Michel Foucault, respectively, to represent each strategy. David Jones believes the poet incarnates cultural signs, "[Poetry] can be said to be occupied with the embodiment and expression of the mythus and deposits compromising that cultural complex" (preface to *The Anathemata* 19). The postmodern, rather than expressing an origin or telos, displays the relations that would name signs as *deposits, myth,* or *culture.* "Archeology" organizes that display and Foucault describes its method in *The Archeology of Knowledge.*

The modernist poet attempts to return signs to their original context. Foucault traces signs to "a *lack,* which, instead of being inside seems to be correlative with this field and to play a role in the determination of its very existence" (110). Jones offers signs as sacrifice to God; Foucault follows signs to a slippery, pervasive will to power that flows out of absence.

Matthias shares Jones's absolute commitment to craft, the masonry that builds culture. The care with which he sculpts sign into poem reflects Jones's belief that art is "the perfecting of the process by which all sort of ends are made possible" ("Art and Sacrament" 151). But like Foucault, Matthias critiques the ends which ideology builds *as* culture. Intertextuality in his poems meets the requirement of archaeology as articulated by Foucault, "It is nothing more than a rewriting: that is, in the preserved form of exteriority, a regulated transformation of what has already been written" (139–40).

"E. P. in Crawfordsville" demonstrates both the modernist and postmodern strategies in Matthias. The poem contains multiple discourses; it is dialogic, intertextual, postmodern—Pound writing "Cino," Pound writing to Marianne Moore (figured as Athena), Eliot questioning Pound, "What asked Possum more / than once, does Ezra Pound / Believe?" The poem is a series of modernist signs put into postmodern play.

Matthias locates himself in a modernist lineage when answering Eliot's question, "What does Pound believe?"

> In light. In
> light from the beginning,
> in gardens of the sun— (*SM* 31)

The postmodern urge to contextualize is temporarily suppressed by a modernist telos articulated aesthetically—the light in form, the light in the line. Next, Matthias recontextualizes in the specificity of place. Metaphysical light is grounded in a precise geographic site—133 miles southwest of South Bend—Crawfordsville, Indiana, city of Wabash College, which fired Pound, the village explainer. Crawfordsville, where Pound's career begins, provides Matthias with the figure that evokes Pound's end: he is lack-land Cino, singing away on his way:

> having sung & sung the sun
> for thirty years in
> every kind of city, light
> converging into one
>
> great ball of crystal
> silent as some Hoosier
> Presbyterian at prayer
> along the Wabash. (*SM* 31–32)

Light is given its final presence in a silent, formal prayer and the prayer's demographics, "Hoosier Presbyterian." Light hovers over a site regulated by discourse, but it shines on a specific place. Where Foucault tracks discourse into the dark of lack, a poet like Matthias traces discourse to the light of place. The great ball of crystal shines beside a river that's running right now.

Rx.: Map

Foucault maps the surface where signs emerge as discourse; he organizes the relations from which signs emerge—not their meaning. Foucault's map allows us to read cultural objects as signs of "discourse" rather than "culture."

64   Matthias needs a more complex map. The map must accurately represent discourse, but it also requires a legend for signs that mark the place from which discourse emerges. In the first way, the map is a representation of a representation; in the second, the map is a representation of something that cannot be represented—the "thisness" of the "here." Perhaps the recipe for this kind of map is a poem.

"Homing Poem" is one such map:

> An acre, a rod,
> and eleven
> perches of land
>
> .   .   .   .   .   .
>
> The stone walls
> The thirteen towers
>
> .   .   .   .   .   .
>
> An acre, a rod,
> and eleven
> perches of land
>
> .   .   .   .   .   .
>
> The stone walls
> The thirteen towers (T 40)

The destination, home, is left unsigned, but we are led to it by a series of signs. "Acre" and "rod" are derived from the Anglo-Saxon, "perch" from the Middle English. The location of the poem is in the derivation of its words. The words come to measure the land they grow out of. England signified; England measured.

England is the ideal place for archaeology—it has been measured and remeasured across a range of discourses. England is the prime meridian; our clocks are set there. There's Stonehenge and Offa's Dyke, Hadrian's Wall, and Marylebone Station. "Sign the whole anatomy of Britain," says Jones in the preface to *The Anathemata*. It is always already assigned, reassigned, and remeasured:

> to his north and east
> the boundary was the sea
> iron pikes were driven
> in the Waveney and Yare
> to his west the fenlands
> forest to the south
> and south as well

> between the trees and fens
>   at Wandlebury here
> along a narrow belt of chalk
>   no more than eight
> miles wide
>   ("East Anglian Poem," *T* 97–98)

The poem grows out of place, a field for invention. The poet composes by setting to play a variety of discourses that intersect at a physical place. The physical reality of location, mapped but never fully represented, enables the poet to create out of the stuff of the world. Matthias recalls in "Clarifications for Robert Jacoby" (*T* 85–89) the way historical deposits serve the imagination as prompts:

> . . . the whole complicated
>   paraphernalia accumulated to suggest
> Authentic weaponry and precise historical dates,
>   not to mention exact geographical places . . .

Poetry is assisted by its orientation to the physical site where discourse emerges. Indeed, so is criticism. In his introduction to *Introducing David Jones,* Matthias orients his location in England to his analysis of Jones:

> a mile away from where I write runs the Roman road to Colchester, down which Boudicca traveled to sack the Empire's British capital. On the same road, in the opposite direction, traveled the Christian religion out of Roman Jerusalem. Over my head fly the American jets from Bentwaters Air Base. (18)

This precise location—assigned England—is the measure of David Jones and the window through which Matthias peers in writing:

> There's a plague pit
>   just to the edge of the village.
> Above it, now mostly covered with grass
>   a runway for B-17s: (American
> Pilots back from industrial targets). Tribes
>   gathered under my window;
> They'd sack an imperial town: I'll wave
>   to my wife at the end of the Roman road.
>   ("Epilogue from a New Home: For Toby Barkan," *T* 104)

66   Both Jones and Matthias exploit the way temporality is stacked in place. "Here" gathers sediments of time—Roman road, aircraft runway, Anglo-Saxon boundary. The liminal properties of place allow multiple temporalities to become contemporaneous: time is nearly recovered in being uncovered. We might be tempted to say that poetry does this as well. "Epilogue from a New Home" chronicles the poem's failure to answer "that ancient charge":

> to read whatever evidence in lives or lies appears,
> In stones or bells—transform, transfigure then whatever
> comedy, catastrophe or crime, and thus
> Return the earth, thus redeem the time. (*T* 108)

Instead of a lively portrait of the dead husband Toby Barkan asks for, the poet responds with a detailed portrait of where he *is,* "I'm but half oriented here. I'm digging down."

Rx.: Bibliography

Foucault notes that texts are produced to become documents, evidence of the "continuing identity" (129) of a culture. Once produced, though, historians transform documents, through an attempt to "memorize" the past that produces them, into monuments. Monuments are the provenance of archaeology.

Certainly Jones excavates texts as monuments: "Part of my task has been to allow myself to be directed by motifs gathered together from such sources as have by accident been available to me and to make a work out of those mixed data" (preface to *The Anathemata* 9).

Archaeology returns the monument to the document. A cursory list of texts gathered around this essay bears the point out: deposits can be found in texts that are already archeological, documents of monuments:

Anglo, Sidney. *The Great Tournament Roll of Westminster: A Collotype Reproduction of the Manuscript.* Oxford: Oxford University Press, 1968.

Binns, Alison. "Pre-Reformation Dedications to St. Oswald in England and Scotland: A Gazetteer." In *Oswald: Northumbrian King to European Saint,* ed. Claire Stancliffe and Eric Cambridge. Stamford: Paul Watkins, 1995.

A Catalogue of Celtic Ornamental Metalwork in the British Isles c. AD *400–1200.* Oxford: British Archeological Reports, 1993.

Ekwall, E. *The Place-Names of Lancaster.* Manchester: The University Press, 1922.

Gelling, Margaret. *The Place-Names of Shropshire.* Nottingham: English Place Name Society, 1990.

Margary, Ivan. *Roman Roads in Britain.* London: J. Baker, 1973.

Payne, F. G. *Guide to the Collection of Samplers and Embroideries.* Cardiff: National Museum of Wales, 1939.

The Proposed Demolition of Nineteen City Churches. P. S. King and Son.

Seaborne, Malcolm. *Celtic Crosses of Britain and Ireland.* Shire: Princes Resborough, 1989.

These texts are the measure of Great Britain: roads, churches, embroidery, place-names, dedications, windows, crosses. They are catalogs of cultural signs remade into poetry. In such poems, a text is a place that recalls the place it textualizes.

Monuments function in Jones as *anamnesis*—a remembering, a "re-presenting" before God an event in the past so that it becomes *"here and now operative by its effects"* (quoted in a note to "Mabinog's Liturgy"—see Matthias, *Selected Works of David Jones* 193 n. 41). Foucault believes that, since the "here and now" are merely ciphers, we should not restore texts to their original meaning, but watch them lose it:

> not to awaken texts from their present sleep, and, by reciting the marks still legible on their surface, to rediscover the flash of their birth; on the contrary, [our] function is to follow them through their sleep. (123)

What Foucault describes here isn't really archeological. What interests Foucault is not the first principles that archeological analysis can recover, but the transitions between the constituents of discourse that analysis reveals. Foucault is not interested in the *archiao* of the logos, but in the protean signification of logos over time. *Transology* is a word more suited to the process Foucault describes. This distinction also serves as the difference between Jones and Matthias. Jones is a poet of archaeology, art grounded in the identity of sacrament. Matthias is a poet of transology: he narrates the wending among discourses. "Turns" illustrates this most profoundly.

The movement among discourses in "Turns" includes: the turn in verse, transitions in language over space, transitions in language over time, development in narrative and the transformation of literary history. "Turns" also acknowledges, with postmodern self-consciousness, the political implication of any such account. The poet is bound on a trip between productive determination and creative obscurity, where each aesthetic move is weighed by a countervailing political analysis:

> While a relationship of cause and effect is established between obscure and lucid organizations emerging from the division of labour and the consequent dialectical evolution of social reality, such becomes, we know, increasingly separated from the actual productive function of society, from sleep. (*SM* 52)

"Turns" is a traverse across a divide of ideology and its slick surface, language. Appropriately, travel is at the heart of the poem:

> All day long it rains. He travels
> All day long. Wiping water from
> His eyes: and twenty miles? and
> Twenty miles? (*SM* 50)

Like "Homing Poem," movement here is rendered linguistically. Theory and poetry weave in and out of the winding path of the poem. "Turns" is a topographic map detailing a postmodern pass. How does a poet write in our critical age, determined as it is to read discourse into the ground? Matthias's solution is to inscribe both epistemology and aesthetic play on a kinetic surface—the poem constantly changes location and is rewritten at each new site. The poet is on a pilgrimage from discourse to discourse. This is a difficult, unnerving process, akin to the trek Foucault proposed:

> instead of providing a basis for what already exits, instead of going over with bold strokes lines that have already been sketched, instead of finding reassurance in this return and final confirmation, instead of completing the blessed circle that announces, after innumerable stratagems and as many nights, that all is saved, one is forced to advance beyond familiar territory, far from the certainties from which one is accustomed, towards an as yet uncharted land and unforeseeable conclusion. (39)

More than twenty years after it first appeared, "Turns" remains a cogent way to articulate the issues that face a poet in the postmodern age. "Turns" opens a space for poetry in a theory-crowded world. The poet opens this space by tracking the trails of signs under the pressure of change—at a certain place.

Rx.: Cart

In "Turns," language is a cart. The cart carries the good, if it is a good cart. It certainly is good at carrying "a pakke of bokes." But what a cart carries, how much reference it ought to bear, is an important question to answer. As he does with historical and political material, Matthias responds by casting the rules onto the surface of the poem, and then includes them as part of the play (which carries those rules to the field of the nonreferential):

> So destination or Destiny: *Quere He Was Boun!*
> And yet to introduce the antecedent place.
> Restrictive clause; sense of the referent noun.
> A tilted cart is a cart with an awning. (*SM* 49)

"Turns" is a poem that interrogates its own efficacy and then turns that interrogation into its efficacy—poetic play weakens the determination of discourse. Whether we accept the figure of the schoolmaster as poet or pedagogue, we understand that the pressure of such interrogation has consequences:

> the schoolmaster is forever an intermediary: the shape of his life is determined by the nature of society: the nature of his art seeks to determine the shape of society by administering to its nature. And intermediacy ultimately tells (1) on his sex life (2) on his health. (*SM* 52)

This last turn is critical to John Matthias's work. He adds "self" to "discourse" and "place." The self is another place where discourse gathers. "26 June 1381 / 1977" shows this. First Matthias excavates a number of strata: the Peasant's revolt; Engels on England; a tour guide's commentary on reredos; Edmund Burke's response to revolution; peasant rhymes and political epistles. Then he follows signs mined from that excavation to their necessary end, at the self's next, living step into place:

> And us with our heads still on our necks?
> With books on our laps,

> Stupid or Giddy, gawking—
> Us with the eyes still in their sockets
>
>
> And tongues still in our mouths—
> Where do we travel, where
>
> Do we think we can go—
> All of us, now, staff, of one, life? (*SM* 47)

III. On the path/ology

The concupiscence of ears
JOHN MATTHIAS, "A Compostela Diptych"

What is the "place" of the "self"? The body. We sign the body in discourse, but like physical place, the sign is lighted from a living place. As he does with signs of place, Matthias transforms signs of the body into poetry. This includes discourse gathered from the hospital and clinic. But we don't have to travel with Foucault in order to excavate systems of relations from the hospital and clinic. We can look to "a man who was [his] teacher once," a poet important to Matthias: John Berryman.

Berryman, who reviewed *The Anathemata* for the *New York Times Book Review*, shares with Jones a belief in sacrifice. Berryman offers his body and mind: psyche and soma. To be sure, a few of his altars are profane, but the poem accepts his sacrifice anyway:

> A hemorrhage of his left ear on Good Friday—
> so help me Jesus—then made funny too
> the other, further one.
> There must have been a bit. Sheets scrubbed away
> soon all but three nails. (*Dreamsongs* 128)

Matthias recognizes this sacrifice in Plath, "A girl / who died for poetry" ("Part of an Answer," *T* 21), as well.

Matthias, though, is more circumspect in his offering. The body is never given completely or madly. It is presented as collateral in social relations. "Elegy for Clara" describes an ear infection similar to Berryman's:

> In the Winter, my poor red ears aflame,
> infected by the complications
> of February strep, I heard
> the gossips saying, "Terrible! it's awful"
> . . . .
> They said the man who'd married you
> demanded you do "awful things"
> and so you left him (*C* 18)

Later, Clara dies young. The narrator, having met her only briefly as a youth, writes an elegy. The narrator's ear infection is the apologia for his lament. His interest in Clara is related to his illness: sex and death intersect at the body's site.

In "Elegy for Clara," the body is presented to show the stake the poet has in writing the poem. "Turns," on the other hand, makes it clear that society has a stake in the poet's body. The poet takes the signs of that stake, written as medical discourse, and translates them back into the poem:

> Dull ache in his hip is probably gout.
> Painful nodes of calcium—(neck & in the ears).
> Palpitations, flutters. Stones in the gland. (*SM* 49)

This is reminiscent of a passage from *The Cantos,* where Pound offers diagnosis as part of the discourse of Renaissance Italy:

> Audivimus venerabilis in Xti frateres ac dilectissimi
> filii . . . (stone in his bladder
>   testibus idoneis) (Canto X)

"Turns" argues that the social order taxes the health of the poet. Certainly, the health of Berryman's Henry can be seen as an economic condition. In a depression, he takes stock and finds himself bankrupt. In *Dreamsongs,* Henry's sex life and health bear the dis-ease of his alienation:

> O empty bottle. Hey: an empty girl.
> Fill 'er up, pal.
> I cough my proper blood. (*Dreamsongs* 250)

> Penniless, ill, abroad, Henry lay skew
> to Henry's American fate, which was to be well,
> have money in the bank
> & be at home. (*Dreamsongs* 314)

Matthias's "If Not a Technical Song American" is a critique of the postin-
dustrial society that would fix Henry's fate. The critique includes the political, the economic, and the pathological:

> Cachectic, cachectic.
> Heart rate grossly irregular.
> Jugular venous distention.
> Systolic expansile pulse.
>
> Right ventricular lift.
> Left ventricular tap.
> Murmur along the sternal borders.
> Pulmonary edema.
>
> All piezometers installed
> In the boreholes.
> Static and dynamic
> Cone penetration made. (*T* 25)

The piezometer in the poem measures the pressure in some obscure
engineering project, as well as the stress of contemporary society on a heart.
The discourse of cardiology and technocracy are linked, as critique and verbal texture, in aesthetic play. Furthermore, the tradition of inscribing social
symbols onto the body, society's tattoo, is also recalled. The tattoos in this
case are texts of internal fault lines, the tape of an EKG, the list of ailments
on an autopsy.

"Spokesman to Bailiff, 1349: Plague" explores the historical relation
between the economic and the pathological. It shows the plague reclaiming,
by the force of its own law, the body of society:

> Let no one approach us.
> Here we make an end
> Of ceremony, custom.

Not surprisingly, the ground for the excavation is fourteenth-century England, where the class system and the plague spread at the same site:

> A birth of avarice and
>
> Powers oblique, unfathomed.
> Leave us bread & ointments.
> Free from obligations, we
> Leave the world to its wealth. (*T* 68)

Yet, short of the moment when affliction claims the body entirely, the body remains what we can offer. The narrator in "For John, After His Visit: Suffolk, Fall" offers his medical history as a sign of empathy. He opens his heart, not its sentiment, but its discourse, as a sign of friendship:

> Hiking on a treadmill
> at the clinic, I tested badly on a
> Winter afternoon myself. I traded polysyllables
> with cardiologists who hooked me to their
> Apparatus, checked my pressures, watched my blips
> on television screens, and asked me all
> The secrets of my heart. . . . (*SM* 18)

This gesture is counterpoised to the narrator's father, who held his secrets close to the vest. The narrator could only read the father's signs obliquely:

> As a child I saw irregularities signaled
> in the pulsings of distended veins
> Running up his temples and across his wrists:
> more affaires de coeur. . . .(*SM* 19)

Even in death the father withholds:

> . . . no dream, even, did he
> send me in my mourning time, no news
> At all. . . .

The sign the father does send marks the son's body. The son inherits the father's illness:

> The bombs my father planted
> Go off in my bones; I am weak
> ("Halfdream in Sickness," *T* 20)

The stare inward necessary to invent from the body's weaknesses distracts the poet from living. Later in the poem this produces guilt:

> Lovely
> The women who gather around: my
>
> Daughters, but nothing to do.
> Love is too hard . . .

The inertia brought on by illness is countermanded by the force of time, where relationships call us out of the solitary confinement of our bodies.

Matthias's use of the discourse of the body, ultimately, recognizes this and recovers a concern for the living from death-drawn confessional verse. Beyond the politics and poetics of the body is a place with its own strong claim, ethos. There, the father leaves his legacy as his body's movement through time—his action, his attention to the living:

> this awkward body
> which, despite its ills,
> manages to do extraordinary simple things
> like walk through heaths of gorse
> with you before the others are awake
> ("Poem for Cynouai," *C* 25)

IV. Across the Stile

The poet, though trailing chains of EKGs, is able to walk through fields of time with his daughter. He is able to act. "Act" is a place in the continuous present, site of the body's sacrament, where what we do and what it means are bound. Here, language moving upon consequence is not the written, but the lived.

What *is* writing's reference to living? For Matthias, as for only the best poets, THIS IS THE QUESTION WE MUST ALWAYS RAISE. Such a question raises anxiety:

> Then I read some simple, perfect
> Poems by someone else and wonder once again
> if ever I'll be any good at
> Writing or at living.
> ("On Lake Michigan—I," *C* 12)

Although a poem is an act, there are differences between writing and living. We revise what we write; we can't revise what we've lived (except, of course, when we write). It is easy to make a boast (in words), "and we do propose to lead a better life this year than last"; it is more difficult to figure out how to complete the deed (in acts), "though we do not tell ourselves exactly how" ("The Mihail Lermontov Poems: Nine," *C* 118). We craft logos; we act ethos. Poiein/praxis; the text/the act.

Matthias's poetry frequently shows the demands of text at odds with the demands of living. In "Edward" the father strikes at the poet through his books:

> . . . when I had no pity, when I couldn't
> stand to hear him say like any eight-year-old:
> *You made me cry,* and when he said just audibly
> enough for me to hear: *Go back to your*
> *God-damned books. (SM* 12)

In "After Years Away" (*SM* 150) the son reads while the father dies, "he lay dying . . . while I sat reading books." The father rings a bell in the poem; the mother listens, "she heard the ringing here" while the son makes texture, "as I said *Gnostic, Bogomil.*" The bell is the sound outside the writing.

The poem "On a Slip of the Tongue," a brief Steinian exercise, relates Imogen Holst's slip when speaking of her late father. Matthias transforms *sound* into *wound* there:

> A sound, a sound
> was in his mind
>
> At the very end
> of his life
>
> But what was found
> in his life & wound
>
> At the very end
> of his mind? (*SM* 23)

The poem prepares the reader for the past participle of the verb "to wind" that rhymes with "found" and "sound." But the word "wound" asserts itself—as the rift in Holst's speech, as the pain of a child, misspeaking and missing her father's death:

> And though I drove one January night
> Through freezing rain into Ohio—
> And though I hurried,
> Seeking the words of the dying—
> All I found was a turning circle of women,
> All I heard was the lamentation of survivors.
>   ("Survivors," *T* 18)

The poet as son sounds an important ethical note in Matthias's work. The tone is elegiac: *this is past, this is lost.* When the poet changes subjects,

76   though, he begins to listen for the bell's tone. We read this in the last four
lines of "Fathers":

> what son will talk
> to me? What stranger
> take my daughter from
> a daughter's house? (*T* 15)

Now the ethical concern has changed. The poet as father anxiously listens. The figure of the daughter, who takes different names—"Cynouai,"
"Laura," "my daughter"—is the call of haeccitas. Haeccitas may be consti-
tuted in discourse, but what it points out is brought by time and set before
us as the present. Attendance to the craft of living is its appeal.

> Sunday, then. In Trumpington. And nearby bells.
> My daughter runs among the village graves
> this foggy January morning of her early youth
> as I lie late in bed
> and watch her from my window.
> ("My Youngest Daughter," *SM* 64)

The daughter plays in a field of bells and memorials. The poet is in a father's
bed, watching. He tells her to stop holding her breath, not to dissuade her
from superstition but to reinforce his faith:

> I tell her
> not to hold her breath in graveyards.
> Watching her red coat become a gaudy blur
> against the brilliant hoarfrost,
> I realize I'm holding mine.

The daughter disappears out of the poem. Her disappearance is the poem's
act; it reclaims the poet's attention while the daughter plays elsewhere. This
stops the father's breath—word without expiration, poem.

The sublime "Poem for Cynouai" attempts to capture the quiddity of
the daughter in a living, breathing word:

> a world
> we both believe in
> and can sometimes share:—
> where names are properties of things
> they name, where stones
> are animate and wilful, trees

cry out in storms, and compulsive
repetition of the efficacious formulae
will get us each his way. (*SM* 82)

But the words get put away while the father goes to work. By the time
the father returns to the words as poet, the daughter has changed. The poem's
"out / of date." The poet updates it with texts, efficacious formulae: tags from
Shakespeare, Piaget, the asobase-Kotoba, Lars Norén, Berryman, Hass, and
Wordsworth. The poet is back in his books, excavating logos, while the
daughter rides around outside.

The poet recognizes that time passes between the poem and the daughter outside: "it feels as if you've been away two years." Not inside the text,
where the words wait, but in the poem's writing. It felt like two years, *"as he
wrote his poem,"* I mean to say, while the daughter played.

The daughter's art heals the father, who once was son unable to heal the
father:

When my father finished playing dying
I began.
You gave me pictures
which I held against a wound. (84)

The wound of the father is healed by the daughter's attention. The cure is
only transitory because, although the poet attends to the daughter in the
poem, the daughter outside continues to move forward in time:

How I stumbled after you with memories & books.
How far ahead you rode. How very
quickly all the books
were closed. (85)

The bookman closes the book, a mimesis of attending to the outside.
But because this poem remembers its origin as writing, because that writing
is a memory of the daughter who rides on, the language remains elegiac,
Wordsworthian. The poet continues to mine texture to find the linguistic
formula that will help him attend to the daughter, on both sides of the stile.

I say *flank, hock, heel, hoof;*
I say *fetlock, gaskin, thigh, stifle, sheath.* (88)

While the daughter grows, the father learns. The daughter "is the father of
the man." In living, the daughter calls, "attend to life." In the poem, the

daughter is "the one who rides away." "Poem for Cynouai" traces the complexities in writing and living. We read there a father attempting to act a life with the care of a poet crafting the text.

Appropriately, in the poem, a book has the last word:

> And the Manual says: *It is interesting to assess the progress and accuracy of the training by riding a circle on ground upon which the imprint of the horse's hoofs can be seen. . . .* (89)

The poem ends as the daughter winds silently around. Time rides away. And we follow out of the poem. This is why Matthias is a poet of ethos: his making points to the doing left undone by the made.

V. Three Pilgrims

The Poet

We are called out of the book to attend to life. "The aesthetic" and "the theoretic," knocked around in a brawl with "circumstance" and "choice," become "the ethic."

Critical inquiry informs but does not conduct "this difficult business of living." The ethical makes its demand at the first step outside criticism into time. Yet we depend on criticism to analyze acts that have already been done. For Matthias, materialist criticism serves as a way to prepare for the ethical and to read past acts for their ethical value: Adorno, Trotsky, Babeuf, Marx, Engels, Nachaev, Bakunin, Lassalle, Lenin, all make appearances in his poems. Matthias uses materialism as critique but recognizes that critique is not a sufficient condition for the ethical.

This sets him apart from many postmodern thinkers in literature. Criticism whose lineage extends from Foucault's *Archeology of Knowledge*—cultural studies, neo-Marxism, New Historicism, call it what you will—uses materialism as a way to prepare a rhetoric: materialism as rhetorical hermeneutic. This practice ignores the agonizing realization (or uncompromising call to action) that materialist determination brings. Indeed, it ignores the place Foucault was thinking near the end of his life, when, in *The Care of the Self* and other work, he began to consider more closely the relationship between the aesthetic and ethos.

Matthias does engage in class analysis with an assumption of materialist determination, but showing the relationship between the means of production and cultural artifact is not his sole aim. If we use the late poet Thomas

McGrath's distinction between tactical poetry (poetry as progressive ideological propaganda) and strategic poetry (poetry that changes consciousness), it
is apparent that Matthias has been mainly writing strategic verse since the
collection *Bucyrus*.

One strategy is to position the poem as the synthesis between two tactics: the poet as ideologue and the poet as artist/magician/clown. This dialectic is captured in the strange bedfellows of Matthias's poems: Lenin/Prospero,
Brecht/Bothwell, Margery Kempe/Will Kemp. Earnest politics interrogates
the playful aesthetic: "While you are singing/who will carry your burden?"
("While You Are Singing," *SM* 135).

But Matthias reformulates this question in a later poem, changing its
effect:

> But while you carry
> your burden who will sing your song?
> Those deciphering your codes,
> grinning at your misdemeanors, those
> who made their case & sent you
> into exile.
>
> ("Public Poem," *SM* 137)

"Public Poem" answers the legitimate challenge in "While You Are
Singing." The subordinate clause "While you are singing" becomes the inde-
pendent clause "Who will sing your song?" Social labor becomes subordinate
to song because ideology that organizes social labor frequently ends as
oppressive and censorious.

"Three Around a Revolution" ends the account of a speech by a political revolutionary with an attack of alliteration and assonance, "palfrey, palindrome, pailing, palinode, palisade." Ironic play undercuts the political function of speech. This does not erase the original political challenge: language
just offers another account.

Because language always offers another account, the role of the poet is
never stable or determined. Matthias's strategy is to move from role to role.
This is reflected in the diversity of his work—lyrics, ballads, odes, found
poems, syllabics, collage, nonsyntactic poems, long poems. In a single poem
we may encounter the confessional, the modernist, the postmodern. Matthias establishes, then transforms. This is the arc of his career: carry a *pakke
of bokes,* then let circumstance reread them. The poet becomes a pilgrim—
orient by text, orient by place, move on by way of aesthetic transformation,
move on by way of living. And because Matthias's political epistemology

gains its vocabulary from the left, he avoids the reactionary pitfalls of Eliot, Pound, and Jones. Matthias is "the scolemayster" who "levande was the toun." The town he leaves is modernism, the village already explained.

Although he moves beyond modernism, Matthias is not an unrepentant postmodern. Happily, his poetry isn't driven by postmodernism's cure and curse, irony. The ironic has a presence but does not determine the poet's relationship to his material. The poet interrogates his own life with the same serious intelligence with which he questions culture.

Matthias's shorter poems are dispatches from a pilgrim on the road. We can find the poet traveling in the company of Langland, Chaucer, Pound, and Jones there, a goliard walking with Duncan:

> Cycles pass him. Cars pass him.
> Busses full of tourists . . .
> Dauncers & Minstrels, Drunkards
> And Theeves. Whooremaisters,
> Tossepottes; Maskers, Fencers
> And Rogues; Cutpurses, Blasphemers
> Counterfaite Egyptions . . .
> ("Turns," *T* 74)

The poet gathers from each text, each place, each other, each self, what is necessary to go on, and then he does.

The Word

Because reference bears meaning across signs, language can allow the poet to move without changing places. The wide range of reference in Matthias's poetry broadens the dimensions of what is being referred to, whether it's the word's own materiality or a specific, nominated site. Language opens place; reference changes place; language and reference travel in time:

> Langland has it "keured"
> John of Mandeville "coured"
> Wycliffe "keuered"
>
> But "covert" in Arimathaea
> ("Turns," *T* 72)

In "Two Ladies" (*C* 38–40) we track the change in nomination of Queen Ethelreda to Saint Audrey. The name traces a mini-history of medieval

Northumbria: *Aethilthryth, Etheldredaea, Etheldreda, Audrey.* Her name and what it means culturally are translated—carried from one place to the next, from one people to the next—over time.

Matthias himself gets translated "Into Cyrillic":

> I'm tangled in Cyrillic and I cannot
> find my way. They'll help me.
> They'll lead me on. I say I want to be
> led out of this, away. (*SM* 144)

Matthias also explores how the poet can change place, reference, or circumstance with language. This is language used as magic, the poet's hermetic privilege. Matthias's use of Gnostic linguistic practices recalls some Language Writing and is supported by techniques from *The Stein Era*. Although a Gnostic epistemology is just one discourse among many in Matthias, it is given succinct and powerful expression in "Six for Michael Anania":

> Qualities tend
> To Perfection.
>
> We may assist. (*T* 61)

Matthias understands, though, that hermetic language is sometimes used as a counterfeit means. Ask the alchemists who translated Hermes Trismegistus:

> antiquorum aegyptiorum
> oh, ... imitatus . . .
> ("Turns," *T* 74)

Translation is the operative word in Matthias as *Incarnation* or *Transubstantiation* is in Jones. Language is the translation of the signified into the signifier. Ethics is the translation of intention into act. Poetry is the record of such transactions and their aporias—what reference carries inside, what reference cannot bear. Seeking the perfect translation—word for the thing, intention for act, poem for being—is akin to the search for the Holy Grail, which is always already covert. Poetry should point this out:

> With Joseph of Arimathaea, turns: to elliptically gloss.
> ("Turns," *T* 77)

The Body

As language fails in allowing "a word for word defense," a perfect translation, so do our bodies fail in time. We see the brightness fall from our hair, acts, and words. Dust to dust is no longer a curious notion; it is our condition. Dust is the sanctuary where the body's pilgrimage ends. So the body is *res* presented to *being,* a thing set aside, anathemata, what we offer as we move through time.

Pilgrimage is a familiar metaphor for this travel. Pilgrimage means leaving the text on the way across another stile, another poem, another year. Out of the text, in the world, the daughter, or any other calls, and demands that we act. We read these acts in retrospect like a text and attempt to revise them, like a passage in a poem, before our next call.

If the pilgrimage is a sacred one, we try to move beyond the previous text to a site we can, upon reaching/reading, profess. There, we can offer a weakening signifier to a receding signified and hope we are translated into something higher, greater than who we know we are. Santiago functions as a metaphor for this place in Matthias. The body will be presented there, a site where the poet desires:

> Santiago, call him what you like,
> Son of Thunder, Good Saint Jacques, The Fisherman,
>
> Or whoever really lies there—
> hermit, heretic, shaman healer with no name—
> will somehow make us whole.
>
> ("Dedication to a Cycle of Poems . . . ," *SM* 154)

This desire takes its place beside the discourse, maps, medical charts, and daughters in Matthias's poetry. It turns signs out from their cultural and personal significance and sets them wending as well. This desire reveals the sacramental space in language, not in determining but in opening. This desire precedes the poem's making. This desire is why John Matthias is a profound poet, a religious poet.

Note

1. Blake says, "The production of our youth and our mature age is equal in all essential points." Though I begin with a quote from one of Matthias's first published poems and end on the last poem from the Swallow collection, I read all the work as part of one long poem. The discussion is thematic, not chronological.

Works Cited

Berryman, John. *The Dreamsongs.* New York: Farrar, Straus and Giroux, 1969.

Eliot, T. S. *The Collected Poems and Plays.* New York: Harcourt, Brace, 1962.

Foucault, Michel. *The Archeology of Knowledge.* New York: Pantheon Books, 1972.

Jones, David. *The Anathemata.* London: Faber, 1952.

———. "Art and Sacrament." In *Epoch and Artist.* New York: Chilmark Press, 1959.

———. *The Roman Quarry.* London: Agenda Editions, 1981.

Matthias, John. *Beltane at Aphelion.* Chicago: Swallow, 1995.

———. *Bucyrus.* Chicago: Swallow, 1970.

———. *Crossing.* Chicago: Swallow, 1979.

———. *Swimming at Midnight.* Chicago: Swallow, 1995.

———. *Turns.* Chicago: Swallow, 1975.

———, ed. *Introducing David Jones.* London: Faber and Faber, 1980.

———, ed. *Selected Works of David Jones.* Orono and Cardiff: National Poetry Foundation/University of Wales Press, 1992.

Pound, Ezra. *The Cantos.* New York: New Directions, 1956.

———. *Personae.* New York: New Directions, 1971.

❧ You Keep the Cart before the Horse, See, So They See It Moving but They Don't Know How

PETER MICHELSON

O n a panel discussing his work, the novelist William S. Burroughs was posed a question the metaphysics of which surpassed his patience. That, he said, was a question as incomprehensible as modern poetry. Coming from the author of *Naked Lunch,* second perhaps only to *Finnegans Wake* in contrived opacity, I thought his indictment of modern poetry on that score somewhat cheeky. Still, he's got a lot of company. A few seasons back the Boulder Music Festival orchestra performed Bach's Brandenburg Concertos to a more than full house. The audience had a good time and likewise the reviewers. A week later, performing Hindemith, Weill, and Webern, the same orchestra played to a house half empty. Why? An answer came in a symposium, where the ostensible subject was completely eclipsed by the familiarly querulous question, "Why is modern art so hard to understand?" No matter how heroically the panelists attempted to address the historical and aesthetic rationale for atonality, abstraction, and other modern tendencies, the audience replied grumpily, "That's all very well, *but why . . . ?*"

And later I myself, a worker in the modern art industry, remarked to my wife that Webern's Symphony, Op. 21, about five minutes in duration, was a bit hard to take. She replied that it was a formally perfect symphony. That may be, I said, but it sounds like a pointillist painting done by a stoned abstract expressionist. She found that a bit hard to take but observed that Seurat invented pointillism, shattering color and line into specks the viewer's eye must reassemble, under the influence of Chevreul's chemical and Maxwell's physical theories on the nature of light. Similarly, she said, it is quite likely that Webern and his teacher Schönberg were aware of relativity theory, and by 1928, when Webern composed his symphony, Bohr and Heisenberg had added complementarity and indeterminacy to the cacophony of things. Not to mention, she added, the situation in *Mitteleuropa,* which was hardly conducive to melodic imaginings. She also had a theory about the abstract expressionists and Henry Luce, which is an intriguing but altogether different story.

What she was getting at, of course, is the artist's engagement with the vexious extension of uncertainty into our lives. The poet is as bemused as anyone else in the face of proliferating perversities, though the fact is often masked by his or her aggressive posture contrary to whatever the prevailing wisdom might be. But even that stance, once a sign of keeping the faith, whatever that was, is not so reliable anymore. What do you do with Dr. Death, for example, or whether to pull the plug on your ailing grandmother, to say nothing of her "duty to die" according to Governor Lamm? From Socrates to rather recently, facilitated suicide was justifiably regarded with moral skepticism, as was killing people for their own good. And where do you stand on the Navajo and Hopi in Arizona, Hutus and Tutsis in Burundi, Protestants and Catholics in Ireland, Tamils and Sinhalese in Sri Lanka, Serbs and Bosnians and Croats in whatchamacallit, etc.? It all defies definitiveness. Which is where the artist enters. An artist's value is in direct proportion to how his or her work gives testimony of engagement with, as distinct from resolution of, life, and clarifies it. Along the way he or she will probably have to entertain us, which I mean in the old Horatian sense. Though that, like clarity, does not necessarily mean we'll be put at ease. The best entertainment clarifies, but the best clarification may be abrasive and make us edgy, as uncertainty is wont to do.

John Matthias is as uncertain as anybody in the house and more engaging with that incapacity than most. Only John Ashbery, who has pushed the relentlessly indeterminate meditation about as far as it needs to go, competes with him on that score. But then Matthias (hereafter designated J.M., as the surname implies an objectivity to which I don't pretend, given my long and close association with him, and the use of John would be a bit cozy) takes a different turn with his art. He does not exploit uncertainty, he wears it like the birthday suit it is. Nor, to be clear, am I talking about some guy who can't make up his mind. Anyone who has read his prose—on the function of Jones or Bunting or MacDiarmid in British poetry, for example—or his incisively reasoned selections for his *23 Modern British Poets,* or certain verses, passages in "Clarifications for Robert Jacoby" for example—knows that, where it's appropriate, he is quite decisive. I am talking about the author of the image from "The Stefan Batory Poems," "Prospero whispers in one ear / and Lenin in the other"(*C* 82). It has been so astutely illustrated by Douglas Kinsey in the Swedish bilingual edition, *Bathory & Lermontov,* that I think of it as a portrait. J.M., hands wringing and eyes popping with quandariness, is caught between the croonings of the old magician over his left shoulder and the reasonings of the old historical materialist over the right. He'd prefer submission to Prospero, but he's too conscientious to ignore Lenin. And the politics of left and right, here, are precise.

J.M. is a poetic instance of what in baseball parlance used to be called "rabbit ears." This meant a batter who did not block out verbal abuse from opposing fans or players but heard everything and just might be rattled by discouraging words. It did not mean the batter couldn't hit; I believe Ted Williams was supposed to have rabbit ears, or maybe it was Jackie Robinson. It only meant that he heard you, and you might get a rise. In fact, the more dangerous the hitter the more frantically shrill the chatter. In my sandlot league days a heavy hitter got epithets from the opposing infield that make Arab *hija,* insult verses, sound like high-tea conversation. While the image of J.M. at the bat may, as the poet says, give us pause, the fact is that he has rabbit ears *and* he can hit.

Which brings me to an anecdote that illuminates the obvious connection between rabbit ears and literacy. A couple of years before John Berryman's death, when I was still teaching with J.M. at Notre Dame, Berryman unexpectedly arrived two days before the reading he was scheduled to give. J.M., who had arranged the reading, fearful lest two idle days leave the notoriously drink-indulgent Berryman too besotted to read, rushed to his hotel and engaged him in forty-eight consecutive hours of discourse on any subject he could muster to keep Jack Barleycorn from suborning the bard—reminiscences of his teenage attendance on Berryman at a Utah writers conference, the history of new criticism, of prosody, of old criticism, Mistress Bradstreet, the Bloomsbury group, Longinus, Robert Lowell, near-eastern kenning, Robert Penn Warren, far-eastern kenning, whatever he had in his arsenal and several dozen things he didn't. It was a performance of improvisational genius. And it worked. Berryman was not only sober but happy about it—charmed, gracious, and upbeat, this man capable of boorish meanness. He gave J.M. his reward, a brilliant reading. After the reading, when Berryman was at last able to slake his thirst, he leaned to me confidentially and said, "John is a most interesting man," I quote him exactly, "but he is *very* literary."

Well, yes, John *is* literary. And also resourceful, as I trust Berryman now appreciates. And as he hears everything, so does he read. And it all becomes grist for his mill, again as productive as any and more so than most. Verse is his primary articulation, occasional prose notwithstanding, and anything goes into it—the high, the low, the expository, quotidian, cerebral, or lyrical. But if I am a fan of his art, I am moved perhaps even more so by his project, wherein poetry is integrated with the passage of a highly individualized consciousness through time and space, as Joyce said of life, everyday day after day.

I. Turns Toward a Poetics

But it is of course his hitting technique that makes his consciousness matter. A convenient poem, because it is J.M.'s analog of Pound's "Mauberley" sequence, for noting how these qualities coalesce into a poetics is "Turns: Toward a Provisional Aesthetic and a Discipline." Its centrality is suggested by the fact that he has reprinted it in several contexts, most conspicuously in his prose book, *Reading Old Friends* (191–95), as the lead piece under the rubric of "poetics." For starters there is that indeterminate *provisional* in the title, and not just that but the tentative *toward* the tentative provisional. Because, while the ultimate aesthetic experience might be lofting a fat pitch out of the park, you can never tell when an inside fastball might tempt you to slash a too-hot-to-handle grounder past that particularly obnoxious third baseman. Circumstances, as the Marxians say, also affect poetics. Characteristically, J.M. teases us through seven relatively short sections with enigmatic bits and images that naturally do not *add up* to anything so imposing as an *aesthetic,* however provisional. Because he tends to write not arithmetically but in some algebraic calculus, where these glyphs are known and those are not; in the dynamics of their interaction their symbolic values shift and merge, inviting us to aesthetically perceive fluid relationships and keep the reduction to meaning on a back burner.

The poem, for example, begins with what appears to be a fourteenth-century narrative of a "scolemayster" (*Reading Old Friends* 191) packing up and leaving town. The language, on the backside cusp of Middle English, sustains its authentic ring for thirteen lines, in which we're told little else— not the schoolmaster's name, the reason for his leaving (though we are told that "sary of hit seemed everuch one"), nor "quere he was boun" (191). The last nine lines focus oddly on the schoolmaster's only article of "combraunce," "(saf a pakke of bokes)," a musical instrument called a "symphonye" (192). It occasions what seems to be a bemusingly trivial fact of the

88 man's biography. And there the image stops, the image of an apparently respected schoolmaster leaving town in a covered horsecart encumbered only by some books and an instrument he'd expected to learn to play, "But the zele woned (zele woned). / He neuer couthe ani scylle" (191).

It's an arresting image. Not the least of its contemplative appeal is its language, at once exotic and familiar. The homely nostalgia of the scene itself is intriguing as much for what it leaves out as for what it includes. But the language is the thing, an interactive *tour de force* teasing us with a few arcane words *(levande, sary, quyt, ferien)* in an otherwise recognizable grammatology. The three repetitions and the free-verse format imply that this is not a Middle English poem *verbatim,* but possibly one touched up for contemporary occasion. The verse itself has a modernist precision somewhat different from what we expect in Middle English rhyming metrics. To this point, we're having a good time with this talking Chaucer doll the poet's set on its uncertain road, so what's next? The narrative disappears, its language and image serving as emblem to the poem in the manner of Quarles, or perhaps more like Herbert's "The Pulley" and similar poems, a verbal rather than graphic image upon which the poem "turns."

The remaining six sections circle elliptically around the emblem like musing quarks in a linguistic proton. Each turn evokes some aspect of poetry and its disciplines. The language and verse, including the discontinuous pastiche of images, are distinctly contemporary but looking backward. In the brief second section, for example, a philological image flashes the French connection with middle and modern English and then modulates to poetics with its last word, "defense," which I take in the sense of apologia, as in Sidney's *Apologie,* alternately called the *Defence of Poesy.* The next section, invoking the "Mauberley" dialectic between historicity and neurasthenic contemporaneousness, punctuates with more philology via the poets. This foregrounds poetics, augmented by an elliptical allegory where the schoolmaster becomes an analog of the poet—bound for "Destiny" with the "personal luggage" of those old signs of poesy, the harp and pipe and that "symphonye" again, as well as the word, that "pakke of bokes." We begin to sense a poetics here that mandates historical attentions to those who've gone before, to the medium, to the tools of craft, to the heft of the personal luggage necessary for the trip. Where to? Well, it's an uncertain prospect, but *destiny* is about all one can say. Keep your eyes open and your ear to the tongue, "'covert' in Arimathaea" (192).

As for the rigors of the poesy road, amplified in sections IV, V, and VI, the poet can expect to be marginalized "at the edge / of the toun" when he or she is not "levande" it altogether (191). There will be aches and pains, to say nothing of palpitations and gall stones, oh yes, gall aplenty . And that old temptation, *in vino veritas*. But J.M. can tell you from experience that, whatever Berryman's muse was, it was not booze. Stick to the prescriptions of "the good-doing doctor": a "covert cart" for the journey, a "bibliography," and a "map" (192). Some roads are less traveled, but none are untraveled. Moreover, there's the old mind/body problem, not always so highbrow as it appears. You've got to keep your "instrument" disciplined. As they say in boot camp: "This is my rifle / That is my gun / This one's for fighting / That one's for fun." Then, too, your zeal wanes ("zele wones") as you're "torn between disgust & hope," fearing you "never couthe ani scylle," your art devolving to antiquarian mimicry, as Plato would have it. And it rains. And everyone passes you in their slick new "units," as the car salesmen say; especially galling are the "tourists" and the "Counterfaite Egyptions" (193), who win all the prizes.

In the final section J.M.'s tone gets edgy, as if he suspects our zele wones for having to putter together his bits of language, bits of narrative, image, arcane allusion, purloined verse, etc., into a very provisional whole, as if our panting brains might be objecting that all this carries rabbit ears, literacy, and uncertainty beyond what the *belle lettristic* laws allow. And he's not altogether wrong. But I, for one, am still reading. Nonetheless, the brief verse opening projects an image of casting pearls before swine, its irony not quite blunting its edge. Then he turns to prose, as if perhaps our dullness isn't up to verse. The first four sentences, two of them French, despite the echo of the earlier "belles" (193) are as elusive as ever. The next contemplates apology, but the flinty syntax withdraws the offer, instead almost inadvertently evoking the earlier "defense." Defensively, he begins to explicate the emblem narrative and the philology of its language. Abruptly he shifts to King Alfred's principles of translation; King Alfred, the foreman of a translating gang that effected a West Saxon renaissance in the ninth century. Translation seems to have become a trope for poetry, elusive or mysterious or something female even when it is beautiful (as he says in the French above) and faithful (as he says in section II). And the tone adopts Pound's most exasperated prose pose, grousing about having to explain something so elementary as poetics. It's "simple," J.M. says for the third time in the paragraph (194): you roast the moon with the sun, a daily occurrence, and you get the word, *if,* of course, *if.* . . .

The next paragraph begins with an irony that drips contempt for, if not us—after all we're still reading—then at least that symposium audience so querulous about the indeterminacy of modern art. Then, abruptly again, he returns to the schoolmaster. Only now, in the poem's final stretch, do we discover, or at any rate those of us no quicker than I am, that the emblem narrative has been lifted directly from Hardy's *Jude the Obscure*. Not in Hardy's language, obviously, because J.M. has been traveling backward in both time and language, toting Hardy's nineteenth-century tragedy back to a fourteenth-century lingo that he has reinvented for a twentieth-century reader. At one level, of course, it is sheer *tour de force,* but bravura as such is not all that pertinent to J.M.'s poetics. If he *purse seines* historical seas, plucking more or less obscure items from his catch (Joseph of Arimathaea, Cursor Mundi, or, one of my favorites, those "Counterfaite Egyptions") and giving them conspicuous display, they have a function. In this case there are at least two. One is to make what Pound called an *homage.* When Pound published the first part of "Homage to Sextus Properitus" in *Poetry,* a reviewer who was a classics scholar complained that it was an inaccurate translation. Pound replied that the various *contemporary* references in the poem should have cued anyone with their wits about them that it was *not* a translation but just what its title indicated, an homage. Similarly, J.M. pays homage to Hardy, for starters, who was so vilified as an immoralist for *Jude the Obscure* that he gave up novel writing in disgust. Even the immortals suffer the rigors of the road.

But the homage extends beyond Hardy, also of course a poet, to the language and its history, the indispensable items of the poet's luggage. Hence the invocation of Langland, Mandeville, Wycliffe, etc., those early shapers of the English word and its poetics. Poetry doesn't just *happen,* it's *made,* and its making evolves. As late as Shakespeare's time, poets felt obliged to defend English as a fit language for high art, credible as Dante's "Vulgar" Italian, which itself had to be wrested from the aesthetic authoritarianism of Latin. Even Pound thought Renaissance England, including Shakespeare, was little more than insular marginalia to true aesthetic, meaning Mediterranean, civilization. People have been laboring long in the vineyard, and J.M.'s antiquing of Hardy's narrative reminds us of and hones that discipline as a necessary question of poetics.

The function of J.M.'s linguistic bravado is structural, to make the emblem so vivid that it, "the given . . . truly equivalent" (*T* 71), shines through and informs the collage overlays of the rest of the poem. It unifies a poem threatened by the centrifugal energy of what J.M. himself elsewhere describes as his "attraction to quotation, commentary, pastiche" ("The Stefan Batory Poems," *C* 81). To effect this, of course, the passage has to glitter like real gold right up to the point where the alchemical trickery is revealed. "A neat linguistic exercise," indeed, which is to say "a discipline" (*T* 76). If one wanted to analyze the difference between lyric and narrative strategies, one could do so much worse than comparing J.M.'s "exercise" with the prose from which it derives. J.M.'s "symphonye," for example, is a "cottage piano" too bulky to be moved in Hardy. But for J.M.'s purposes the instrument must be both a "combraunce" and portable, imperative in what will become the poet's "personal luggage." For Hardy, the troublesome piano serves primarily to introduce Jude, his protagonist. For J.M., the "symphonye" serves the figural transmutation of the "scolemayster" into the poet, his emblem.

As for the moment of the trick's revelation, it "makes the art available to the vulgar," which is us (76). But, while it's a cute turn, it also "turns: to elliptically gloss" us (77) in the context of Dante's transmutation of the base vernacular into the precious language of poetry. It's precious in a couple of senses, of course, as J.M. turns the joke on himself as well as us. To this point the poem has featured Prospero's legerdemain. Now J.M. tries to turn to Lenin, but Prospero won't let go. He induces J.M. to parody Marxian critics, absurdly entangling them in their own distinctly unaesthetic language. He also, again, extends the joke to himself by including his own schoolmaster in the parody. This compounds the uncertainty by having the effect of partially redeeming the Marxian analysis while undermining its pompous high seriousness. So, if we're peppered with J.M.'s provisional aesthetic and discipline, we're also reminded that a sense of humor salts its indeterminacy, to say nothing of Prospero's magic show. You keep the cart before the horse, see, so they can see it moving but they don't see how.

In another context, J.M. has said, "the cost to a contemporary of not sufficiently understanding his tradition will be conventionality and mannerism" (*Reading Old Friends* 171). This applies across the board. What is inadequate luggage for the poet's trip into uncertainty is likewise so for his or her reader. I have dwelt on "Turns" because its poetic—in its historical consciousness, its elliptical musing of the obscure into sudden lucidities, and its linguistic enterprise—is not only bedrock Matthias but also reveals the demands serious art makes on author and audience alike, eschewing conventional gratifications in order to address elusive realities. Elliptical complexities are only an aesthetic virtue when that's what it takes. In committing prose on "Turns" I've articulated more semantic bridges than I do when I read it. But sooner or later one does articulate, interpret if you will, semantic bridges. And we know nowadays that we all make our meanings, like archeologists trying to assemble scattered shards. The more we're obliged to do so, the more intimately we come to know them, our ignorance notwithstanding. That, I think, is the epistemological premise of J.M.'s fragmentational poetics. He ranges from that pole to, say, the elegiac directness of "Fathers," which explores his fatherhood in relation to his wife's father and his own, concluding,

> And if I'd known them,
> either one, if I'm a
> sailor now and should
>
> have been a judge,
> what son will talk
> to me? What stranger
> take my daughter from
> a daughter's house? (*T* 16)

But the more thematically ambitious the poem, the more J.M. inclines to kaleidoscopic structures.

II. Poem in Three Parts

At their extreme of elliptical pastiche, J.M.'s poetics depend maximally on aesthetic, as distinct from semantic, apprehension. One must keep the faith that, as in "Turns," eventually the apparent hermeticism will tip its hand. "Poem in Three Parts" (*B* 67–98), which at about its midpoint asks, "Hermes Trismegistos, where?" (85), is such a work in spades. Because the poem is dedicated to me, and because J.M. has publicly included my *Pacific Plainsong* among its "influences" ("Afterword," *BA* 194), there are some who suppose I have the inside dope. In fact, what I can add to J.M.'s notes is minimal if pertinent. In 1968, when both those works were being written, J.M. and I were probably more preoccupied with antiwar politics and agitation than with poetics. But there was a connection. The Vietnam war induced many of us to see the present in terms of the past. I, for example, saw the war as an extension of the nineteenth-century American doctrine of "manifest destiny." While the Vietnam war as such makes only a couple of cameo appearances in *Pacific Plainsong,* my sense of the correlation between the two historical periods is pervasive in that work about the nineteenth-century Indian wars. At the time in question, when J.M. and I were in our closest proximity and association, I was experimenting with voices, both those from history (for example, Gen. O. O. Howard, Chief Joseph) and those from nineteenth-century historians (for example, H. H. Bancroft). The idea, obvious enough, was that those historical voices, their actual language, could be made to reflect the present or, depending on perspective, the future. One way that I attempted to make them do so was by repetition, looping words and phrases with slight variations that gave the original language a distinctly different music and resonance. J.M. was both intrigued by and encouraging of my explorations, enough so that he was stimulated to his own address to history and its voices. That there were already luminous models, such as Stein, Pound, H.D., and Olson, is another matter. We were desperate, youngish guys in parlous times, when you don't look primarily to literary models. You tend to refashion, if not reinvent, the wheel for your own purposes. That stimulus, I think, is the extent of my "influence" on "Poem in Three Parts."

It's also the extent of my privileged information about the poem. Its voice montage, whatever influences he ascribes, is pure Matthias. I suspect that Part One was the model for "Turns," in the sense that our negative capability is tested to the end, when a peculiar revelation lets the pieces click together like a Chinese puzzle. En route, however, historical—not to say hysterical—voices from the Aberdeen witch trials of 1597 croon in our ears as from a perverse Prospero in a sequence of, as J.M. will later say in "Batory," "quotation, commentary, pastiche" (C 81). The witchy testimony of the several Agneses before the ecclesiastical court describes Satanic doings, with particular emphasis on salacious sex:

> Somtym he vold be
> lyk a stirk
> lyk a bukk
> lyk a rae
> lyk a deir
> lyk a dowg
>
> He vold hold up his taill
>
> Lo! We kiss his arce. (B 68)

The court, nothing if not thorough, strip searching the witness/defendant, "founde upon her cunt a lump . . . and then they wrung it with their fingers there and moisture came like lee" (69). Further testimony—

> in the kirk yard / with her daughters adoring

his member

> exceeding great and long / no manis
> memberis so great and long / is abler for us then
> than ony man could bee (70)

—of course requires further strip searches. And so it goes. Quotation evolves to commentary, as the poet's voice situates juridicial porn as a social disease:

> Current of an inclination
> imperceptible contagion
> vaporous insinuation

> . . . .

> Rigidity at first
> Convulsionary epidemic in the end. (72–73)

As the section moves toward its conclusion, history is abruptly juxtaposed with a contemporaneous "I" on an erotic quest that ends in interruptus, but not before he reveals the sign of Satan: "I recited like a bull and like a dog" (74). This I, the messenger, the poet's function, "rigid, scared," inclined to refuse illumination like anyone else, is nonetheless obliged to mediate the recognition of the past in the present, "we shall (they did) assemble" (74). And in the final image we get the "shades" of Aberdeen hysteria in spades, as the United States frets its nerve gas deficiency, its puny capacity to kill the world's population 30 times in the face of Russia's to do it 160 to 190 times. Thus, appropriately via nerve gas, the present is put in the legacy of the witch trials' "convulsionary epidemic."

Part Two is perhaps the most exasperating sequence of verses in J.M.'s corpus. Hermes Trismegistos, where are you when we need you? J.M.'s notes to the poem identify his sources, and the reader wanting comprehensive explication should go directly to them. I prefer going by J.M.'s own "general advice" to readers of David Jones's work *(Introducing David Jones),* that the reader should get what he or she can from the verses themselves and only in subsequent readings consult Jones's extensive notes. Moreover, J.M.'s notes, unlike Jones's, are generic. They do little more than confirm the poem's invocation of the Cabala and alchemy, though they do indicate the Jungian interpretation that informs the poem, the cue that rescues it from antiquarian indulgence. For the reader, the implication of J.M.'s poetics here is that, while the poem and its sources inform one another, reading each is a discrete activity.

Rather than historical voices, the pastiche of this section features the historical context of the renaissance, when the European mind was simultaneously reaching back to its humanist sources as well as its pre-Christian Jewish and Egyptian spiritual influences and reaching forward to the sciences, especially chemistry and psychology. Because it was a peculiar mixture of myth, Cabalism, mysteries, empiricism, and often enough anticlericalism, alchemy was a principal agent. And it serves "Poem in Three Parts" as a kind of Warbling Pivot. Where Parts One and Three have a semantic drive, Part Two invokes alchemy as all but pure incantation. Even where semantics are foregrounded they serve more to inflect the chant, as in enchantment, than to stabilize meaning. The overall effect, which I take to be J.M.'s intention, is a celebration of alchemy. This peaks in sections V (incidentally, a conspicuous instance of language looping) and VI. Section V tells us, "(Tripod over Flame) Doth not attempt to transmute / into gold but summon Thot o ibis-headed god o Mercury" (82), highlighting the Jungian interpretation of alchemy as primarily a quest for spiritual transformation and as such the historical missing link that Jung came to feel validated the connection between Gnosticism, neo-Platonism, and his own psychology of the unconscious. Hence, the "sublimation" of VI—also of course a quintessential alchemical function—and its concluding appeal to Thot-cum-Hermes-cum-Mercury-cum-Hermes Trismegistos, the multicultural deities of secret knowledge and authors of the Hermetic Writings.

Knowledge—even unto the sublime that so captured the fancy of a late-eighteenth and early-nineteenth-century Europe where science struggled with theology for epistemological ascendance, mirroring the situation of alchemy in the renaissance—and its tribulations is the theme. One variation on the theme is "mortification," which functions in several senses. It frames the chant of II, which concludes "because they mortified / until they died" (79). "They," presumably the alchemists in I and III, mortify nature high ("one the ram," etc.) and low ("visit the inward / parts of the earth") in their esoteric researches and produce a logic (as in Basil Valentine's syllogism) that apparently mortifies those (for example, the Inquisitors, as per Part One) who are obliged to "reply," to say nothing of "submit" (77, 78). The cameo appearance of Oedipus to conclude section I gives us pause, but he certainly is an authority on eternal triangles, and he learned something about perspective, how an apparently "straight" line turns out to be "curved" if not altogether circuitous. As the poet says, a little knowledge is a dangerous thing. And of course, as in III, the truth may well be mortified. I don't know exactly how these men "lied," but it's easy enough to surmise how they might. Paracelsus and Agrippa were not only notoriously anticlerical but also confronted superstition and received wisdom aggressively enough that they spent much of their itinerant lives as *personae non grata*. Roger Bacon and Albertus Magnus, formidable theologians as well as empiricists, were clerics at once admired and suspected by the church. And Part One contextualizes the ecclesiastical hysteria that might well compel seekers of nature's secrets to lie. Gilles de Rais (de Retz in *Bucyrus*, 1970, an alternate spelling or a different person?) gives us pause as the spokesman for truth. Possibly more remembered from J. K. Huysman's novel *Là Bas* than from history, he presumably told the truth about his sadistic homicidal pedo/necrophiliac habits. A perverse truth, to be sure, but one that reveals the dark side of knowledge. As Sade said, nature is a sublime Vesuvius of contradictions.

As were the alchemists themselves, whose peculiar experiments are speculatively connected with the canonical songs in IV. Of course, the connection "cannot be determined with any degree of certainty" (81). But then what can be? And "matter, he said, / expresses mysterious sound" (82). The alchemists were nothing if not hell-bent on plumbing the mysteries of matter. If plainsongs harmonized with "the words of the epigrams" (82), why not give it a shot? Which is precisely what J.M. does in the next two sections, full tilt into the uncertainty. Poet and alchemist alike share a "discipline," and,

> for Thot [the invention of writing among his credits after all]
> will sweat
> > whole days and nights before that
> > > furnace until face explode in boils
> > > > and running sores (Tripod over Flame). (82)

Where the sublime ("sublimation," "ascension") is the object, it is not unlikely that the price will be "mortification" not only of the seeker's self (as per Hardy and the schoolmaster/poet) but also of conventional wisdom and morality. Being is—witness the contest of Prospero and Lenin for the poet's ear—dialectical. The temple, in VII, arises from the fetal ash, "Yang & Yin / Yin & Yang" (85). That is the Dao of things. On that way to "god in / the vowels of the earth," the alchemical poet is often enough "feared" as a "public menace" (86). J.M.'s not talking Spiro Agnew's nattering nabobs here: "ascribe unto / these metals, / Hermes, / need" (86). For, be the indeterminacies of IX and X what they may, the situation is that "The still-providing / world is not / enough: we add" (88). And, faces exploding in boils and running sores, we sing.

And, like Nargajuna, we dream. This south Indian Buddhist dialectician, usually transliterated Nagarjuna, held that Nirvana is not "non-existence" but rather an engagement with worldly being that dispels "ignorance." His Middle View reconciles empirical reality with the metaphysical by way of a duality. Thus the recognition of suffering as at once absolute and relative, permitting us to both experience and transcend it, is an occasion of "happiness." Then again, it is a consummation merely "dreamed" (88). J.M.'s admittedly recondite image evoking this super subtle ontology punctuates Part Two on a peculiar upbeat which carries into but does not survive Part Three, where secular jurisprudence echoes its ecclesiastical counterpart in Part One. If the secular sort is less lascivious, its legacy seems about as shaky, built upon the shifting sands of North Carolina's coastal banks.

J.M.'s choice of material here poses a poetic challenge. Witch trials and alchemy are well-documented world-historical facts prominent in cultural memory, whereas the Atlantic Beach incident of Part Three is local and comparatively obscure. J.M. has to give local and family history (his father is a lawyer in the case) a signifying resonance. One tactic is to evoke the local history in the context of its three-hundred-year connection to the colonial settlement of the New World, prominently repeated through the poem and concluding it. Another tactic is to obscure the parochial particulars of the case and highlight its past as an archetypal analog of the violent settlement of the New World. The third is to transform the legal property description into a chant that is repeated three times to become an emblematic chorus grounding the poem in a peculiarly literal way.

The poem begins *in medias res* with this chant. It establishes particularity of place and a legal conflict. Pedestrian real estate is promptly expanded by invoking semiexotic place-names of the surrounding area, raising both the geographical and lyrical ante. This is intercut by two abrupt images alerting us to the long- and short-term histories that will unfold as the poem develops. The long-term history is teasingly enhanced in the first two of the three numbered sections that follow, an inauspicious beginning in storm and near mutiny confirmed by the inhospitable conditions on the dunes. But the headlines punctuate with short-term history and impending violence. The third section counters the drifting dunes with the lush appurtenances of high society apparently made possible by development, the law, the state, and the army. But this pacification is promptly interrogated by images of murder and atavistic rites, presumably perpetrated by those long-time "squatters." Well, Lenin having again caught the poet's ear, we know that *they* certainly don't own the newspapers or banks behind civilized development. Turning on the earlier "Bogue Banks for the Bankers," the poem sharpens its sardonic focus, as it juxtaposes what will turn out to be the judge's metaphysics with what in its second recitation becomes not so much a chant as an ironic psalm of real estate.

The irony hovers over the "judgment," which reconciles the "rights or privileges" of both parties to the complaint—that is, the holders of rights and privileges (93). We know, Lenin again, that these do not include squatters, whose bloody voice in the matter would seem to make the rights of the privileged somewhat precarious. At any rate, did they not when Alice Hoffman was cavorting among her mountains and French harpsichord with her fancy foreign friends? Meanwhile, the judge, "the man of great wisdom" (94) transcends the dubious judgment with a meditation on the metaphysics of indeterminacy and Buddhist acceptance of the world's duality. In the face of that ontology about all you can do is measure the immeasurable and run a title search. Surely the squatters didn't bother with a title. On the other hand, as the third variation on the chant tells us, they did survey the property boundaries with implements of butchery and destruction, raping, pillaging, murdering, and otherwise reducing the estate to world-historical reality. Not exactly revolutionary reality, the decadent Alice Hoffman escaping with her skin, whereas the workers did not. And drinking the blood of those pink Parisian maids would certainly be beyond the pale of Lenin's analysis, more tribal madness than class struggle. Still, it *was* a matter of haves and have-nots. And the future lies ahead: "ends and beginnings / cannot be regarded / as fixed" (93–94). Does it lie with Lenin? If from the perspective of the sixties it seemed it might and to some that it should, that was not J.M.'s take nor is it that of his poem. It ends with the uneasy pacific image of Davy John Willis sitting on an ancestral legacy of piracy and murder, of which he "Remembers little" (97). Revolutionary or otherwise, the atavistic cycles of tribal-cum-class violence would seem to have a future. J.M.'s politics were always quite clear that, whether you were Mandelstam in Moscow or four college kids in Kent, Ohio, "The other guys are faster and they draw" ("May 4, 1970," *T* 27).

The question of just who the other guys are and how fast they draw not only punctuates Part One of "Poem in Three Parts" but informs the whole. From the poet's perspective the army, the ecclesiastical courts, the secular courts, and possibly even the misfortunate Alice Hoffman are the other guys. From the perspective of what in the sixties was called The Establishment, the witches, the Soviets, the alchemists, the squatters, and the poet are the other guys. There are plenty other guys to go around, hence the volatile condition of being that the poem diagnoses. In the matrix of Pound's useful distinction between the art of diagnosis and the art of cure, between an address to ugliness and the address to beauty, "Three Parts" is essentially diagnostic. Parts One and Three reveal how the institutions of social order in fact facilitate hysteria. Part Two, the fulcrum on which past and present balance precariously, lyricises the figure of the alchemist/poet, but neither Nagarjuna's dream nor alchemical incantations sublimate the ironies of mortification. If the alchemist/poet's enterprise is one way to curative memory and consciousness, its prospects seem bleak. Neither the Bankers nor Davy John Willis are likely to read or remember. As for the judge, he is lost in a metaphysical haze where his determination of rights and privileges is predicated on a self-serving version of indeterminacy and misappropriation of Buddhist acceptance. It's a bit more civilized, as befits its time, but it's not appreciably different from the Inquisition's proposition that justice is irrelevant because God will know His own.

III. On the *Batory* and the *Lermontov*

By Watergate in 1974, which marked the transition from the sixties to the seventies, otherness was epidemic. Nixon, a long-time other guy to liberals who in turn populated his famous list of other guys, joined Agnew in comprehensive otherness. Meanwhile, Nixon's own band of sleazy advisers, to say nothing of that slapstick gang of Watergate burglars, did their best to upstage him. Everybody wanted into the act. Meanwhile, too, in Vietnam several sets of other guys continued killing one another and sometimes even themselves, as was confirmed in *Friendly Fire*. Back home, of course, the war had divided the American house against itself several times over. This was the house to which J.M. was returning aboard the good Polish ship *Stefan Batory* in the summer of 1974. In the winter of that year he had written that he was "seriously contemplating" staying in England, would I "argue against it"? I replied with the letter from which he versifies in "Batory" Five (*C* 81).

Its feisty tone was what—I see retrospectively scanning our correspondence of that time—he wanted to hear. The late sixties and early seventies had pitched our private embattlements in the matrix of America's third great domestic agon of this century. He was seeing the country in terms of both personal and historical apocalypse. During the year he'd been in England, for example, Swallow Press, which had contracted to publish *Turns,* went all but totally under, casting his manuscript upon the waters, along with his editor and friend Michael Anania. Further, my sanity as well as that of my ex-wife had barely survived a divorce and custody crisis in which the court—where "the man of great wisdom," remember, sits in judgment—had threatened to

100   possess our two daughters, a nightmare through which John and his wife, Diana, had wrenchingly seen the both of us. Then I had been fired from my teaching job for a supposedly obscene style of writing and, presumably, of life, the third such incident in six years. His letters reflect his pleasure, or perhaps relief, at life and the literary scene in England, as opposed to his anxiety about the lives and careers of his friends, to say nothing of his own, in the American maelstrom. Like Pound, he spent no inconsiderable energy carting books around to English bookshops and publishers, as if he might somehow transplant at least our careers in a saner culture. Small wonder he was tempted to stay there.

His reply detailed his phobia. I cite it because it is behind the ostensibly comic scenes of both "Batory" and "Lermontov." "The point is really," he wrote, "that I'm *afraid* of America and that I don't (can't) write there. I've written nothing at all in America for over five years." He worried that this paralysis might extend to teaching, which turned out to be premature but prophetic. "And I don't think I should submit Diana [born in Britain, where her family lived] . . . or Cynouai & Laura [daughters] to American madnesses unless there's a damn fine reason why I *must* be there . . . . But I thought you'd say just what you've said, and I think that's what I wanted to hear. I don't know what I'll decide in the end, but I think we'll come back for at least another year, look around, and think things over." And that's what he did, came back on the *Batory* and left again two years later on the *Mihail Lermontov.* Hence the scenario of the two poems, sailing from Old World to New and back again, in a large sense the story of his life and work. J.M. says that "both poems aim at comedy in the broadest sense, not satire." Though there is apparently more satire than he wished, I take his "aim" at face value. And he hits the mark brilliantly. His considerable comic gift, however, is still subject to not only his history muse and Lenin but also "The heavy and judicial German / In me called Matthias" (92).

I knew that J.M. had Prospero whispering in one ear and Lenin in the other long before his own incisive self-caricature in "Batory." So did anyone else who happened to be paying attention. But, since he knew that I was paying attention, that's why he wanted to hear from me what he expected to hear, though I didn't know that then. In fact, we'd both been grappling with Prospero and Lenin. It seems to be the curse of our generation or writers, more for some than others. I reinforced Lenin's pitch, notwithstanding that "gringo baiting" was about as close as either of us ever came to Lenin(*C* 81). No doubt his consciousness of that induced the antic disposition of "Batory." Still, while J.M. amuses himself by logging his voyage day by day, the poem is what he originally called it, a "comic lament" (73). It's not so much "for the decade of the sixties" (73) as he put it, as for himself as an American of that decade, which confirmed for a young American a *personal* loss of national coherence. The poem throughout evokes the innocence of children, but in the very evocation reflects the poet's sense of its loss for both him and his daughters. In Part Four, for example, where Diana teaches the girls how to ask a new shipboard friend her name and J.M. then imagines a slapstick drowning, he doesn't end on a ridiculous note but with a haunting insistence: "Was ist Ihre Name, bitte? / Was ist Ihre Name?" (79).

The poem opens with an oddly edgy gesture of lightheartedness, where the poet teases us with the possibly ominous fate of Katarsky and then dismisses it by self-consciously appealing to the needs of the poem. That strange psychic dialectic informs the whole poem. Part Five's comical Prospero/Lenin image punctuates a "serious" meditation on J.M.'s return to America that devolves to brilliant parody where "serenity" rhymes with "Pastrami" (82) before returning to introspective interrogation. And if J.M. engraves his own emblem as comic bemusement, he is after all returning to "The banalities and rhetoric of power" (80). The future lies ahead, as Mort Sahl said, but it's rather like the iceberg in Part Six lurking in the ship's foggy path, unrecorded by the radar but luckily caught by the spotlight. Anxiety devils comedy throughout the voyage. J.M. may not be whistling in the dark, but he is whistling, and even in the sunrise there's an "eerie morning haze" (88). On that last day, as "New Poland steams toward Old Quebec," J.M. has heard the news of Nixon's resignation and contemplates contradictions in several histories, his guilt in "obscure complicities . . . The ugly birthright of / My sinking class" (88, 89). He rereads an unanswered letter from his daughters' "beloved nurse." She echoes his anxieties, "afraid to set out on the porch / Any more." "It's real cold here," she concludes (89, 90). Meanwhile, an earlier image presides: "Western / Nations dress themselves / To dream a dull apocalypse" (89). As Molly used to say to Fibber, it ain't funny, Magee.

"Lermontov" is rather more relaxed than "Batory," more dominated by play, parody, anecdote, and less informed with an anxiety of American "exile." Now J.M. is returning to England and the Old World. England had already provided him a brilliant and beautiful wife, extensive inspiration for his work, and a public forum in several of its magazines and the Anvil Press. And he was and is, of course, an Anglophile, not uncritical but an Anglophile. His *Another Chicago Magazine* column, "Not for Sale in the U.S.A.," continues to be the most persistent and perceptive American address to modern British poetry. As for the Old World, it would command

102   much of his attention in the next few years. The Swedes would translate and publish "Batory" and "Lermontov," and he would collaborate on ambitious translation projects of modern Swedish poets and the classical Serb epic *The Battle of Kosovo*. It was as if J.M. were aware that he was steaming toward what was to be perhaps the most productive period of his career.

For the first seven days of the trip he does a nifty stand-up comedy act, somewhere between Mort Sahl and Lenny Bruce on an upbeat day. The hi-jinx begin with the peculiar "Dog-eared Proem," where he invokes his enterprising and social activist maternal ancestors to upstage the "heavy and judicial" legacy of his paternal name (92). Under their name and aegis Prospero prevails. But on the eighth day, as the ship nears England, the comedy takes on a more diagnostic edge. J.M. assumes kinship with the ship's namesake, the Russian poet Mikhail Lermontov. It's not just that they are fellow poets. J.M. tries on the Russian poet's mantle as he tries on the name and élan of his maternal ancestors. Lermontov's life was, as J.M. concludes in section VI, "a little bit Byronic" (106). As a young hussar he wrote a vitriolic elegy on Pushkin's death that was considered subversive and got him exiled to a regiment in the Caucasus. He survived two exiles there as well as several battles. But he had a habit of satirizing his contemporaries, which led to duels, which led, as with Pushkin, to his very premature death.

Section VIII begins with one of J.M.'s patented etymological tropes elaborated to the convergence of poet *(scop)* and ship in their common "Resistance" to contrapuntal waves, and then the poet evolves to Shelley's "legislators unacknowledged" (109). Under this elevated Poetic banner, J.M. proceeds to a fantasy of Lermontov's "exile . . . In my America" (109). The fantasy parodies both Russian and American history and is largely comic. But from behind the comedy, where the poet is figured as "An alien-seditious Natty Bumpo," J.M. tips his hand: "Cousin, your ambivalence about all things / matches even mine" (110). That ambivalence carries to the last day, as the *Lermontov* heads up the Thames to dock. In the concluding ninth section, J.M. kicks "Thames Head" and "the Thames heads" like poetical footballs around the field of English history (112), especially its history of patriotic humbuggery. Like those, these are parlous times, and J.M.'s ironizing brings him to the Scot George Learmont, soldier of fortune, namesake, and distant kinsman of the poet Lermontov. Lermontov's parlous times impinge, and J.M. configures him as a sacrifice to those patriotic gods about whom he and Lermontov are so ambivalent, those gods who turn "poetry to prose, roubles into dollars . . . and revolutions into resolutions and détente" (115–16).

A pox on both their houses, as those gods and parlous times impinge
anew. For J.M. it is,

> this time of jokes & parodies, pastiches.
> An inbetween
> when I don't know precisely what I want to do in time
> but only where I want to go
> again. (116)

Well, he's there, waiting for the "sixties / to arise again" (116). "Middle class for life," J.M. caricatures himself as a kind of Walter Mitty (116). His stand-up routine at an end, it's time to shed the *sprezzatura* of his kinship with Lermontov as well as the guise of his own admired kin. He's kept the comedy gamely going. But by the last two days of this second of the two voyage poems he originally billed as comic lament for the sixties and celebration of national anniversaries, J.M. is rather more logging a moment of self-mockery and bemusement. After that, comic patter notwithstanding, the future lies dead ahead.

Works Cited

Matthias, John. *Beltane at Aphelion: Longer Poems.* Athens, Ohio: Swallow, 1995.
———. *Bucyrus.* Chicago: Swallow, 1970.
———. *Crossing.* Chicago: Swallow, 1979.
———. *Reading Old Friends: Essays, Reviews, and Poems on Poetics, 1975–1990.* The Margins of Literature Series. Albany: State University of New York Press, 1992.

John Matthias's England

JEREMY HOOKER

In "For John, After His Visit: Suffolk, Fall," a poem in *Turns,* John Matthias asks: "how / can I speak generously enough / About the life we've shared?" (*SM* 17) Speaking generously characterizes John Matthias's poetry. He is a poet of friendship, and of family love with its pleasures and anxieties, its happiness and grief. He is also a poet who knows the mental and emotional turmoil of the America that gave us "confessional" verse. In this essay I shall be concerned with the Matthias who is close to David Jones and Robert Duncan; but he is the same man who, on another side, is drawn to John Berryman and Robert Lowell. There is a good deal of fraught personal and generational *angst* in Matthias's poems of the 1960s and 1970s; feeling engendered by the Vietnam War and the difficulties of maturing as a man and a poet in a fragmented, materialistic, and aggressively competitive society. Matthias's anxious self-making contributes to the variety of his lively, experimental poetry. It both completes and helps to account for the strong impulse toward homemaking, which is my main concern in this essay.

I should explain at once that I use the expression *homemaking* in two senses, and am concerned with the connection between them. The first sense is the ordinary one: making a home, establishing the conditions for a shared life in place. The second sense has metaphysical and ontological implications, and is well summarized by Karl Kroeber's comment on Wordsworth and Constable that "their art makes us feel not that we would enjoy Cumberland or East Anglia but that we are at home on the earth" (quoted in *Reading Old Friends* 43). In describing John Matthias's poetry as a homemaking, therefore, I wish to indicate both his concern with place as the ground of a shared life, within a historical community, and his quest, in unsettling times, for a sense of wholeness, which involves being "at home on the earth."

In the same poem from which I have quoted above, Matthias writes: "'I must have savagery,' a wealthy British / poet told me, leaving for the States. / I've gone the other way" (*SM* 19). It is evident that in choosing England, therefore, Matthias was choosing something other than "savagery"—which I would gloss as meaning not only brute energy but naked egoism. It would be too simple, however, to say that what he was choosing, as one might expect of a student of Yvor Winters, was "civilization." The problem with writing about Matthias in a short space is that he is highly conscious of the variety of choices facing him as a poet in the late twentieth century, and of the need to make himself and his "world." Consequently he has opened himself to different and even opposing streams of modern and postmodern influence; and it is difficult for a critic to get the balance right in acknowledging both his originality and his eclecticism and syncretism. Certainly we cannot discount influences (Yvor Winters among them) in discussing Matthias's reasons for going "the other way." What I would suggest, however, is that for Matthias, England represented an answer to his strongly felt personal need for a poetry of relationships, of generous sharing.

Stephen Fredman, in *The Grounding of American Poetry,* has detected "a myth of exile at the core of the American character" (69). He reads American poetry in "the Emersonian tradition" as an attempt at "grounding" in "the basis of tradition" (vii). "Grounding," in this larger sense, relates to what I have said above about homemaking, and I want to keep it in mind while discussing more intimate and particular things that Matthias seeks to share. These include specific relationships (with his wife, daughters, friends), and a sense of home and a sense of neighborhood. It is not, however, of a secure "rootedness" that we have to speak in this context. The sharing entails an admission of vulnerability and an opening of the self to human qualities that are traditionally thought of as "feminine" rather than "masculine." Coming to feel at home in England meant for John Matthias a self-discovery and a self-making, the corollary of the latter being a shedding of competitive, "male" attitudes to be seen in an earlier generation of American writers (and perhaps exemplifying the "savagery" to which the British poet was drawn). What might be called the feminizing of the American male poet is by no means a universal process, of course, although it may be seen in other poets of John Matthias's generation, including Robert Hass. It has developed parallel to a new confidence among women poets and to the ecological crisis which reveals, on a global scale, the disastrous effects of human "savagery" upon the earth as our home. The remaking of the "masculine" ego by male poets is, I think, a major example of poetic courage in our time.

John Matthias himself has told the story in *Reading Old Friends* of how during the 1960s, having become "sufficiently caught up in the machinery of protest and the language of neo-Marxist analysis to feel in the end both confused and inauthentic," he had gone to Wordsworth for his "healing power" (40–41). What Wordsworth led him to was "a place of my own." It was through his wife, in fact, that Matthias was led to Hacheston and the Aldeburgh coast in Suffolk. Over several years of summer visits in the late sixties, while Suffolk began "to do its work" on Matthias, Wordsworth made him "consciously aware of what I had begun unconsciously to feel—namely, that whatever I was and whatever I was going to write that might have any merit was bound up, for the present at least, with a place I had come to love, and that I was going to have to learn, somehow, to write *from* that place as well as *about* it" (*Reading Old Friends* 43). It is clear from his autobiographical accounts that prolonged stays in Suffolk, and later in Cambridge as well, from 1967 to the early 1980s, enabled John Matthias to discover himself as a poet. That this was also a self-discovery, a revelation of the self to the self, is shown by the poems he wrote, and by the fact that his life in England taught him ultimately how to make poetic use of his American experience.

Writing *from* place in England was John Matthias's way of "grounding" himself. It is significant in this context that his relationship to place in Suffolk was "that of a spouse." He tells us that, through the influence of his wife and of his mother-in-law, he "slowly opened . . . to the full geological, topographical, natural, historical, and social context of the region" (*Reading Old Friends* 47). His poems and prose also tell the story of the influence upon him of his daughters:

> The child is father of the man
> but not the child the poet meant.
> The child of flesh and blood
> and not the ghost of former selves
> is father of the man—
> ("Poem for Cynouai," *SM* 89)

He has said that, "If my own route to the responsibilities of being an adult was through my children, it was also through my children that I found the route to childhood. And one thing that I wanted to learn on my way to childhood and back again had something to do with the meaning of play" (*Reading Old Friends* 50–51). This is a crucial point, to which I shall return. It is equally significant that as he came to know, through women, the materials from which he made his English poems, David Jones and Robert Duncan —the modernists with the keenest awareness of and respect for female creative powers—were the major poets who showed him ways in which he could shape them.

John Matthias acquired his sense of historical place in England from cultures in which poetry has always been closely bound up with a sense of history; there were Basil Bunting in *Briggflatts* and Geoffrey Hill in "Funeral Music" *(King Log)* and *Mercian Hymns*. As editor of the *TriQuarterly* anthology, *Contemporary British Poetry,* John Matthias brought together some of the most formally innovative British poets. In this anthology and in his criticism he has been one of the few Americans to show an informed interest in British poetry during the past thirty years. Indeed, a larger claim has to be made, as Matthias is one of the few critics on either side of the Atlantic to show an appreciation of the centrality of the modernist tradition in postwar British poetry, a tradition that includes Roy Fisher and Charles Tomlinson and Christopher Middleton, as well as Bunting and Hill and Jones. *Contemporary British Poetry* was a groundbreaking anthology; it is the scandal of English criticism that its achievement has scarcely been superseded. The truth of the matter is, however, that innovative British poetry responds to modernism and tends to engage creatively with history and tradition, opening lines of communication to the past, whereas the dominant fashions that rise and fall are culturally parochial and take their ideas of "newness" from the world of the media.

It is not, of course, the same past that preoccupies British poets, nor is it necessarily history that engages them, since myth is also a vital shaping influence. The same is true of American poets drawn to England. According to Stephen Spender in *Love-Hate Relations,* the quest of American writers in Europe, "in search of the past, to connect with its energies," has finished. In Spender's reading of history after 1920, "The European decline meant the shrinkage of the sense of the tradition as associated with particular places. The cathedrals became like pit-shafts of exhausted mines, old architecture and scenery whirled round by the shining, rapid, shabby circulation of tourism" (219). This is not, however, good history, at least as far as the sixties and seventies are concerned, nor is it good prophecy. John Matthias and John Peck are among the American poets who have followed Ezra Pound and T. S. Eliot in exploring the cultural riches of Europe, while notable American poems about England (whether in its insular or European dimension) include Edward Dorn's "Oxford" (in *The North Atlantic Turbine*) and Ronald Johnson's *The Book of the Green Man.* A brief comparison of these poets' English poems with Matthias's will indicate that American poets have continued to connect with "energies" in their explorations of England.

Dorn's view of England might seem to accord with Spender's idea of "scenery whirled round by the shining, rapid, shabby circulation of tourism." In fact, in Donald Davie's words, Dorn's subject is the North Atlantic as "a landlocked ocean," where "the swirl around it (imaged as the pulse from a dynamo at its center) locks together and makes virtually identical, in one pointless round of activity, all countries that have a North Atlantic seaboard" (185). Dorn, however, perceives energies in the geology of England, energies that an exhausted culture belies. In his version of an Olsonian politics and poetics, he urges movement, the capacity of a man's mind to use physical space in order to imagine anew and break the circuit of political and economic exploitation and outworn ideas. A surprising alliance (probably unconscious on both sides) may be seen in Dorn's exposure to view of England's geology and David Jones's invocation, in *The Anathemata* and *The Sleeping Lord,* of dormant cultural powers embedded in the very land, and capable of release.

Whereas Dorn maintained that "A seer is what England needs" (35) Ronald Johnson, in his book-length poem based on a year spent in England and Wales during 1962–63, uncovers the indigenous visionary tradition and reveals that seers are native to English ground. Johnson reawakens the dormant power of the tradition by reestablishing the connection between vision, in music and painting and natural history as well as literature, and nature, and place. In the stone-carved leaves at Southwell Minster, for instance, he discloses "a kind of greening speech" form "mouths // all but winged—each leaf / cleft & articulate" (59). In Christopher Middleton's view, Johnson "presents an image of England, or, to be precise, of sundry English scenes, with a vividness and a strangeness beyond the reach of any English poet." Middleton's precision is necessary, for Johnson unearths an English poetics of place, in Gilbert White's Selborne as well as Samuel Palmer's Shoreham, for instance. As Middleton says, Johnson's "observation is microscopic, but his sense of place drills through to the mythic substrata" (Middleton's jacket copy for *The Book of the Green Man*).

John Matthias does something rather similar in his English poems, but with differences arising from the personal needs he brings to his historical and mythic materials. The ground he shares with Johnson is a sense of imaginative energy latent in English places—energy that has quickened poets and painters, musicians and naturalists, to speak of the earth as home. In his historical poems set in England, such as "Brandon, Breckland: The Flint Knappers" (*SM* 38) and "26 June 1381/1977" (*SM* 44), Matthias shows a keen political awareness which recognizes the cruel and grotesque and ironical aspects of historical continuity. But he is also, like Johnson, a celebratory poet.

Crucial to Matthias's historical sense is an element of play, which is also a primary agent in his own self-knowing and self-making. He is quite explicit about this in his poetry and prose. In "Double Derivation, Association, and Cliché: From *The Great Tournament Roll of Westminster,*" for instance, he writes of

> illuminations:—
> where, o years ago, say twenty-two or
> say about five hundred,
> cousins in the summertime would
> ritualize their rivalries
> in sumptuous tableaux.
> Someone holds a camera. Snap.
> In proper costume, Homo Ludens wears
> Imagination on his sleeve. (*SM* 74)

The personal reference to experiences of twenty-two years ago is evidently to what he writes about to his cousin in "Clarifications for Robert Jacoby": "all those games / we used to play: the costumes, / All the sticks & staves, the whole complicated / paraphernalia accumulated to suggest / Authentic weaponry and precise historical dates, / not to mention exact geographical places" (*SM* 78–79). There are, I think, several important outcomes of Matthias's imaginative playacting. One is that he has a mind quick to empathize with historical figures and to enter imaginatively into the parts of the play. Significantly, in several poems Matthias establishes an "I-Thou" relationship with his subject, and he is particularly sensitive to those vulnerable in their human relationships, or wounded by love, like Sir Thomas Browne grieving over the death of his son Tom. Imaginative play is thus not an escape from history but a means to understanding human feeling and behavior, whether twenty-two or five hundred years ago. It is also a cause of merriment. Characteristically Matthias prefers the Shakespearean comic actor Will Kemp, "who Morris-danced / from London" to Norwich, to the "frenzied Margerie Kempe" (*SM* 43). And, with his penchant for word play, Matthias has a quite wild sense of humor (see for instance the third part of "The Mihail Lermontov Poems" *BA* 68–69).

According to George Steiner in *Real Presences,* it was "in Mallarmé's disjunction of language from external reference and in Rimbaud's deconstruction of the first person singular" that the "break of the covenant between word and world" was first declared (35). It seems to me that John Matthias and the American poets (all students of Yvor Winters) with whom he is most closely associated, Robert Hass, James McMichael, John Peck, and Robert Pinsky, all feel the need both to re-create a covenant between word and world and to defend an idea of integral human personality. Consequently they all devise different poetic strategies to these ends, but without falling back on outworn notions of a correspondence between word and thing or a naively conceived ego. Their resistance to postmodernist assumptions about the nonexistence of "reality" or "self" is germane to what Matthias has called "the wholeness and tenacity and coherence of their work" (*Reading Old Friends* 174)—qualities present in his own poetry of relationships and generous sharing, in the homemaking that he first accomplishes in his English poems.

It is in this context of resistance to postmodernist assumptions that I understand John Matthias's art of naming and his gathering of materials. "East Anglian Poem" begins:

Materials of Bronze and of Iron—

    linch-pins and chariot wheels, nave-bands
and terret-rings: harness mounts, fittings, and
bridle-bits: also a sword, an axe: also a
golden torc
        But the soils
        are acid here

    and it rains

Often there's only the mark of a tool on a bone
Often there's nothing at all (*SM* 93)

The method resembles Geoffrey Hill's in *Mercian Hymns,* but the impulse behind it seems much simpler. The poet is unlocking his word-hoard, and like an archaeologist he is poring over his trove. It consists of words that name materials and things, words the poet relishes and sets down with a sense of wonder. Wonder, too, that the things vanish. We may read "East Anglian Poem" as a poem of homemaking, in which, with scrupulous objectivity, the poet considers the ground he has entered upon and what lies under it. It is also a poem about the materials with which other settlers in East Anglia made their worlds and about the relation between culture and nature, which both creates and destroys. Unlike other poems by John Matthias, however, it is relatively static: more a gathering of materials than an imaginative shaping. A major difference between it and the later "An East

Anglian Diptych" is that the latter charges its language and rhythms with an energy that corresponds to mythic and natural powers embodied in the land. "An East Anglian Diptych" is also, it seems to me, the major poem in which Matthias realizes the relationship between his impulse to settle, to make a home in place, and his necessarily unsettling experience.

"Poem for Cynouai," one of Matthias's finest and most moving poems, is also concerned with names and things. His daughter argues to keep "every one of thirty watercolors":

> How luminous their rendering of a world
> we both believe in
> and can sometimes share:—
> where names are properties of things
> they name, where stones
> are animate and wilful, trees
> cry out in storms, and compulsive
> repetition of the efficacious formulae
> will get us each his way. (*SM* 82)

The point is not, I think, that names are properties of things, stones are animate, and we live in a world in which "the efficacious formulae / will get us each his way." It is rather that adult and child can "sometimes share" the world rendered luminous by their belief. The belief is, as it were, an imaginative truth, which the child reawakens in the mind of the adult poet, her father. There is consequently a difference between the names in "East Anglian Poem" and the names in this poem, for here they have a magical aura. They correspond, in fact, to Robert Hass's idea of images:

> Images are not quite ideas, they are stiller than that, with less impli-
> cation outside themselves. And they are not myth, they do not have
> that explanatory power; they are nearer to pure story. Nor are they
> always metaphors; they do not say this is that, they say this is. In the
> nineteenth century one would have said that what compelled us
> about them was a sense of the eternal. And it is something like that,
> some feeling in the arrest of the image that what perishes and what
> lasts forever have been brought into conjunction, and accompany-
> ing that sensation is a feeling of release from the self. (275)

Images that say "this is" also convey a feeling of closeness yet distance, and therefore of troubled longing:

What I had wanted to say was: *red, ocher,*
orange, blue, green, violet.
What I had wanted to say was: *grass, sky,*
sun, moon, child, forest, sea.
I had wanted to say:
English village (SM 86)

The poet had wanted the world as it cannot be, except in a child's imagination or a poem that denies the reality of human life. But the counterpart of Matthias's magical propensities is a stern sense of the actualities they cannot transmute. This poem, like all Matthias's playacting, brings the ideal to the test of reality and shows reality in the light of the ideal.

It may be that Matthias's England had a magical luminosity that could not survive either the passage of time or a closer acquaintance with actual historical experience. He remained, of course, an American poet, writing about an England which he saw as an American, and with a vision that inevitably, to some degree, compensated for what he did not find in America. His England was where he found healing; it was a place which he shared with his family and which helped in his maturing process. It gave him what America at that time did not: a sense of being at home on the earth. Yet a significant part of his life was lived in America, which was not only the country where he made a living, but a shaping influence upon his mind and art. For all his affinities with certain British poets, he saw England differently. In my view, the purely celebratory elements in Ronald Johnson's and John Matthias's visions of England derive in part from their freedom from complications of feeling, which have beset native English poets in the twentieth century, and especially since the Second World War. Seamus Heaney has described Geoffrey Hill, Philip Larkin, and Ted Hughes as "afflicted with a sense of history," and argued that "English poets are being forced to explore not just the matter of England, but what is the matter with England" (see Heaney's "Englands of the Mind" and my *Presence of the Past: Essays on Modern British and American Poetry,* especially 9–32). Hill, who reveals a strong attraction to the idea of a long-settled England, also sharply diagnoses English social ills and agonizes over the condition of "Englishness," as Matthias is under no compulsion to do. The reality of living in England in modern times has been a profoundly unsettling experience for poets, confronting them with problems of social and national identity. Matthias's England, by contrast, offered him a more settled experience. He is not however a sentimentalist, and if at times he has been tempted to express an illusory sense of belonging, his experience of England ultimately brought him a greater sense of reality. Indeed it has been in incorporating his experience as an unsettled American in his apprehension of England that John Matthias has written some of his finest poetry to date.

Stephen Fredman has spoken of "the construction of an idiosyncratic tradition or the creation of a poetic community" which, for American poets, "represents the hope of finding a place to stand while on the open road" (5). This offers a suggestive formulation of what I believe England ultimately was for John Matthias: a place in which he was able to make a home (and to create a poetry that is, metaphorically speaking, a homemaking), not in spite of his nomadic existence between England and America, but because he recognized that he was necessarily "on the open road." The truth of Matthias's own position that is manifested in that of others—Edward Thomas and John Constable—is "An East Anglian Diptych."

"Images," Hass says, "are powers" (303). In "An East Anglian Diptych" *this* is a word charged with power. The reference is to the "pinch of earth" Edward Thomas picked up in answer to his friend's question after his enlistment in the army: "what are you fighting for over there?" (*BA* 115). The words refer to an actual instance which Eleanor Farjeon recorded in her memoir, *Edward Thomas: The Last Four Years.* John Matthias gives the same word to John Constable in answer to the question: "what are you drawing landscapes for out here?" In each instance the single word has the force of an image; it says "this is." The word is a haunted one; it implies "This England" (the title of Edward Thomas's anthology published in 1915). Its burden is a love of country mediated by particular places, which are numinous even in "a pinch of earth." The simple word *this* fulfills the desire of the poet who "had wanted to say . . . *grass, sky, / sun, moon, child, forest, sea.*" It is a word containing a whole world, but its power is made possible not by wishful thinking but by sacrifice and loss—the kind of loss experienced by poet and painter, who fully realized a vision of place only in their removal from it—Thomas by the war, and Constable, in another period of historical crisis, by the necessity of making a living in London. Another way of putting this would be to say that poet and painter gain their rootedness only in movement, their nearness in distance, and their sense of the whole through an experience of being broken.

Something similar has to be said about John Matthias in his homemaking. The cycle of poems to which "An East Anglian Diptych" belongs was first published as *A Gathering of Ways,* a book of pilgrimages in which what is "gathered" is won from movement and struggle "on the way." Matthias

114   concludes his selected shorter poems, *Swimming at Midnight,* with "Dedication to a Cycle . . . ." It is a poem of shared experience in which he speaks of
his daughter struggling "to a Compostela of her own / in pain & torment"
(*SM* 153). The poem ends with a prayer for wholeness. This fact should
underline what I have attempted to show in this essay: that the cost of generous speaking includes a painful openness and an admission of the weakness
as well as the power of words. This is also as much as to say that a place can
only be gained by losing it, and a home made on earth only by moving on
and letting go. It is not only that we cannot hold on to the past or to the
security of childhood or any stage of a relationship, but that love requires us
not to. This, I believe, is something John Matthias learnt from his attachment to England. Out of the experience he made poems that are a kind of
"home," both a generous, shared space for living in and a way of being on
the earth.

Works Cited

Davie, Donald. *The Poet in the Imaginary Museum.* Manchester: Carcanet, 1977.

Dorn, Edward. *The North Atlantic Turbine.* London: Fulcrum, 1967.

Fredman, Stephen. *The Grounding of American Poetry.* Cambridge: Cambridge University
   Press, 1993.

Hass, Robert. *Twentieth Century Pleasures.* New York: Ecco, 1984.

Heaney, Seamus. "Englands of the Mind." In *Preoccupations: Selected Prose 1968–1978,* 150–69.
   New York: Farrar, Straus, Giroux, 1980.

Hooker, Jeremy. *The Presence of the Past: Essays on Modern British and American Poetry.* Bridgend: Poetry Wales Press, 1987.

Johnson, Ronald. *The Book of the Green Man.* London: Longmans, 1967.

Matthias, John. *Beltane at Aphelion: Longer Poems.* Athens, Ohio: Swallow, 1995.

———. *Swimming at Midnight: Selected Shorter Poems.* Athens, Ohio: Swallow, 1995.

———. *Reading Old Friends: Essays, Reviews, and Poems on Poetics, 1975–1990.* The Margins of
   Literature Series. Albany: State University of New York Press, 1992.

Spender, Stephen. *Love-Hate Relations.* London: Hamish Hamilton, 1974.

Steiner, George. *Real Presences.* London: Longmans, 1967.

❧ Between Revolutions, or Turns *John Matthias and the American Avant-Garde British Experimentalism*

R O M A N A   H U K

I've formulated my title to this chapter in part as a division problem because that's where I picture John Matthias's work—if not in terms of its composition, then in terms of its reading, or reception. In other words, while it's hardly problematic that Matthias's poetry demonstrates a range of modern and postmodern influences, it has nonetheless been to some extent caught, or left uncategorizable, within the unsolved divide opened between American and British experimentalisms after the great packing up and lighting out for "postmodern" territories that happened during the formative stages of his development as a poet. Even though he was among the very first to read and anthologize, in *23 Modern British Poets* (1971), those who have become known as the "first generation" of postmodern British experimentalists, the lack of familiarity in this country with that corollary to what would slowly emerge several years later as the American L=A=N=G=U=A=G=E revolution in poetry meant that Matthias's work, which shares many concerns with both, couldn't be read here as developing between them. Instead, because of his almost single-handed critical championing, for some years, of the key British modernist David Jones and his sympathetic reading of mid-century and contemporary writers as divergent as W. H. Auden, Robert Duncan, Roy Fisher, and Geoffrey Hill, he is often thought of as a kind of "neo-modernist," or some such variant of writer still limed by the projects of a revered but past past, removed from our newly established "posts."[1] And too often the most knowledgeable of his critics couple him too intimately with those loves—particularly Jones and Duncan—when his own sense of the historical contingency of certain poetic possibilities would preclude any sort of unexamined nostalgic practice. John Matthias's work is all about contemplating complex historical contingencies as they impact upon—*by*

116 *providing apocryphal text for*—the necessary "making" that results in every-thing from notions of poetry and place (the latter of which tends to be over-essentialized or mystified in readings of his work) to notions of self; its inter-est in competing historical discourses and its lack of interest in full syntactic disjuncture signal its relationship to British as opposed to American avant-garde writing. I want to argue in this chapter that by the early 1970s Matthias had already made this experimental project clear in his poems, and that in some ways the early work predates the avant-garde's *current* preoccupations, on both sides of the ocean, with imagining a postmodern but "located" rather than an ahistorical, "authorless" art.

It would be impossible in this space to compare the respective trajecto-ries of American versus British experimentalism in any responsible way, but a very brief look at the kinds of informing ideas and correlative formal strate-gies developing here in the 1970s to which the British did not necessarily adhere might help readers understand the distinctions I've been drawing. Let's take just two strains: those ideas that evolved into conceptions of where the poet stands in the work—"post-," say, Roland Barthes and the "death of the author" (that is, new theories of the writing self)—and those ideas that evolved into conceptualizations of "the word" itself and its extricability or inextricability from reference. I choose these two because both have much to do, ultimately, with any poem's awareness of its own positioning in history, which, I would argue, differs on either side of the Atlantic.

For example, in an essay that volunteered explanation for some of the new practices that had become apparent in American experimental work during the seventies, Charles Bernstein, one of the most respected of the first generation of L=A=N=G=U=A=G=E apologists (and indeed one of those to coin the term), writes that the new poetry departs from modernist projects of "mapping consciousness" because, while such earlier writing "does in fact break the monologic spell of writing seen as a transparent medium to the world beyond it, . . . it does so only by making a projection of itself central to its methodology. In the end, this practice leaves the reader as sealed-off from the self enacted within it as conventional writing does from the world pictured within it; . . . while it critiques the suprapersonal transcendental projection [of nineteenth-century writing], it creates its own metaphysical fiction of the person."[2] Concerned to break the spell of what is considered "romantic presence," and to foreground language as the constructive med-ium in which "[t]here are no terminal points (me—> you)," only "a sound-ing of language from the inside,"[3] the new poetry would call for work that empowers the reader, according to a loosely Marxist model of revolution, by not offering "the product of the 'author's' projection/memory/associative process, . . . but work for the reader's (viewer's) projection/construction . . . . The text formally involves the process of response/interpretation and in so doing makes the reader aware of herself or himself as producer as well as consumer of meaning" (1982, p. 233). This displacement of the "author function" releases the text into variable space, in other words, dislocating it from any one point of entry in order to allow for multiple points of entry. To accompany this breakthrough in rethinking the relationship of medium to meaning is the description of words themselves as being released from conventional bondage in reference: "[t]hey do not sit, deanimated, as symbols in a code, dummies for things of nature they refer to; but are, of themselves, of ourselves, whatever is such. 'Substance.' 'Actuality.' 'Presence.' The very plane through which we front the world, by which the world is."[4] Asyntacticality and disjunctiveness have become important strategies in American poetry because they signal such reapproaches to "words [that have never had] any history," as Laura Riding once put it when discussing Gertrude Stein's work; the argument has been made that America, an immigrant nation, is especially able to engage in these pioneering new directions because traditional baggage from "Island English" fades before the prospect of language as the new frontier, disconnected from its "imperial sovereign's" past by the many pasts that continually arrive to reassemble it.[5]

Although "[t]he stimulus of American poetry is a constant factor in the new poetry" of the United Kingdom, as Eric Mottram (the well-respected British teacher/critic/poet and proponent of international avant-garde trends) wrote very recently,[6] there are aspects of even the bit of the American project described above that translate differently into the British context simply because there are different things at stake in either arena. Hopefully one needn't rehearse the contrasts that arise due to differing constructions of "nation" and cultural nationalism; it might be enough, anyway, to quote Peter Jay from his introduction to Matthias's *23 Modern British Poets*: "Williams [as opposed to Eliot and Pound] was specifically trying to evolve a poetry in an American idiom, free of historical-literary associations which he considered irrelevant for American literature . . . . [I]t was a problem which could not affect English poets in the same way. At any rate, there have always been these two diverging strands of modernist poetry—the Europeanizing and the Americanizing; the one (to oversimplify rather brutally) 'making new' the past, the other responding to the texture of language and things around it" (xviii). In short, the former historicizes rather than dehistoricizes in order to revolutionize—*especially* after the late-fifties' "linguistic

118 turn" into postmodern philosophy, whereas thinkers like Fredric Jameson have famously targeted American postmodernist artists for dispensing with great modernist concerns about time, temporality, and memory in a rush to inhabit the synchronic rather than the diachronic.[7] In Britain, interest in the collisions of historically influential discourses in contemporary frames occupies more time in experimental texts than does fully disjunctive assemblage or words made into material objects; the work of J. H. Prynne, which has had such an extraordinary influence on experimental writing in the latter part of this century, is perhaps the most important case in point.[8] Mottram remarks in his contribution to *New British Poetries* that in the British context, "[o]riginality combines exploratory behaviour *with a cultural accumulation*" (36, my emphasis); in other words, the project of *locating* language rather than "releasing" it from particular places and speakers also might be said to differentiate British from American work.[9]

In a recollection of a 1973 talk given by Roy Fisher, an important postwar experimentalist of particular interest to Matthias, Mottram stresses that Fisher was at that time interested in "precision of language, often located in precise place," and in how "'the consciousness is charted' so that it is neither abstract nor autobiographical"—that is, so that there is commerce between them (38). Rather than jettisoning the idea of charting consciousness, then (or "mapping it," as the section of the book in which Mottram's essay appears refers to it, almost in direct opposition to Bernstein's dismissal of such activity above), the differing emphases of British experimentalism often necessitate the location and historicizing of language in such a way that it betrays its current point of issuance from place and memory even if (Matthias quotes Fisher as writing) "the poem has always / already started."[10]

Matthias has written that Fisher's cycles of "verbal structures," like Paul Klee's visual ones, "stalk up on 'a perceptual field jammed solid with sensory data' and break it up into mobile, unstable parts"—though in the end, in Fisher's work, this does turn out to be a "sufficiently systematic," "convoluted treatment of cognition" from which, Matthias suggests, such play with the materials cannot be separated.[11] He explains by quoting Francisco Varela's conclusions about M. C. Escher's etching "Print Gallery," in which "the observer, a man at an exhibition of prints, is ultimately found to be standing inside the same work of art he is viewing":

> We find ourselves in a cognitive domain, and we cannot leap out of it or choose its beginnings or modes . . . . In finding the world as we do, we forget all we did to find it as such, entangled in the strange

loop of our actions through our body. Much like the young man in
the Escher engraving "Print Gallery," we see a world that turns into
the very substratum which produces us, thereby closing the loop and
intercrossing domains. As in the Escher engraving, there is nowhere
to step out into. And if we were to try, we would find ourselves in
an endless circle that vanishes into an empty space right in its middle.[12]

The vast difference between, say, Robert Duncan's reimagining of numinous places, his "opening of the field"—which becomes "a property of the
mind that you can return to"—and the recognition of self in this space is that
you don't "return" to this one; you're always already there. The problem of
seeing it is definitely a postmodern rather than a modern one; "you" as a fictive or textually generated but nonetheless obstructive entity can't get out of
your own way here; "you" certainly can't look out onto that language/textual
tradition that constructed you, either, from any newly generated modernist
position of objective transcendence. Therefore in Fisher's cycles, as Matthias
describes them, the subject is "the 'I' that perceives, creates, moves among his
images, and, finally, becomes itself an object in an overall design" (41). There
is no discreet "empirical" self there, but there is also no escaping the nonetheless located and limited, limiting, cognitive self that you can only "try to steer
a sufficiently agile course [around so that you] may be able to see the back of
your own head" (Fisher 1975, 33). Matthias equates this idea with Rimbaud's
notion of locating the "I" that is being thought, rather than the "I" that is
thinking; he then goes on to quote from Fisher's partly comical "Of the
Empirical Self and for Me," which at its beginning sounds a bit like a send-
up of the notion of fully erasing "(me → you)" separations in language:

> In my poems there's seldom
> any *I* or *you*—
>
> you know me, Mary;
> you wouldn't expect it of me—[13]

It is the "I" that is being thought as the conceptualized one which, in its discreet outlines, along with the "you," can be abandoned—though here not
without recognizing that that still leaves us with the back of the head of the
"me" doing the disbanding, the "me" that can never be fully seen or separated
from the "etching" though its presence is recognizable, that behaves as it
must in its intimately worn con*text*, that does as Mary "expects." The poem

120   ends with the reminder that the poet's own writings, like the "lightning-strokes repeatedly / bang[ing] out their own reality-prints / of the same white houses / staring an instant out of the dark," demonstrate at best an elliptical connection between what is empirically out there (including the material word as world—which constructs us each specifically in our discursive spaces, as do the places that locate us) and the internal linguistic landscape whose *limits* order the elliptically perceived. The persons drinking milk by a lit window on a dark porch in the poem look out on white fences similarly lamplit; the man in the dark, walking "what looks like a black dog" from the milk-drinkers' perspectives, believes them to be drinking coffee, and is gone in an instant of history after having uttered a universalizing text—italicized like the "I" and "you" negated earlier: *"It's nice to be able / to drink a cup of / coffee outside at night . . . ".* For Fisher, the pronominal fictions and their utterances are all the texts we have, each flawed in its peculiar perspective on "the real," and from their emergence at certain fleeting lightning-strokes, or the (dis)locations of apperceptions that make up history, we make up the universal. All universals. Including the ones that suggest "there are no terminal points (me → you)," "only language sounded from the inside," etc., which have their glancing place in history all the same.

Though swiftly drawn, the rebalancing sketch offered above suggests the historical poetic/philosophical context within which John Matthias's poem "Turns: Toward a Provisional Aesthetic and a Discipline"—composed shortly after *23 Modern British Poets'* anthologization of work by Fisher and other experimentalists appeared (1972–73; published in England in 1975)—must, in its "turn," be read.[14] The title suggests that the poem's seven sections turn upon themselves, striving for a look at the back of their own head as they present lightning flashes—elliptical views—of a purely fictive textual/discursive landscape that nonetheless "ultimately tells," as the final prose sections put it, on the poet's "sex life" and "on his health"—"entangled [as we are] in the strange loop of our actions through our body," as Varela put it in his comment on the Escher etching, suggesting the interconnectedness of texts and embodiments in the world. I want to suggest that Matthias's poem, one of the most notoriously difficult to read in his *oeuvre,* is, like Fisher's cycles, a "verbal structure" composed of discursive planes (as opposed to a discursive poem), and that its subject, like Fisher's, "perceives, creates, moves along his images, and, finally, becomes itself an object in the overall design." Along the way it accumulates pictures of other texts (along with variants of words lifted from other contexts), bits of mysterious modernist encodings or harangue, whole paragraphs of other kinds of politicized discourse, as well as sudden revelations of its own elliptical architecture within comic asides to the reader. In this way it negotiates between the kind of place-and-consciousness mapping one finds in Fisher's work, the kind of purely discursive parataxis one sees in British experimentalist work such as J. H. Prynne's, the "personism" and tonal humor of Frank O'Hara and the New York School of poets, and what Matthias referred to in the seventies as "nominalism," or nondiscursive attention to the word itself, as American experimentalists were beginning to describe it—all of which he continually returned to in his critical writings in the seventies as he considered the strengths of these various approaches to making poems in a postmodern landscape. The result is not a poem in defense of its own obscurity, as some have read it, nor a departure from obscurity or hermeticism, as others, noting its scaffolding inherited from Ezra Pound's "Hugh Selwyn Mauberley," have read it; both interpretations subscribe to modernism's starting points for reading, which hunt down formal coherence and transcendence of contingency, when this particular verbal structure calls for another sort of take. It is instead a poem so highly self-reflexive in its movement through the mine-fields of language and poetic ambition that it all but implodes—like the "self" itself, in contemporary philosophy, though this subject remains within the etching instead of opting for what would be the truly neo-modernist ending of transcendence out.

"Turns" demonstrates an awareness of its inevitable location in the pages following influential modern texts by writing itself into that picture too, though with a postmodern difference. Pound's "Hugh Selwyn Mauberley," that great modernist sequence that justified his transition from imagism to vorticism, begins with an image of Pound himself as Odysseus lingering too long on Circe's isle and "pass[ing] from men's memory" into his self-made tomb; it then progresses through a scathing portrayal of the time's uninspired mass culture toward an "envoi," dated the year Pound left London for Paris, before finishing with an equally scathing portrayal of the sort of "hedonism" that his ghostlike persona, Mauberley, representative of the dead movement, practices as hermetic continuance of his "subjective hosannah," unconcerned by his "social inconsequence." Matthias's sequence resonates with echoes of Pound's and also twists itself inside out in an attempted answer to his forebear's indictments of "obscurity." But the differences between what Pound *could* indict (as well as later be indicted for) and what Matthias's persona might in his "turn" are what emerge as important in "Turns"—which is not an homage but rather the only response possible: another sketch in the series (or perhaps *upon* the series, in the manner of David Jones's endlessly receding painting/palimpsests).

First off, Matthias's initial image of being "out of key with his time" and of "leavetaking"—rendered as a translation of Thomas Hardy's first paragraph of *Jude the Obscure* into fourteenth-century English—effects a trajectory in terms of movement or "progress" quite opposite to Pound's. Whereas Pound pulls Odysseus and the mythic past into the present, as the moderns tended to do—thereby suggesting both the transhistorical presence of certain universal, essential forces and structures of experience, and the discovery of their currency by artists in a decadent modern age—Matthias takes a modern text *back* in time, through an act of testy translation that exposes its "backstage" or choice of variants and asserts its "equivalency" (despite having taken at least one notable liberty in changing the story: the schoolmaster in his version takes the piano along as he leaves, the "onelych thyng of combraunce," even though his zeal to learn to play wanes—"[h]e neuer couthe ani scylle" (or skill); he is always "out of key," by metaphor, like Pound's buried imagist):

I

The scolemayster levande was the toun
and sary of hit semed everuch one.
The smal quyt cart that covert was and hors . . .
to ferien his godes. To ferien his godes
quere he was boun.

The onelych thyng of combraunce (combraunce)
was the symphonye
(saf a pakke of bokes)
that he hade boghte the yere
quen he bithoght
that he wolde lerne to play.

But the zele woned (zele woned).
He neuer couthe ani scylle.

II

And so the equivalent
            (the satisfactory text.

> squ'elles sont belles
>> sont pas fidèles. rough
> west-midland, hwilum andgit
> of andgiete: the rest is not
>> a word for word defense. . . . (*SM* 48)

In other words, instead of "making it new," according to Pound's famous modernist injunction, Matthias is conspicuously "making it old"—thereby suggesting at least two things: (1) on the one hand, the necessity of "introduc[ing] the antecedent place," as he puts it in the third section (quoted below), in the same way that he has noted his own poem's place within the unerasable legacy of modernism and Pound's work; and (2) on the other hand, the obvious impossibility of translating current (con)texts backward toward "origins," resignaled by such willful (or subjective) changes and choices being announced as "the equivalent" text—in other words, the impossibility of viewing past texts or myths or language in anything but Jude-like ways: appropriatively, and through the lens of the present's desires and self-definitions (which *have,* nonetheless, evolved out of that past). The sideswipe taken here at Charles Olson, through the use of his signature deployment of opened parentheticals that never close to signal the poet's recognition that his own translation might not be *exactly* equivalent, suggests an inheritance of somewhat suspect "archaeological" principles from this other modernist forebear as well. The complexity of the situation—that is, the necessity/impossibility of seeing what the "antecedent" (history) affords as a "gloss" on the present (as the end of the poem will put it)[15]—calls for an aesthetic of "turning," of looking at what one writes (or thinks one has written) from the back of one's head, or from another historical/discursive angle, and even of opting to play devil's advocate against one's own assertions. Therefore, "[T]he rest is not / a word for word defense" of what he has begun to do, though on the outside the next section looks like one:

III

And make him known to 14th-century men
Even when everything favors the living?
Even if we could reverse that here
I know you've read and travelled too.

So Destination or Destiny: *Quere He Was Boun!*
And yet to introduce the antecedent place.

> Restrictive clause; sense of the referent noun.
> A tilted cart is a cart with an awning.

> Langland has it "keured"
> John of Mandeville "coured"
> Wycliffe "keuered"

> But "covert" in Arimathaea (*SM* 48–49)

Instead of a defense, what forms here is a kind of opposition to the seeming project at hand—a Trojan horse that both "covers" and displays its "covert" intentions in the building/undermining of its own structure. (That the variant comes from the apocryphal "text" of St. Joseph (who never wrote a word) is key; I will return to it at the end of this reading, as the poem does). This because what we have, in the second stanza, is the injunction to return to the antecedent place, given that *"Quere He Was Boun!"* is a restrictive clause that gives us only a sense of the referent noun. But the antecedent here offers no suggestion of the destination except—the cart; and the movement into translating the cart's particulars suggests in turn that the destination is, in a very real way, the cart, the covered cart. It is critical to note the various references to textual circularity through tragedy in these first few sections ("the rest is not"—the line end and white space suggesting Hamlet's "silence" (or textual closure) not granted; the sense of being *"Boun"* to "Destiny" and to forever introducing the antecedent place that always already knows you as you don't know yourself, as in *Oedipus Rex*), all of which reverberates in our recognition here that our Jude/Judas/poet is "bound" nowhere except to that cart:

> This is personal luggage / destination / travel

> Harp and pipe and symphonye

> (saf a pakke of bokes)

This, then, is the pilgrim's progress: into his own "baggage," his "fictive verbal structure," as Fisher would describe it, the cultural etching—here, the portable cart/head full of texts and instruments and the doctor's orders: "Rx.: bibliography / Rx.: map." The place and its texts—neither of which he can return to—and the instrument (which he can't play), nonetheless entrap him, as they do Jude in Hardy's text (the instrument becoming, in the novel and in this poem, a metaphor for the body, too, ultimately held at all but an impasse by all the uninterpretable imperatives/intertexts that bind it in its place):

> The metaphysicality of Hermetic thought—
> Let him think o' that! (Problem is he
> Still enjoys cunt . . .)
>
> . . . instrument was ay thereafter
> Al his own combraunce . . .
>
> Sary of hit semed everuch one.
>
> Torn between disgust & hope
> He simply never couthe . . .
>
> antiquorum aegyptiorum
> oh, ... imitatus . . . (*SM* 50)

The ellipses (and allusion to the equally elliptical history left us by our antiquities held from ancient Egypt) remind us of Pound's descriptions of Mauberley's similarly fragmented, destinationless departures—in his case, out of fading Greek roots into Latinate abstractions and imitations emblematic of his diminishing potency as he

> Drifted . . . drifted precipitate,
> Asking time to be rid of . . .
> Of his bewilderment; to designate
> His new found orchid. . . .[16]

(with the pun on "orchid" depending on the reader's remembering that in the Greek the word means both the flower and "testicle").

But this is not to suggest that the poem so far has been a simple or, in imitation of Pound, ringing condemnation of Jude/Judas/the poet traveling amidst

> Greek, Arabic, Medieval Latin,
> Mis-translated, misconceived. (*SM* 51)

And it is necessary to understand that the initiating translation, on the same score, has been effected

More than just for his disport

who loveth daliaunce

who falleth   (o who falleth)

far behinde . . .

But it is *also* crucial not to take at face value the first two prose sections of part VII that seem to too strongly defend, by snide "apology," the project in section I. We have, in fact, been told that "the rest is not a word for word defense," which should make us wary of this sudden defensive line-by-line *re*translation or gloss on the gloss, as it were, and encourage us to look at this block of prose, this plane of prose, otherwise. And the fact that words like "defense" (used at the beginning of the poem) and "apology" (used at the end)—seeming opposites but also, in some instances, synonyms—depend entirely on context for their meaning alerts us to the slipperiness, or the instability of reference, and therefore the possible collision of discursive vectors in this poem. It's difficult, first off, not to hear a surfaced and therefore more rancorous version of Eliot's ironic footnotes to *The Waste Land* echoing in this supposed "revelation [of] the art." Like Eliot's jokey/condescending directions to the readers to make imagistic connections between allusions, or his hilariously irrelevant autobiographical notes about locations in which he heard certain birds singing and their preferred habitats, etc., Matthias's notes give the reader more than they want—"what is idle and boring to rehearse." In a sense, Matthias is—like Eliot, it could be argued—challenging his reader to read a poem that uses its materials differently than they might expect, but this echo of Eliot is no more an indication of homage than are the ones of Pound, and so its deployment as "defensive" tool must be called into question. Particularly if one considers its peculiar "translation" of Eliot's famous scientific metaphor for the creation of modern poetry minus the poet's "personality," which calls for comparing it to "the action that takes place when a bit of finely filiated platinum is introduced into a chamber containing oxygen and sulphur dioxide" (producing sulphurous acid with no trace of the platinum, the catalyst).[17] Matthias's "explanation" of his translation, in keeping with his project, gives Eliot's formula a medieval, somewhat alchemical twist that robs it of its modernist yoking to the new science and all that such historical contingency afforded, ironically, in terms of "transcendent," impersonal authority:

Let me simply indicate the manner. Take sulphur from Sol for the
fire and with it roast Luna. From which will the word issue forth . . .
If the given appeared in a verifiable text. *If* the given was truly equivalent. (*SM* 51)

The demystification of Eliot that happens here through *re*mystification
of his principles (or through their possible "translation" back into another
context) is key to our understanding of Matthias's project as it happened in
section I, and the ways in which "turns" to the past can provide glosses for
the present. Eliot's claims for universal authority via dismissal of his own
autobiographical input and its dependence on the contingencies of history is
called into question in this verse paragraph "aside"—especially as the latter
gives us the voice of the current poet revealing not only the "idle" facts of his
translation to chastise us, but also admission of his quite idiosyncratic
choices in the same with regard to his change in the narrative and his own
particular reading that informed his use of the dialect. And Eliot's project of
being our Hieronymo-cum-Hamlet, in *The Waste Land*—the one able to see,
under the seeming "majestical roof fretted with golden fire . . . what is [our]
quintessence of dust," and therefore "catch [our] conscience" through playing within the play, or enacting our situation for our recognition in the
wasteland—*is* happening here too, through enactment of our situation in
language, but the final verse paragraphs throw us back from Hamlet's dying
fall (or even Eliot's mysterious/ambiguous closure) into another play within
the play within the play, viewed from the back of the poet's head, enacting
exactly those messy arguments that stymie poetic action.

Their severing enactment happens in several colliding planes of recognizable political discourse that arise in response to the climactic question
asked following the "apology":

And such a revelation makes the art available to the vulgar. Who will
abuse and discredit? *Keeper of secret wisdom, agent of revelation,
vision, and desire:* THIS IS THE QUESTION WE MUST ALWAYS
RAISE. (*SM* 52)

The one who abuses and discredits—responds tellingly to the play within the
play—is the poet himself, of course, who is also the "agent" of revelation in
mysterious italics as the repetition of the word in the above quote makes
clear. Three arguments against revelation follow; two of them, the first and
third, mirror one another and demonstrate again the circularity of seeming
opposites. The first implicates the poet directly (if we know that he is him-

128 self a university professor); its elitist response is the strongest of the discred-
itings, though it ends ambiguously:

> Now some of the obscure, like some of the lucid, do not become
> proletarianized. . . . Perhaps they hold teaching jobs in public
> schools or universities; perhaps they have an inherited income. In
> any case, some maintain their Hermetic privilege. They are not
> obliged to live by their art or to produce for the open market. Such
> unproletarianized obscure are revolted by the demands of a com-
> mercialized market, by the vulgarity of the mass-produced com-
> modity supplied to meet it. And revulsion ultimately tells (1) on
> their sex life (2) on their health. (*SM* 52)

Pound's indictments against the "social inconsequence" of Mauberley's art
take a blow here as we remember that his revulsion against the masses, who
had received "press for wafer; / Franchise for circumcision" (63), qualifies his
call for "social consequence" in poetry. What are the (linguistic) "roots that
clutch" when it comes to thinking of socially consequential art—the kind of
art Matthias has always wished to write? The next verse paragraph of quasi-
Marxist discourse again defends the social efficaciousness of the obscure and
unpredictable existing in dialectical relation to lucidity, but ironically widens
the gap between the "vulgar" and the "elite" with its depersonalized—indeed,
doubly ironically dehistoricized—abstraction, which calls to mind Mauberley's gravitation into "inconsequence":

> While a relationship of cause and effect is established between
> obscure and lucid organizations emerging from the division of
> labour and the consequent dialectical evolution of social reality, such
> becomes, we know, increasingly separated from the actual produc-
> tive function of society, from sleep. This gives us pause. "The point
> is that the notion of invariancy inherent by definition to the concept
> of the series, if applied to all parameters, leads to a uniformity of
> configurations that eliminates the last traces of unpredictability, of
> surprise." This gives us pause. (*SM* 52)

The repetitiveness of sentence structure here, with its "sleep" lodged in the
center (and sleepy pauses as punctuation) is both formally comic and
indicative of the difficulties of choosing an "efficacious" language for radical

writing since the *effect* of this political discourse—made systematic and co-opted by "organizations" of speakers, through which it becomes safe, defused, a narcotic, "the opiate"—has slipped back into collusion with the *cause* for it. And such circularity gives us to pause again as we enter the penultimate verse paragraph, which circles 'round on its mate (quoted at the top of p. 128 above). A third modernist, Auden, enters here with his vocabulary of heroes, conspiracy/spies and villains, which rhymes with that of Hamlet's tragedy to suggest the entire sequence's "necessary murder" as suicidal mission:

> And so the system and its adherents are the villains; license, conspiracy, and nihilism are the virtues of the heroes: *or:* The system itself becomes a context for heroics; license, conspiracy, and nihilism become the crimes of the villains; acceptance of convention and austere self-discipline become the virtues of the heroes. The schoolmaster is forever an intermediary: the shape of his life is determined by the nature of society: the nature of his art seeks to determine the shape of society by administering to its nature. And intermediacy ultimately tells (1) on his sex life (2) on his health. (*SM* 52)

The fictive figure of Jude and those poets holding teaching jobs in the previous verse paragraph seem to morph here into characters, along with the poet, among Auden's schoolmasters and his other "orators": the self-imploding middle-class intelligentsia on their way to Spain in the 1930s, where the "system" of revolution had already begun to work against itself. Against whom, then, is the "necessary murder" (a phrase edited by Auden himself out of the 1930s version of his deeply partisan poem, "Spain") directed? The palindromic dynamic of the penultimate line in the passage above signals the complicated "turning" upon oneself as a fictive "shape" that must take place and why: because the mirroring afforded by the sentence's structure equates the seeming "naturalness" (or "nature") of society with that of the poet's own life, and the vague referent for what he subversively "administers to" suggests he must act against himself as well as "it." The "nature of his art"—which Pound in his modernist rendering of it would attribute to the contouring of numinous figures made essential forces, like the Aphrodite that haunts his Mauberley sequence—is, for Matthias, as compromised by historical as well as contemporary social and linguistic structures as is Jude's love for Sue Bridehead, and their "sex life" or "natural" course of feeling fatally strained by their context's visible and invisible webs of conventions and social "intelligence." The last line in the above passage, repeated like a final refrain in photo-negative, places the positions of "revulsion" and "intermediacy" in a hall of mirrors; neither escapes ensnaring by contextual ills and we are left without simplistic or binary distinctions to be drawn between them.

But we *are* left with a re-"turn" to the imperative to make this figure "known to 14th-century men," and are asked to effect, "[w]ith Joseph of Arimathaea, turns: to elliptically gloss." Another refrain or repeating element in the poem, Joseph is that historical figure who "turned" against the authorities who crucified Jesus Christ (though he was himself a member of the Sanhedrin) in order to give the body burial. But it is crucial to the poem that he is more famous as an apocryphal figure, in medieval legend, where he is made the keeper of the Holy Grail, and, in other legends, the builder of the first Christian church in England, in Hardy's Wessex. In Matthias's poem, this "figure" is the supposed source for the key word in the poet's translation, his "verifiable text"—"covert," the word for "covered," as in Jude's/the poet's cart, as in the covered body of Christ. That the unrecoverable "body" of non-scriptural history is guarded by apocryphal text is a theme that runs through a number of Matthias's poems. In "Turns" what we *do* uncover, by extending our textual etchings back to "14th-century men," are the "covert" intentions/dilemmas of the immediate text/context, and of the "translator"—both of which depend upon and add to that "fictive verbal structure" which, by necessity, becomes our "bibliography" *and* our "map" to place and selfhood.

One of the differences, then, between John Matthias's work and that of his experimenting contemporaries on this side of the Atlantic is that, within its confining frame, the option of jettisoning "self" and its imaginings due to its/their fictionality could simply never even be contemplated; instead, the fiction of them is pursued to the extent that it can be within their own "virtual reality," their textual history. And instead of relocating the "origin" of that history and the operation of its words in a "real" space—say, America— his poetry grapples with postmodern redefinitions of "location" that must situate each of us differently in a complex virtual body of language that bleeds backward, in terms of mediated inheritance, to a text of the equally complex past. In Matthias's "experiments" the words come out of their frames no more easily and with no less cost than does their "viewer"; it's a matter, as Varela put it in his commentary on Escher's etching, of having nowhere else to step out into. And so—one turns.

Notes

1. It is true that some have compared Matthias to quasi-Language poet Susan Howe, given the deep interest in historical discursive terrains that both "walk through" in their long poems (see, for example, Howe's *Singularities,* Wesleyan University Press, 1990); and in the spring of 1996 there was also a conference at Notre Dame that brought together papers on Matthias and Lyn Hejinian.

2. "Writing and Method," collected in *Content's Dream: Essays 1975–1984,* (Los Angeles: Sun & Moon Press, 1986), 231–32.

3. "Language Sampler," *The Paris Review* 24.86 (fall 1982): 75.

4. From the 1976 essay "Stray Straws and Straw Men" in *Content's Dream,* 43-44.

5. I'm quoting bits and pieces from Bernstein's essay "Time Out of Motion," in *A Poetics* (Cambridge, Mass.: Harvard University Press, 1982), 109–10 (by "Island English" Bernstein is of course referring to British English); Bernstein quotes Riding out of Peter Quartermain's essay "Actual Word Stuff, Not Thoughts for Thoughts," *Credences* 2.1 (1983): 11, 121. Quartermain's introduction to his important book, *Disjunctive Poetics: From Gertrude Stein and Louis Zukofsky to Susan Howe* (Cambridge: Cambridge University Press, 1992), makes the argument alluded to concerning America's immigrant rather than European sensibility which has become so enabling as (I would call it) part of a new American poetic mythos.

6. "The British Poetry Revival, 1960–75," in *New British Poetries: The Scope of the Possible,* ed. Robert Hampson and Peter Barry (Manchester: Manchester University Press, 1993), 39.

7. I am of course thinking of Jameson's "Postmodernism, or the Cultural Logic of Late Capitalism," which first appeared in the *New Left Review* 146 (July–August 1984).

8. Though it's true that Bob Cobbing and his fosterings of concrete and sound-text work represent a deeply respected community of writers in the United Kingdom which this assertion would seem to overlook. And certainly it's true that today there are in the experimental community important new figures such as Miles Champion, whose influences are almost entirely American.

9. Much more could be said about the differences between American and British poetry's interpretations/deployments of twentieth-century philosophies, such as phenomenology, for example, or use of models such as those provided by Marxism; the latter, by way of illustration, has not been overtly employed in the United Kingdom as a revolutionary model for avant-garde poetry's own functioning, as it was (and for some still is) in the North American context, but rather will enter poems as a discourse, etc.

10. "The Poetry of Roy Fisher," *Contemporary British Poetry* (see note 4 above); the lines come from Fisher's poem "If I Didn't," in *The Thing About Joe Sullivan,* collected in *Poems 1955–87* (Oxford: Oxford University Press, 1988), 152.

11. In this quote, from the essay noted above (p. 53), Matthias is also quoting Fisher himself from an interview done by Jed Rasula and Mike Erwin, in *19 Poems and an Interview* (Pensett, Staffordshire: Grosseteste Press, 1975), 21.

12. Francisco J. Varela, "The Creative Circle: Sketches on the Natural History of Circularity," in *The Invented Reality: How We Know What We Believe We Know: Contributions To Constructivism,* ed. Paul Watzlawick (New York: Norton, 1984), 320; Matthias (1988), 54.

13. Roy Fisher, *Poems 1955–1987* (Oxford: Oxford University Press, 1988), 125.

14. Matthias has always been suspicious of unifying readings of a poet's *oeuvre* that pull up poems written decades apart for comparison, as though they were "timeless."

15. The relationship between language and history made apparent in my attempted explication calls up a famous suggestion made in the early 1950s by Geoffrey Hill—"Etymology is history"—which links many concerns in Matthias's work to those in Hill's and explains his admiration for this poet too often pegged as a "conservative" writer in England. For essays on Hill's relationship to postmodern thought, see James Acheson and Romana Huk, eds., *Contemporary British Poetry: Essays in Theory and Criticism*, (Albany: State University of New York Press, 1996).

16. Ezra Pound, *Selected Poems of Ezra Pound* (New York: New Directions, 1957), 72.

17. See Eliot's essay "Tradition and the Individual Talent," in *The Selected Prose of T. S. Eliot*, ed. Frank Kermode (New York: Harcourt Brace Jovanovich, 1975).

A Gathering of Proper Names
The Onomastic Poetics
of John Matthias

BROOKE BERGAN

Sheboygan by any other name . . .

From Chicago it is an easy summer pilgrimage north to the land of the Potawatomi; that is, to the land they inhabited after being pushed from one peninsula to another by the Iroquois and before being pushed into, and out of, Illinois, Indiana, Kansas, and Oklahoma by the French, the English, the Americans, by the trader, the farmer, the cowboy. You can head your Winnebago toward Winnebago and count sheep—I-90, 94, 43, 42—straight through the Door Peninsula, where the Potawatomi hunted and fished, then ferry to Washington Island, where they grew corn, and on to Rock Island, where they lived and built domed wigwams and long bark houses. You can see a *baye verte* where La Salle's *Griffon* is said to have sunk, and even stay in an inn called the Griffin. But first, there's Bristol for cheese, Milwaukee for beer, Cedarburg for strawberries, Port Washington for chubs, and Sheboygan Falls, where my friend, who is driving, veers off because he wants to "see the falls." There are none, I explain, just sausages. And "not a Potawatomi in town" ("Facts from an Apocryphal Midwest," *GW* 26). My friend is Indian—not Potawatomi, not Native American, but from that land Columbus sought, and even, given his dreams of a northwest passage, La Salle. Perhaps in India names mean what they say. (*Indian* means "from India." His means "teacher.") More likely, in a land not your own, a name has several registers, including descriptive. The state we drive across is a part of the terrain that John Matthias covers in the second poem of his collection of pilgrimages, *A Gathering of Ways*. I read aloud, as from a travel brochure, *"It's all so beautiful and fertile, free from forests / full of meadows"* (38), and the land seems to shimmer with the obsessions that vivify the poem.

Many of the obsessions that propel the three poems in *A Gathering of*

134   *Ways* are obvious in the first few pages of the first poem: the ways themselves—both water and land routes; the ways of the people who traveled
them, "their weapons and their coins" ("An East Anglian Diptych," *GW* 8),
their burial mounds and sacred places, their gods and goddesses; the light
that embodies good as well as evil in Bel and Beltane and "phosphorous
lucifer" (4) evolving to nuclear reactor. Obvious as well are proper names,
which both embody and radiate these obsessions: Tom Paine, an Englishman
who helped colonize, then nationalize, a country; the Beakers, who introduced copper and therefore the Bronze Age, and who also introduced individual burial rites; Queen Victoria, whose potteries industrialized one of
mankind's most ancient crafts; the "Pascal wick" (5) lit for the latest in a long
line of sun gods. Such cultural epiphanies are also among Matthias's obsessions. In *A Gathering of Ways* they are tied to a palpable source, a name that
roots them in time and place.

There are, in fact, some fifteen hundred instances of proper names in *A
Gathering of Ways*. They belong to people "now known to all or . . . now
known to none" ("Notes from an Apocryphal Midwest," *GW* 43), to gods
and goddesses both well known (Allah) and not so well known (Epona), to
heretics (Priscillian) and saints (James) and heretical saints (Bonaventure), to
churches and abbeys, paintings and painters, songs and their singers, chronicles and their chroniclers, ships, cars, constellations, rivers, lakes, mountains, mounds, roads and the towns they lead to, nations and the battlefields
that created them. There are nicknames (El Cid, from *as-sid,* Mozarabic for
lord), surnames (Cooper, Joliet, Picaud), fictional names (pseudo-Turpin),
and mythological ones (Wiske), and names that are both (*Terpsichore,* the
ship and the muse; Roland; and the actual Turpin, who appears in *The Song
of Roland* but was apparently miles from the historical battle). There are
eponyms like "the Studebaker & / the Bendix" (35), anachronisms like "the
Frankish Blitzkrieg" (67), acronyms like "E.T.A." (69), and adjectives "Devonion and Trenton" (34). Perhaps most interesting are the names that are never
named or are named belatedly: Edward Thomas, "the young man soon to die
at Arras" ("An East Anglian Diptych," GW 5); Robert Frost, the "friend who
tries to show him how to turn his prose to verse" (5); Francis Parkman, "The
man who followed [La Salle] . . . and read his words" ("Notes from an Apocryphal Midwest," *GW* 43); Mary and Aphrodite, "who rose up on [the] scallop shell" they share iconographically ("A Compostela Diptych," *GW* 60).

Inevitably, these proper names enact the concerns of onomastics—the
study of proper names—which involves anthropology, history, geography,
linguistics, and philosophy, concerns that Matthias exhibits here and in his

other work. The more obvious of these concerns sometimes gather at the surface of the poem:

> brides among them turned their heads
>
> to gaze at Golliwog, Sheila-na-gig.
> Whose giggle, then, this
> gog-eyed goggle goddess, ogling back
>
> above the portal near the Wandlebury
> Gogmagog?
>
> ("An East Anglian Diptych," *GW* 8)

This "fit of alliteration" (118) comes from one of Matthias's sources, T. C.
Lethbridge, who is arguing for an etymological descent of Sheila-na-gig from
Gogmagog. An even more explicit etymology uncovers the literal meaning of
"Framlingham: 'Framela's people'" (14), its suffix revealing an Anglo-Saxon
ancestry. Etymology becomes archaeology when Matthias explores the history embedded in names and in name changes, usually a history of invasion
and colonization. "Beodricsworth became / Saint Edmund's town" (10) in
the eleventh century when it was named after the Benedictine abbey built
over the remains of St. Edmund, an East Anglian king slain by the Danes in
869. The *bury* of Bury St. Edmund's is correctly translated from Old English
to modern English as *town,* not as one might initially suspect, something
related to graveyards. "[E]very local Fosdike, every local Waller" (17) is a testimony in reverse chronology to the influx of Normans after the conquest
and later of the Dutch, who came to trade. The lost name of the Deben, an
old map seems to indicate, was Adurnus, called that by the Romans who
came before the Dutch, and the Normans, and the Vikings, but after the
Celts.

In America the imprint of invasion and colonization is equally vivid,
though the effects are somewhat different. The Mississippi River and its tributaries are exemplars of American onomastics. Like *Mississippi,* many Native
American names have been filtered through the language of invaders, in this
case the French. The Indians who traded in Montreal referred to the "great
water" *(Mitchi-sipi)* of the great river (Balesi 7). A French missionary soft-
ened this to Mesippi (8), but the river was known through most of the
French colonial period, and through most of "Facts from an Apocryphal
Midwest," as the Colbert, after one of Louis XIV's most powerful ministers.
According to a Matthias source, Colbert was actually against colonizing the

136   valley of the river that bore his name (Sauer 142), adding another category to onomastics—the ironic name. Midwestern tributaries of the Colbert/Mississippi are variously called the Kankakee or Seignelay; the Illinois or *"Rivière des Illinois, ou Macopins"* ("Facts from an Apocryphal Midwest," *GW* 28); and the St. Joseph, "which the French called the River of the Miamis" (119). Without Matthias's notes at the end of the book, even a Midwesterner might be at sea here. But the rivers reveal two additional features of American place-names: the habit colonizers had of commemorating someone or something back home and the frequency with which Native American place-names fail to correspond to actual tribal homelands, partly because of the often-forced movement of tribes across the American landscape and partly because the rivers that bore their names flowed from place to place as well.

At this largely etymological level, onomastics is play, though serious play to the onomastically obsessed. Just how seriously playful can be seen from the titles of a few representative articles in the journal of the American Names Society, *Names:* "Prufrock / Smufrock," "The Origin of NYC's Nickname: *The Big Apple,*" and my particular favorite, "Looking Back to Beaver and the Head: Male College Nicknames in the 1950s." Play is, of course, a serious matter to Matthias's poetics, as he makes explicit in "Three Poems on Poetics," a chapter in *Reading Old Friends.* This collection of reviews and essays examines both poetics and the nature of reading, which for Matthias are intimately related. The first of the three poems on poetics, "Turns: Toward a Provisional Aesthetic and a Discipline," executes "a neat linguistic exercise" (194) in obscurity, a game whose rules are explained later in the poem, albeit somewhat obscurely. The game in "Double Derivation, Association, and Cliché: From *The Great Tournament Roll of Westminster*" is mock war, as in chess or football or backyard dress-up battles on a hot summer day in Ohio, for "out of revels" comes "revelation" (199)—and, if you are lucky, revolution in the form of cultural epiphany. The tournaments, after all, marked the commemorative end of one way to make war. "Clarifications for Robert Jacoby" defends this devotion to play, to "a world of imagination, / Lovely and legitimate" (203), and to happy accidents like poetry's most famous misprint: "brightness falls from the air" (201).

> *A rose would smell as sweet*
> *is a rose would smell as sweet*
> *is a rose would smell as sweet.*

Less obvious (and less obviously playful) than these etymological issues, but even more important and integral to the poems in *A Gathering of Ways,* are the philosophical and linguistic implications of proper names, which have become something of a cause célèbre for philosophers from J. S. Mill to Bertrand Russell to Gottlob Frege to Saul Kripke to Jacques Derrida. Naming provides interesting answers to the question of how language relates to reality, a question that has obsessed twentieth-century linguists, philosophers, literary theorists—and poets, who arguably should be first, not last, on this list. Proper names in particular are the hinge for a whole series of philosophical and linguistic polarities: necessity and contingency (and by extension, essentialism and nominalism), sense and reference, a priori and a posteriori knowledge, truth and falsehood, identity and significance, connotation and denotation, description and ostension, singularity and multiplicity, parole and langue, presence and absence, signifier and signified—all of which are at play in *A Gathering of Ways*.

John Stuart Mill helped initiate the modern controversy about proper names by suggesting that they are purely denotative. Going a step further, Bertrand Russell insisted the demonstratives *this* and *that* are the only true proper names because they are purely ostensive, not merely "abbreviations for descriptions" (quoted in Gardiner 59) like "Hortulanus in his garden" ("A Compostela Diptych," *GW* 6). Proper names are "words for particulars" (58), and "a name . . . can only be applied to a particular with which the speaker is acquainted, because you cannot name anything you are not acquainted with," says Russell (quoted in Gardiner 59).

> and talking with a friend who'll ask:
> *And what are you fighting for over there?*
>
> he'll pick a pinch of earth up off the path
> they're walking and say: *This!*
> *For this,* he'll say.
> *This This This*
> *For*
> > *this*
> > ("An East Anglian Diptych," *GW* 6)

"This" is what "the young man soon to die at Arras" (5) is most familiar with, the land he walks and writes about, a land both palpable and fertile with the bones of his ancestors. Ironically, according to his biographer, Jan Marsh, Edward Thomas's actual answer to the question posed by his unnamed friend Eleanor Farjeon was, "Literally for this" (155). His insistence on literalness paradoxically makes the statement figurative; that is, less ostensive than synecdochical.

Gottlob Frege countered the ostensive Russell and Mill by maintaining that proper names have both sense and reference; that is, both connotation and denotation, figuration and actuality. (Venus is the morning star and the evening star; the reference is the same, the sense different.) For Saul Kripke, proper names are, by contrast, "rigid designators" used to "fix a reference" (5), however wide the scope (Venus is the morning star, the evening star, the second planet from the sun, but not the planet with the rings). Kripke also concludes that "identity statements between names" (99) are logically "necessary," not contingent. But unless they are tautological (Venus is Venus), and therefore trivial, they can only be known a posteriori; that is, after investigation provides knowledge to fill in the second half of the equation, as Babylonian astronomers did when they discovered both the morning star and the evening star were Venus. Successive use of a name amounts to a "causal chain of reference" (King 183). In other words, once a name has been bestowed, its reference remains stable no matter how often it is used or by whom—or how much information is added to it (Venus = second rock from the sun).

Kripke published *Naming and Necessity* in 1972, but as early as 1953, drawing on what he described as "recent linguistic theory," Alan Gardiner was maintaining that "the category of proper names is a category of Language, not a category of Speech" (6). It was a way of grappling with the problematic properness of names with multiple referents (Venus the goddess and Venus the planet), of multiple names for the same referent (Venus and Aphrodite), of plural names (the Venuses of Arles and Willendorf), and of singular entities like God and the sun that might be categorized as Speech rather than Language. The sun, says Gardiner, is only properly proper when personified, as Sol, for instance (28)—or "Bel," or "Belus" ("An East Anglian Diptych," *GW* 4), or "Helith" (19), or "the King of all these Frenchmen [who] *was* the sun" ("Notes from an Apocryphal Midwest," *GW* 32), or the Light of the Manichees, the Albigensians, the Eleusinians. Other such singular entities not usually considered proper names in spite of their singularity include "moon, paradise, hell, . . . zenith, nadir . . . zodiac, demiurge, . . . polestar" (Gardiner 28). These questionable proper names, often cited by philosophers of language to prove or disprove various theories of proper names, appear with interesting regularity and under various guises in "A Compostela Diptych": "Polestar's daughter urging / them to Finisterre" (57); "was it *zenith* now or *nadir* in the Latin Arabic" (84); "the moon on his shoulder, the pole star in his eye" (90); "Everyone a step-child to some devotee of Sol Invictus" (107); "the demiurge / was author of this world" (71). Polestar is especially intriguing because Matthias uses it in different contexts as a personified, and therefore proper, name, and as a common, albeit singular, one.

Two decades after Gardiner published *The Theory of Proper Names,* Roland Barthes would devote much of *S/Z* to what could not be named:

> All the signifieds which compose the portrait are "true," for they are part of the definition. . . . but even taken together, they do not suffice to name it. . . . The connotative signified is literally an *index:* it points but does not tell; what it points to is the name, the truth of the name; it is both the temptation to name and the impotence to name. (61–62)

Truth, connotation, the signified, ostension, and description are gathered here, as they are in Derrida's *Signéponge,* where the contradictory "temptation to name and . . . impotence to name" become the simultaneous self-encoding/self-erasure of the poet Francis Ponge in his own work. Derrida goes on to echo the surprising if subtle essentialism of Mill, Russell, and Kripke when he says, "The proper name . . . should have no meaning and should spend itself in immediate reference" (118). Even more surprising, nothing much new has been added in the way of real theory to the discourse on proper names by either Barthes or Derrida. Gardiner, for example, had already recognized that the "signified points to" its name when he suggested "the direction of thought is opposite" (7) for words and names. The sound of a word causes us to think of what it means; for a name the "raison d'être" (7), or "connotative signified," comes first.

> *I love you, Peter, Alex, Adam, Brian, whatever your name is.*
> —AUDREY HEPBURN TO CARY GRANT, *Charade*

All of these theories are cleverly summarized by Umberto Eco in *The Name of the Rose* when his medieval and monastic Sherlock Holmes explains how he deduced the name of the abbot's runaway horse (28). But in spite of Brother William's scholastic certainty, no one has yet come up with a philosophic, linguistic, or semiologic theory of proper names that "solves all the known problems . . . and . . . is free of difficulties of its own" (Linsky 18). In any case, Matthias's investigation of proper names is framed "in the language of the Castilian *juglares,* which is not, God knows, the language of the Latin clerks" ("A Compostela Diptych," *GW* 114) or the French theorists or even an Italian semiologic novelist. The play of theoretical opposites in *A Gathering of*

140   *Ways* constitutes a *poetics,* both as theory and as practice, making the poem experience not epistemology. Especially important to this onomastic poetics are necessity, reference, truth, identity, a posteriori knowledge, presence, and sometimes their inverses. Of course, necessity as Matthias presents it is not an equation from modal logic but a "force by source of sun" that takes three long poems, three circuitous journeys across two continents, and time travel that begins in prehistory to play out:

> . . . *& flint by salt by clay*
> *by sunrise and by sunset*
> *and at equinox, by equinox*
> ("An East Anglian Diptych," *GW* 3)

By flint the people of the Neolithic era, some ten thousand years ago, were able to make the tools that made farming possible. *By clay* they could fashion bowls to store their water, and *by salt* preserve their food. They could, in short, settle down with some hope of a less contingent future—at least until the flint, or clay, or salt gave out or the land became barren from overuse. When it did, they dug beneath the earth for flint with "antler picks" and "a shoulder bone" (4) in a mine now called "Grimes Graves" (7), or "scoured [the] long chalk man" (3) to renew the land by way of sacred rite, or moved, or traded. Trading, they became "walkers who / brought flint, brought salt, brought clay, / paved the way in footprints over peat / and grasses with their animals before them" (7), pacing out a road about which Edward Thomas could later say, with some etymological support, "It may someday be proved . . . the Icknield way . . . was an ox drove" (21). Passing their "flints as far down time as Waterloo / . . . Flushwork on Long Melford Church / . . . Queen Victoria's potteries" (5), they were taking the first steps toward what is known as civilization. The steps are arguably contingent, but the near tautology of "at equinox, by equinox" seems to justify this overdetermined reading.

    With settlement also came the necessity for "the tumulus, the barrow, and the grave" (9), which now mark the places of settlement as well as the places along the road made sacred by the bones beneath the earth. Such a demonstration of "religious care for the dead," says David Jones, defines us as human (*The Anathemata* 61). And this human necessity becomes a poetic one for both Jones and Matthias. In an essay titled "Robert Duncan and David Jones: Some Affinities," Matthias in fact describes Jones's understanding of his own *"materia poetica"* as having "everything to do with the channels through which the ancestral burial mounds, the stratified cultural deposits, were opened" (*Reading Old Friends* 111). For Jones they were opened by Wales; for Matthias, by his British wife's East Anglian "dear site" (Jones, *The Sleeping Lord* 55). "I slowly opened myself to the full geological, topographical, natural, historical, and social context of the region where I came . . . to write," he explains in "Places and Poems" (*Reading Old Friends* 47), an essay that is subtitled "A Self-Reading and a Reading of the Self in the Romantic Context from Wordsworth to Parkman." In opening himself to the place, he opened himself as well to the names of what was now also his own dear site: "Orford, Framlingham, the rivers Stour and Alde and Orwell and Deben and other places the names of which are utterly *resonant* for me now but which, at first, *meant* nothing" (43, emphasis added).

Matthias's resonance and meaning—meaning connotation and significance—counter the distrust of meaning expressed by Mill, Russell, Kripke, and Derrida. But the fertile connection between proper names and dear sites alluded to by Matthias had been noted by Alan Gardiner:

> The proprietary instinct is the seed-ground of proper names. Every man has his own home and family, his own goods and chattels, his own neighbors and town, his own country. According as these are dear to him, and according as they are too individually distinct to be grouped in a mere class, he gives them names which enables him to foist them upon the attention of the linguistic community at large. (57)

What Gardiner says here prefigures Derrida's "two stems" of the proper, "*propriety* and *property*" (*Signéponge* 28), and recalls Bertrand Russell's generally discredited assertion that proper names are only applicable "to a particular with which the speaker is acquainted." It is closest, however, to David Jones's seed-ground of poetry: "the actually loved and known" (preface to *The Anathemata* 25). For Jones, knowledge and love are what vivify all "effective signs" (25), which should be read as efficacious signs, sacramental and incarnational, not mere communication or propaganda or names foisted on the linguistic community.

Matthias clearly shares with Jones this reading of effective signs, as he does other affinities between Jones and Robert Duncan, poets to whom he dedicates "An East Anglian Diptych." He also shares their singularities. Like Duncan, he can be described as "an erudite conglomerate of all that [is] half or totally heretical in the course of Western cultural history," a comment made by Ekbert Faas that Matthias tellingly quotes in "Some Affinities" (*Reading Old Friends* 109). This love of the heretical is especially obvious in "A Compostela Diptych," where Matthias's sympathies, if not his beliefs, seem to be firmly with the Priscillians, the Albigensians, and even the Mithraists, all of whom participated in local cults forced underground by *Imperium,* a Jones word that Matthias appropriates. Like Jones, Matthias is intensely committed to the local, which creates a problem noted in the preface to *The Anathemata* for "the artist working outside a reasonably static culture-phase" (15). Matthias puts it this way: "If the goddess who would restore us does appear, but calls herself Rhiannon, what if no one acknowledges that name? And if she says her name is Kore, are the chances really better?" (*Reading Old Friends* 123).

"Who are you, *Khora?*" (*On the Name* 111) asks Jacques Derrida in an essay bearing the name "Khora." For Derrida, this *khora* of Plato's *Timaeus,* which is incidentally the source text for the Albigensian demiurge, is a place without a proper name and thus "a receptacle [that] *gives place* to all the stories, ontologic or mythic" (emphasis added, 117). Neither wholly logos nor wholly muthos, *khora* and the *Timaeus* nevertheless "[tell] what is necessary on the subject of necessity" (126), both philosophic and poetic, and on the subject of causality, both "necessary" and "divine" (127).

Kore, both divine and properly named, is part of Duncan's pantheon. Rhiannon, another name for Epona, rides through "An East Anglian Diptych" and through Jones's dear sites. The problem they both present is the other side of Derrida's problem. They are proper names with unknown, or at least unfamiliar, referents. The solution to this problem helps configure the poetics of Matthias as it had that of Duncan and Jones. Jones used prefaces and extensive notes both to elucidate the obscurities of his *materia poetica* and to make them immediate. Unlike Eliot's ironic and unconvincingly self-deprecating notes to *The Waste Land, The Anathemata*'s notes are meant to be genuinely helpful. Their companionable tone provides the "requisite nowness" (preface to *The Anathemata* 15) Jones is always aiming for, however culturally or historically distant his content and vocabulary. In Russell's parlance, the notes acquaint the listener with the "particular with which the speaker is acquainted." Matthias uses endnotes and a list of his sources to accomplish something similar. The technique invites participation in the glossing of the poem, reading as a medieval reader would, leaving the text for other texts and returning with an expanded sense of both.

This act of leaving the poem to explore the referent of a proper name foregrounds the a posteriori nature of identity statements involving names and initiates an epistemological game. For in spite of Matthias's careful and daunting listing of source texts, the materials he uses are not necessarily easy to find. It is not simply a matter of checking an index for Epona. Sometimes, it is true, the phrasing in the poem is nearly identical to the original, but as a curious result, what is not included from the source becomes part of the referent as new knowledge, and consequently part of the poem as well. When Matthias draws globally on a text rather than quoting exactly from it, the pilgrims who follow him must find their own way. That they are expected to do so is clear from the central image of *A Gathering of Ways*: the ways only exist because walkers, traders, dowsers, dodmen, colonizers, invaders, hunters, explorers, saints, heretics, pilgrims, troubadours, and chroniclers followed each other along them. And, of course, they followed each other because the ways were there to follow. Geoffrey of Monmouth reports that *"no one seemed to know / the rules or lines whereby the boundaries / of the roads had been determined"* and then "consults the works / of Gildas" for verification ("An East Anglian Diptych," *GW* 7). Francis Parkman "read [La Salle's] words, and read the words and followed all the trails of others who had passed this way before he did himself" ("Notes from an Apocryphal Midwest," *GW* 43). Arnauld du Mont transcribed "the writings of Picaud" ("A Compostela Diptych," *GW* 64), whom everyone read and followed and quoted.

Reading the ways and walking them become "by necessity" contiguous: "Whichever way / they came they sang. / Whichever song they sang they came" ("A Compostela Diptych," *GW* 57). And so to understand how "Matrona, Bel, and Wandil gather in the mist / upon the hillside" ("An East Anglian Diptych," *GW* 10), it is necessary to read all of T. C. Lethbridge's strange little book *Gogmagog: The Buried Gods.* Even with Matthias's notational hint that Lethbridge is himself a dowser (117), it takes some digging to recognize "his sounding rod" is the one that "bites into chalk" to discover figures carved millennia ago into a hill just off the Icknield Way ("An East Anglian Diptych," *GW* 10). Lethbridge, who it turns out is actually an archaeologist, or modern-day dowser, begins his book with "a fairy tale" and proceeds with digressions and false starts that read like a handwriting exercise constantly looping back on itself before making headway. But with each loop, something new is added to the names in "An East Anglian Diptych." Buried in the text is even a suggestion that elucidates "A Compostela Diptych": "[T]he Norman kings, down to the Plantagenets, were devotees of the witch cult" (139). Did "the song that found the south for Eleanor of Aquitaine" (75) find its way to England through her marriage to a Plantagenet, or was it the other way round?

In *A Poetics,* Charles Bernstein suggests that leaving Olson's *Maximus Poems* to read everything Olson had read would not be much fun. Perhaps fortunately, George Butterick has already done that for us. But dipping into Matthias's sources *is* a part of the fun, especially the more arcane and quirky ones. To read Lethbridge, Joutel, Picaud, Jacobus de Voragine; to reread *The*

144   *Poem of the Cid* and the *Song of Roland* is to revel in "the nonuse value of language" Bernstein praises Stein for (144), in David Jones's "extra-utile," and in
Matthias's own notion of *"play"* (*Reading Old Friends* 118). Referents prolif-
erate, existing by "necessity" in the proper names themselves, in the texts that
shelter them, and in the knowledge found in these texts. They cascade off
names like the glued-together cards in a trick-playing deck, distinct yet
metonymically contiguous. The distance between a name and referent can be
measured by its relevance to the immediate moment of the poem and by the
time it takes to "look it up."

> But distances are tricky
> and it often takes
> you longer
> than you think. ("Notes from an Apocryphal Midwest," *GW* 25)

To give the game more torque, Matthias sometimes delights in Barthian
"snares" that further delay, sidetrack, or confuse by separating name from referent, playing on multiple referents with the same name, or presenting multiple names for the same referent. In the last category, Rodrigo Diaz de Vivar,
also known as Ruy, or el campeador (the companion), or El Cid, wins hands
down. Matthias also calls him Rodrigo Diaz El Compeador, Don Rodrigo,
Don Rodrigo Diaz, and just plain Rodrigo, and if that isn't confusing
enough, he explains that the Cid's anonymous chronicler "sang the life of
Don Rodrigo while El Cid / yet earned the fame to warrant song" ("A Compostela Diptych," *GW* 102), making Don Rodrigo sound as if he were a different fellow altogether from El Cid. He was, of course, as a comparison
between the fictional *Poem of the Cid* and the historical Cid described by
Ramon Menendez Pidal demonstrates. Yet it is the legendary nickname, El
Cid, not the given name, Don Rodrigo, that lives in the "real" world, earn-
ing the right to both the legend and the alias.

At least the exploits of the Cid are familiar enough to make spotting him
somewhat less difficult than sorting out the various generations of Onan-
gizes, Pokagons, Alfonsos, Sanchos, and Abd-al-Rahamans, the last of whom
is formally introduced this way:

> . . . the hungry Umayyad, hunted in the streets
> and alleys by the Abbasids, was going there:
>
> the young man hiding in the rushes of Euphrates
> then a silhouetted horseman riding through the desert
>   in the night,
> the moon on his shoulder, the pole star in his eye.

> Landing north of Malaga, he wrote his laws.
> Having *crossed the desert*
> *& the seas & mastered both the wasteland & the waves,*
>
> He came into his kingdom, for he was Abd-al-Rahman
> ("A Compostela Diptych," *GW* 90)

The many names for El Cid might be categorized by Roland Barthes as an *"equivocation"* (75), a wavering between truth and evasion that creates narrative delay, which in turn heightens the desire for narrative resolution. The three-stanza piling up of referents before the utterance of Abd-al-Rahman, the proper name that embodies them, is a *"suspended answer"* that defeats disclosure (75). "Anna and . . . Ethelreda, queen and saint" ("An East Anglian Diptych," *GW* 8) is a *"partial answer"* (Barthes 75), for although grammatically the appositive applies only to Ethelreda, as it does historically, the usually female referent for the name *Anna* creates the expectation that Anna is the queen, rather than the father of Ethelreda, saint and queen, that he in fact is. Such expectations created by narrative delay are related, says Barthes, to the expectation of recurrence that structures poetic rhyme, a balance of distance and proximity that plays on similarity and identity.

> *The man's the same even if the name isn't.*
> —CARY GRANT TO AUDREY HEPBURN, *Charade*

Distance courts identity, and identity distance. "If the near is impossible, then the nearest, insofar as it is entirely other, also becomes the most distant. This happens through the proper name," says Jacques Derrida (*Signéponge* 98). On the other hand, "all the signs rime," says Robert Duncan, in a segment from "Structure of Rime" (*Bending the Bow* 4) cited by Matthias in "Some Affinities." Not coincidentally, the proper names in *A Gathering of Ways* rhyme in great profusion. Ezra Pound's nicknamed friend, Arnaut (Eliot), rhymes with Edward Thomas's unnamed friend, Robert Frost. The beheaded saints—Honoratus, James, and Denis—rhyme, for each carries his own severed head, as does Bertran de Born in Dante's hell. The cathedrals on the road to Santiago rhyme, for "the houses of St. James aligned / themselves from north of Arles into Spain" ("A Compostela Diptych," *GW* 71), each with its own holy relics, its shared vision of Romanesque magnificence. Vortigern in "An East Anglian Diptych" (19) rhymes with Charlemagne (66), the sons of the Visigoth Witiza (89), and Franco (111) in

146   "A Compostela Diptych," for each makes war against one enemy by way of a dangerous liaison with another. Nicholas Perrot, "picking up a clod of earth and brandishing his sword" ("Notes from an Apocryphal Midwest," *GW* 33), is an off-rhyme with Edward Thomas and John Constable, who both pick "a pinch of earth up off the path" to a different end ("An East Anglian Diptych," *GW* 6, 13).

When rhymes are assimilated to refrain, one of Matthias's most frequent poetic practices, they move from similarity to identity, which is apparently a far more interesting concept to him since he largely eschews metaphor unless it comes from a source text. His obsession with historical proper names veers the poems away from figuration as well, exactly because these names have fixed referents in a real world of event, however slippery its truth value. If the poem is caught in a "mimetic hallucination in order to describe political reality," as Derrida describes the Socratic argument against poetry (*On the Name* 118), at least the terms of the description are identical. And if proper names are not descriptive at all, then there is no hallucination, merely pointing, or pointing out.

Tellingly, the most obsessive refrain in *A Gathering of Ways* is Charlemagne's recurring "mimetic hallucination" translated from the Oxford *Song of Roland* attributed to Turaldos. It is a dream within a dream; that is, a dreamed vision sent by the angel Gabriel. As such, it is paradoxically both doubly distant from the natural world of "political reality" and, in the ancient tradition of dreams, a place where the natural and supernatural merge. It is also a dream of the classic medieval battle between our alleged animal and spiritual natures. On one side is "Li angles est tute noit a sun chef," the angel Gabriel, who spends the night watching at Charlemagne's head (154), then actually enters it through the dream. On the other side are the "bears and leopards" that "walked among the men in Charles' dream" ("A Compostela Diptych," *GW* 66). In the *Song of Roland* (156), they first try to devour the men, then actually "parolet altresi cume hum," speak like them and fight like them, all exercises in absorbing identity.

The dream, then, is the divine announcement of a battle to be fought with a known and brutish enemy but with an unknown outcome that will include the loss of a beloved comrade in arms. In the first two instances of the evolving refrain, it belongs to the original dreamer, Charlemagne. This fictional dream within a dream is followed in the poem by references to historical artifacts such as Charlemagne's own sometimes savage capitularies as well as to alternative fictions like "the Cluny version" (67), falsely attributed to Turpin in the *Codex Calixtinus* that is misnamed for Pope Calixtus.

Historically, it was the Gascons who retaliated against the famous rearguard, not the Saracens, according to Einhard. As Charlemagne's contemporary and official biographer, Einhard represents "the facts" (68) as opposed to a tale several removes from its referents and encrypted in fiction, dream, and vision by layers of pseudo-authors. These ever-more-distant referents jostle as each of the chroniclers offers a version of truth that can only be tested by other equally problematic versions, for the factual is not privileged over the poetic, in defiance of Socrates. By the time the real but fanciful Aimery Picaud has the dream in the twelfth-century "Cluny version," the golden age of Abd-al-Rahman's tolerant rule of Muslim Spain is long over and *"there were times when all was war"* (95). This generalized warfare further undercuts Socrates' harangue against poets, which, Derrida points out, is a self-indictment. As inherently placeless outsiders, neither poets nor philosophers can ever "be capable of celebrating as one should this city and its citizens [in war]" (quoted in *On the Name;* the bracketed addition is Derrida's) or by "proper" naming. But when war is everywhere, it loses its localizing force. It is unbridled entitlement rather than a celebration of the "actually known and loved."

Two variations of the Roland refrain shift completely from Charlemagne to other dreamers. Bernard of Clairvaux dreams the recapture of Jerusalem by the Saladin, who had already retaken Tyre. His bad dream turns to an even worse nightmare, the desecration and dismantling of Cluny during the French Revolution, followed by Napoleon's violation of Spain, where in Galicia lay Saint James, whose bones had conjured Clunaic abbeys from Paris to Santiago. The final dreamer, British general John Moore, sees his own "high requiem" (110) as his troops fight to victory over the French in Galician La Coruña, where they had retreated to await evacuation by the British navy. Moore would indeed be fatally wounded in the battle there, which was one of the turning points against Napoleon in the Peninsular War, as Trafalgar under the fatally wounded Nelson had been against the Napoleonic bid to control the seas and eventually invade England.

If Charlemagne's recurring nightmare suggests that all wars are the same war, the "circle of dancers / who will help achieve the spring" ("An East Anglian Diptych," *GW* 20) suggests that all dominant gods are the same sun god. Behind this idea are T. C. Lethbridge, Eleanor Monro, and Guy Davenport, to whom "A Compostela Diptych " is dedicated. Lethbridge's book *Gogmagog: The Buried Gods* argues for a circle of identities, a confluence of person and place etymologically and physically. The name *Gogmagog* derives from a biblical reference, "Son of Man, set thy face against Gog, the land of Magog" (Ezek. 38, quoted in Lethbridge 10). Gog and Magog, person and

148   place, are collapsed into one name, first used by Geoffrey of Monmouth. It now refers both to a hill in Wandlebury and to the giant that "fairy tale" and legend connected with it. In the 1950s Lethbridge actually unearthed *three* giant figures on the hill. Invisible for more than a century, they were "Gog, Magog and Wandil" (72). Gog, a sun god, is the son or husband of Magog (167), who is the earth mother and the moon goddess (164). Wandil is he who "stole the spring" and was transformed, by way of punishment, into the constellation Gemini (Lethbridge 71; "An East Anglian Diptych," *GW* 10). Wandil, of course, gave his name to Wandlebury, as Gog and Magog had to the hill. The earliest of these giants goes back to the third century before Christ, and there is evidence the figures were "scoured," or cleaned, in an annual ritual up to the seventeenth century (Lethbridge 174), etching them more and more deeply into the land that bore their names even as the referents to these names became more distant and more dim. They are testimonies to the power of names and of rites.

   Each of these hill divinities has other pertinent referents as well, according to Lethbridge. Magog is also both Matrona and Epona, who in turn is related to "the Greek [horse] goddess 'Hippa,' the mother of Apollo, the sun god" (68). Gog is related to Helith (92), who is identified with Belenus, also known as Bel (165), "the equivalent to Siva, whose consort Kali . . . is the counterpart of Magog" (165). These pairs are all "deities of fruitfulness" (165). Their figuration in the hillside was the effect, not the object, of rite, says Lethbridge (23). Cut into the turf year after year until they bit into the chalk subsoil, they are like the roads that lead to them, a result of process, an implicit necessity. But the gods they represent, Gog, Magog, Wandil, Siva, Kali, are a mixed blessing that "remained at the back of medieval Christianity, and may almost be said to be an underlying principle of modern civilization. . . . Light and darkness must always be at war" (98).

   Light and darkness are most clearly at war in "A Compostela Diptych," as orthodoxy, which would unite their creation under one God, battles with medieval Gnosticism and its heretical offspring. "There was, [Bernard of Clairvaux] thundered, darkness in the light. And light in the darkness of the fastness, of the desert, of the cave" (81), arguing against the Gnostics, for whom Logos, the First Light, *degrades* into the darkness of the material world and the song that breaks the silence of the unsung Word "in the stillness / before anything was still, when nothing / made a single sound and singularity was only nothing's / song unsinging" (114). Bernard's cave is the cave of Mithra, an Iranian sun god who entered the Roman pantheon in the second century but was later suppressed by Imperial Christianity. Mithraism is connected to Gnostic Christianity by the shared iconography of the cave, in which, according to an apocryphal gospel attributed to Saint James, Christ, like Mithra, was born. In this place of darkness, Mithra "by slaying the Bull of Heaven . . . releases the blood of life" (Gervers 592). The bull he slays is the bull Goya and Picasso paint, the bull on the frieze of Saint Maria del Camino under which Moore's troops camped, the bull that is sacrificed at Pamplona by Manolete and mass blood lust.

Mithra's sacrificial bull drags through Europe, and through "A Compostela Diptych," uniting time and place. But like the gods Lethbridge describes, Mithra himself is an ambivalent figure. He is, says Eleanor Monro, "the Warrior-god who slew the cosmic bull and so let evil into the world" (147), a rhyme with the Gnostic demiurge. His worship, like "the contours of the worship of Demeter and Persephone [also coincides] with grain-producing terrain, and with the contours of Catholicism" mapped by Guy Davenport in *The Geography of the Imagination* (10). Worship of sun gods with rites of bloody sacrifice to restore the land is thus a "force by source of sun" ("An East Anglian Diptych," *GW* 3) and fruitful organic decay. If Wandil stole the spring, then Mithra, or Christ, or some other sun god must "bleed the wheat they'd make into their bread" in order to restore it ("A Compostela Diptych," *GW* 113).

The polestar, not the sun, is Eleanor Munro's guiding light and guiding metaphor. It shines over pilgrimage routes in India, Indonesia, Jerusalem, and Compostela, for unlike other stars, it is singular, fixed in the sky over the North Pole, the *"father, risen into myth"* (56) and proper name. The polestar and the Milky Way point to the route to Santiago, to Saint James, whose "body is Galicia; [whose] soul a field of stars" ("A Compostela Diptych," *GW* 67), a conscious rhyme with Jones's "Sleeping Lord," whose body "is the wasted land" of Wales (96). Munro describes the road to Compostela as "one more of those 'heavenly rivers' like the Ganges, Euphrates, Jordan, and Nile that flow down from the sky across the earth to the sea, only to rise back into *identity* as the River of Stars" (179, emphasis added), as do the rivers in "An East Anglian Diptych." Trailing this heaven-borne river (or field) of stars are Saint James, in his reincarnation as sun god, and the Black Madonna (Munro 183), the chthonic goddess who rises again and again out of the fire of the poem or falls "from very heaven" ("A Compostela Diptych," *GW* 57). She is both Polestar's daughter, "who rose up on a scallop shell" (60), and the mother of his son, says Munro, "destined for cosmic instrumentality from the time of her fourth-century designation as Theotokis: generatrix of God himself, the Father" (203). Riding her scallop shell, the emblem of female

150 genitalia, she provides James with vicarious sexuality, like Ginger Rogers dancing with Fred Astaire. She is Matrona, Magog, Kali, Aphrodite, and Mary as James is Gog, Bel, Siva, Apollo, and Christ. "If *Belus* is spelt *Bel*" ("An East Anglian Diptych," *GW* 4), and even if it isn't, the gods and goddesses have begun to actually "merge and absorb one another" (Monro 148), becoming the one, "true," singular God of Christianity, the Divine Logos.

This god has only one referent, a self-generating trinity—father, son, and the love that unites them—a holy identity in three parts from which there is no escape. The danger of dualist religions—Mithraism, Priscillianism, Albigensianism—is potential reversion to polytheism, to multiple and local gods, always a threat to Imperium. What follows in the name of the Word is Crusade, Auto-da-Fe, religious war, all to ensure "As it was in the beginning . . . it will be in the end" ("A Compostela Diptych," *GW* 115). Language becomes teleological, folding back on itself. Naming, in the absence of local deities, is dislocated from its seed ground. New names for people or places can be pulled out of a limited wardrobe of saints' names, like second-hand clothes passed on to a poor relative. But no *"midonz"* (77) can pour from the throat of some light-dazzled worshipper to honor a new goddess riding the numinous seashell of her self-generation, ashimmer with extra-utile meaning. This thwarted impulse to name a local god explains the cult of Saint James. The very lack of detailed referentiality makes him, like Derrida's *khora* "a receptacle [that] gives place to all the stories." *Khora* is a referent without a proper name; Saint James is a name without referent. Together they exemplify the "temptation to name" Barthes speaks of, a temptation to take possession of what is named, to know it and love it, or at its worst extreme, to own it.

> *I don't like my name. I won't have*
> *a name and I'll just be a girl.*
> —Cynouai Matthias, quoted in "Epilogue for a New Home"

Naming "monumentalizes," says Jacques Derrida in *Signéponge* (4). It can, by extension, even confer divinity, as it does particularity. In fact, the two are related. "The place is the [W]ord," Derrida quotes Angelus Silesius, a seventeenth-century German poet whose work hovers between mystical Christianity and pantheism (*On the Name* 57). But when we cease to be able to deify what rises out of our "dear site," and then to name and celebrate our deities locally, proper names lose some of their numinous power. Using a name is a "renaming," and repeated use confers "renown," to apply Derrida's vocabulary. Perhaps because the extent of this renown is inevitably circum-scribed by monotheism, some of the most crucial names in *A Gathering of Ways* are never spoken. Like Derrida's *khora,* they are signifieds with no sig-nifier.

Most noticeably, it is women who are unnamed—in the poem as they are in history. Evoked only as goddesses or the occasional queen, they become conspicuous by their absence. Equally conspicuous are the singers of the ways, the chroniclers, who are also unnamed, or named belatedly, or anonymous and therefore nameless, or so little known their names require renaming: Edward Thomas, John Constable, Ezra Pound (and their friends); Henri Joutel and Francis Parkman; Aimery Picaud; the singer who "sang the life of Don Rodrigo" ("A Compostela Diptych," 102); those who sang "the song that found the south for Eleanor of Aquitaine" (75); and Matthias him-self. The poems offer everything of them *"sauf le nom,"* save the name. In an essay so titled (*On the Name* 35), Derrida plays off the various meanings of this phrase: except the name, protect the name, preserve the name, withhold the name. Matthias plays this game as well, conjuring, as does *khora's* "absent body," unnamed presences "more 'here' than any 'here'" (56). For Derrida, the paradigm of such absent presences is the rhetorical figure *apophasis,* which affirms by denial, encoding a contradictory desire to be universally understood and to preserve a [Gnostic] secret only revealed to those who "are capable or worthy" of understanding it (83). For Matthias, the paradigm is the cenotaph, a burial monument without a body, a disembodied tomb that can be reembodied only "in a man's imagination or before him on this page" ("Notes from an Apocryphal Midwest," *GW* 48). The content of the imagi-nation, of the song itself, thus takes precedence over the unnamed singer. But the singers are far from forgotten or erased. They are often named outside of the poem in the notes, bringing the outside inside to resolve another binary opposition and to reveal the apophasic secret. For the reader willing to fol-low Matthias outside the poem to his sources, the Gnostic secret is revealed as well.

The closing lines of "Clarifications for Robert Jacoby," one of the three poems Matthias designates to represent his poetics, also make the case for the incarnational power of imagination incarnated in the written word, as it is in the proper name. While the poet writes, outside his window a child in a field imitates a wren and enters the poem. She is "here in the poem as surely as there" (*Reading Old Friends* 203). "[I]n the world / of her imagining . . . / She is a wren" (204). In the world of the poet's imagining she returns to a home that is unhappy "because [he says] so" (204). But the poet who has the power to imagine her unhappy also has the power to return her to her world of fantasy. And so at the end of the poem, he does: "She is a wren— / She remains in the field" (204)—of her imagination, of his imagination, of the poem. Like Duncan's famous meadow in "Often I Am Permitted to Return to a Meadow," it is a field you can revisit "as if it were a given property of the mind" (*Selected Poems* 44) because *"the place is itself in you,"* says Silesius (quoted in *On the Name* 57). This internalized *khora,* or place, is Silesius's internalized Divine Logos, Jones's dear site, Duncan's meadow, Matthias's field, an actual "property of the mind" that is "so near to the heart" (Duncan 44), it is a proper name even when it is not named.

Matthias ends *A Gathering of Ways* by placing himself in the field of the poem, naming at last his own name and his wife's:

> I, John, walked with my wife Diana
> down from the Somport Pass following the silence
> that invited and received my song
>   ("A Compostela Diptych," *GW* 115).

Like all the namings in the poem, this complicated gesture incorporates ostension, ownership, particularization, identification, and their opposites. It is signature ("I, John") and introduction ("my wife Diana"). Affirming both self-identity ("I, John") and otherness ("my wife Diana"), it balances identity and distance through an echo of the marriage rite. Giving only given names, it balances familiarity and specificity as well. Finally, it counts Matthias among the poem's many singers, while, through a rhyme with Picaud's transcriber ("I, Arnauld du Mont"), leaving unanswered the question of textual ownership that Derrida poses in *Signéponge* and *Glas.* As always, more interested in medieval than contemporary discourse, Matthias does, however, suggest an answer to the Gnostic quandary regarding the creation of the material world. Silence, he says, invites speech. Secret invites telling. Place invites name. The "singularity" that was unsung and unnamed nothingness (114) invites the gorgeous, generous, and generative polyphony of the poet's song. Like the "dapple of reflected cloud" (21) that ends "An East Anglian Diptych," song is always more than mere "mimetic hallucination." It is reflected cloud created by evaporation off reflective water replenished by cloud moisture in the form of rain. This complex image defines both Matthias's poetics and his own theory of proper names. As the dappled water that reflects the cloud constitutes it, the imagination constitutes what it imagines, and the proper name constitutes its referent.

Works Cited

Balesi, Charles John. *The Time of the French in the Heart of North America, 1673–1818.* 2d ed. Chicago: Alliance Francaise, 1996.

Barthes, Roland. *S/Z.* Trans. Richard Miller. New York: Hill and Wang, 1974.

Bernstein, Charles. *A Poetics.* Cambridge: Harvard University Press, 1992.

Brault, Gerald J., ed. and trans. *La Chanson de Roland.* University Park: Pennsylvania State University Press, 1984.

Davenport, Guy. *The Geography of the Imagination: Forty Essays.* San Francisco: North Point, 1981.

Derrida, Jacques. *On the Name.* Trans. and Ed. Thomas Dutoit. Meridian, Crossing Aesthetics. Stanford: Stanford University Press, 1995.

———. *Signéponge / Signsponge.* Trans. Richard Rand. New York: Columbia University Press, 1984.

Duncan, Robert. *Bending the Bow.* New York: New Directions, 1968.

———. *Selected Poems.* Ed. Robert J. Bertholf. New York: New Directions, 1993.

Eco, Umberto. *The Name of the Rose.* Trans. William Weaver. San Diego: Harcourt, 1980.

Gardiner, Alan. *The Theory of Proper Names: A Controversial Essay.* 2d ed. London: Oxford University Press, 1954.

Gervers, M. *Mysteria Mithrae.* Ed. M. J. Vermaseren. Études preliminaires aux religions orientales dans l'Empire Roman, 16. Leiden: Brill, 1979.

Jones, David. *The Anathemata: Fragments of an Attempted Writing.* New York: Viking, 1965.

———. *The Sleeping Lord and Other Fragments.* London: Faber, 1974.

King, Debra Walker. "Reading the 'Deep Talk' of Literary Names and Naming." *Names* 42.3 (September 1994): 188–99.

Kripke, Saul A. *Naming and Necessity.* Cambridge: Harvard University Press, 1980.

Lethbridge, Thomas Charles. *Gogmagog: The Buried Gods.* London: Routledge, 1957.

Linsky, Leonard. *Names and Descriptions.* Chicago: University of Chicago Press, 1977.

Marsh, Jan. *Edward Thomas: A Poet for His Country.* London: P. Elek, 1978.

Matthias, John. *A Gathering of Ways.* Athens: Swallow, 1991.

———. *Reading Old Friends: Essays, Reviews, and Poems on Poetics, 1975–1990.* The Margins of Literature Series. Albany: State University of New York Press, 1992.

———. *Turns.* Chicago: Swallow, 1975.

Munro, Eleanor. *On Glory Road: A Pilgrim's Book about Pilgrimage.* New York: Thames and Hudson, 1987.

Sauer, Carl O. *Seventeenth Century North America.* Berkeley: Turtle Island, 1980.

Thomas, Edward. *The Icknield Way.* London: Constable, 1913.

❧ "To Find the Song"—
John Matthias and the
Legacy of David Jones

KATHLEEN HENDERSON STAUDT

There is only one tale to tell even though the telling is patient of end-less development and ingenuity and can take on a million variant forms. I imagine something of this sort to be implicit in what Picasso is reported as saying: I do not seek, I find.
—DAVID JONES, preface to *The Anathemata*

The geste says this and the man who was on the field . . . and who wrote the book . . . the man who does not know this has not under-stood anything.
—DAVID JONES, closing lines of *In Parenthesis*

The work of John Matthias mines an important vein in the modern poetic imagination—opened by David Jones in *In Parenthesis,* in "Rite and Fore-time," and in the multivocity of the voyage sequence in *The Anathemata.* For both poets, the making of a poetic shape is an affirmative act of discovery, of listening, of process and survival—a faithful effort, as Jones put it, "to make a shape out of the very things of which one is oneself made" (*The Anathemata* [hereafter *A*], 10). In Jones, the process of finding and making a poetic shape, however costly, always ends in offering and imag-ination in the face of loss and historical forgetfulness. In some of his earliest poetry, where he echoes the language and style of Jones, and most strikingly in *A Gathering of Ways,* Matthias's poetry pulls together personal and historic, letting modern language and image play against fleeting, elusive historical insight. Light comes, in his work, when poetry, a sense of corporate history, and personal pilgrimage meet.

The opening sequence of *A Gathering of Ways,* "Ley Lines, Rivers," is dedicated to David Jones and Robert Duncan. In these two poets, Matthias recognizes an approach to poetic making that appeals fundamentally to him. As he observes in his essay on the two poets, both recognize the act of making as a fundamentally human act, and both see affinities between the poet and the priest, as makers of signs who offer what they have made in a ritual, communal gesture. What he finds most congenial in them, perhaps, is their shared commitment to what Jones calls "the actually loved and known" (*A* 24) as the material of poetic making (*Reading Old Friends* 109–14). Like Jones and Duncan, Matthias uses allusions to poets, artists, warriors, and makers from other times in history, belonging to places that he has lived in and loved. Like them, he writes poetry that may seem erudite and elusive, but which is in fact built of things that have interested and formed the poet—that he has found ready to hand. Reading Matthias, and especially following his engagement with various cultural materials through the three poetic sequences that make up *A Gathering of Ways,* one can also discern a growing and deepening personal voice, as the poet clarifies and illumines his own relationship to the things and places that have formed him, and seeks through his poetic materials to give new expression to his own lived experience—"to find the way. . . . to find the song," as he puts it in "A Compostela Diptych" (*GW* 75).

Some of Matthias's earliest lyric poems, and most notably the "East Anglian Diptych: Ley Lines, Rivers" in *A Gathering of Ways,* employ self-consciously the Jonesian discipline of "digging down" through the strata of place and history as a way of situating the modern poet's own experience. In his "East Anglian Poem," published in *Turns* (1975), Matthias adopts as a poetic discipline Jones's habit of interrogating artifacts and geographical sites, asking in his own way, "Who were they?" (or more often, "Who was he?") who lived and worked on this land before—and what story can be reimagined out of the faint traces left behind? The poem focuses on artifacts believed to have belonged to an early East Anglian chieftain, and beginning from them, imagines what his people felt about him, and what he saw in his day. A few lines from this poem typify the homage to Jones that is implicit throughout it. Reflecting on the warrior's artifacts, and on the people and cultures that came before him, Matthias writes:

> Within his hornworks
> Behind his stone and timber walls
> Below his towers and beneath his ample crop
>
> these early dead

> (he saw the Trinovantes destroyed
>   who later saw Caratacus in chains)
>
> Their armlets and their
> toe-rings will adorn. Bronze
> bowls, amphorae, still provide.
>
>
> . . . .
> Before him and unknown to him and
> southward came the stones: dolerite-blue
> with tiny bits of felspar. From the Mt. Prescelly
> outcrops—Carn Meini, Foel Trigarn (*NS* 70–71)

Readers familiar with Jones cannot fail to hear echoes in Matthias of Jones's careful attention to details of artifact and place-name. In Jones, this is reflected in the well-known passage from "Rite and Fore-Time" on the maker of the prehistoric female figure the Venus of Willendorf (*A* 59), in his interrogation of another prehistoric figure "Who was he, who? Himself at the cave-mouth" (*A* 66), and the recurring series of questions about what came "before" that organize "Rite and Fore-time" (see *A* 67–74).

The interrogation of a shadowy, quasi-mythic human figure and his actions in the history of a place is an identifiably Jonesian strategy. In the section of *The Anathemata* entitled "Angle-Land," for example, Jones's poem follows the journey of this shadowy forbear through the Celtic, Jutish, Saxon, Viking, and Roman phases of culture on this island, using resonant place-name and multilingual verbal texture to evoke the strata of history underlying "these isles" (see especially *A* 110). Matthias pays homage to this Jonesian technique in "East Anglian Diptych: Ley Lines, Rivers," the first sequence in *A Gathering of Ways,* when he evokes the shadowy figure of the prehistoric "Dod-man" who surveyed the land of East Anglia and laid out prehistoric tracks, still visible today, called "ley lines." Present-day dowsers, looking for water, follow the ley lines laid out by the dod-men. Thus near the beginning and end of the poem, "the dowser leans by Dod-man's / ley alignment and / against some oak by water now" (2, 20). In the companion poem, "Rivers," this continuity across the strata of history is expressed through a shift in language and social experience on a geographical site that has remained largely unchanged. Toward the end of this sequence, the poem reflects on the individual, named personalities who built the dams and walls to drain the seawater from the land around Deben. Beginning from a photograph from around 1850, the poet imagines what the speech of these men would have sounded like and portrays in the verbal texture of the lines a historical shift that has taken place, on this site, in language, culture, and material life:

> The bird that flies above them angling toward
> the Orford Ness they call a *mavis*
> by the time it reaches sprawling spider webs
>
> of early-warning radar nets it's lost its name,
> and anyone at Chantry Point
> looking with binoculars for avocets or curlews
>
> would only see, if it passed by, a thrush.
> Along the ley-alignment point
> at Sizewell, Beltane fires in the reactor
>
> are contained by water drained out of the sea. (16–17)

The imaginative movement from the nineteenth-century workers to the modern nuclear reactor on the same site, draining the sea for different purposes, in the service of civilization, is made by following the flight of the thrush, across time, its name changing from the old word *mavis,* with the echoes of the ley lines and "Beltane fires" recalling once again the antiquity of the land and of the history of human habitation on it. The use of language and words in this way, and the conjunction of contemporary present with time long past, is a hallmark of Matthias's work, as well as an homage to David Jones. Jones's work is characterized by an imaginative leaping between "strata" of history, revealing a typological continuity between phases in the story of human artifacture, and of human redemption, the underlying theme of all of *The Anathemata.* Matthias takes this Jonesian discipline in a different direction, pursuing in a linear, storytelling way the "continuities" that connect one moment in history to another, and especially the human personalities and experiences that connect the artist and poet in his own time to those who have gone before. Through his own vision of the lines that connect past and present, and his ear for language, he has learned to perceive and render in language what Jones calls "the inward continuities / of the site / of place" (*A* 90).

At the end of "Ley Lines, Rivers," the poet follows the sight lines from

158 the figures from zodiac and gogmagogs at Thetford abbey, following this surviving contemporary artifact back through history over the topography of
the land and the ancient ley lines, to bring the shadowy "he" of the poem to
life:

> Beyond the Roman camp, the Saxon mound.
> Beyond the Saxon mound the Viking
> outpost in the Celtic forest with its secret paths.
>
> Along the paths, the route to tributaries
> creeks, the sweetest hidden wells. Above the wells
> a dowser with his twig, a Dod-man
>
> with his sighting staves. . . . (*GW* 20)

These verbal and thematic echoes pay deliberate homage to Jones, as signaled
by Matthias's dedication to Jones and Duncan. They also reflect the subtle
and pervasive influence on Matthias of Jones's imaginative discipline of
exploring and interrogating. Places, place-names, archaeological sites, artifacts, and chronicle.

For an American, the continuity between present places and remote,
prehistoric civilization is troubling because the earliest human inhabitants of
the land had their cultures destroyed by European invaders. This theme
becomes a background or "ground bass" in Matthias's account of the history
of an American place in "Facts from an Apocryphal Midwest," the second
sequence in *A Gathering of Ways*. Faint echoes of their culture survive in some
Native American place-names, but most often the names are all that survives,
left behind by people who have been thoroughly dispossessed by the race and
civilization of the contemporary United States. Similarly, the brief empire of
the French in this part of North America is echoed in many of the family
names and commercial products from the region, and Matthias makes eloquent use of these names to suggest the additional loss that comes with the
disappearance of the French from the North American midwest. The cultural
loss is expressed in farcical wordplay on the Native American and French
names that survive, uprooted, into contemporary culture, in the part of the
sequence where Matthias first introduces the Old Sauk Trail, whose history
becomes the primary "way" through the Apocryphal Midwest of the imagination in this sequence:

> The old Sauk trail, they say
> still runs under U.S. 12
> north from Niles to Detroit.
> U.S. 20 takes it west through
> Rolling Prairie to Chicago.
>
> You can drive a car that's named
> for Cadillac up U.S. 12
> to Ypsilanti, turning north
> at 94 to a port named for the Hurons.
> You can even drive
> your Pontiac to Pontiac.
> But only trickster Wiske's brother
> Cibyabos ever drove
> in a Tecumseh to Tecumseh. (*GW* 29)

Weaving voices from Native American legend with the chronicles of La Salle and Father Hennepin, Matthias's poem brings to life the human encounter between these two cultures, how they saw each other, and subdued one another in their own ways, and how both ultimately had their histories buried by the ancestors of contemporary American culture, histories that now survive primarily in names and language.

Matthias reports in his endnotes that the writing of "Facts from an Apocryphal Midwest" began as "an act of will"—an effort to dig down into places that he had lived in but never attended to in the American midwest—and gradually became "something else," a more personal pilgrimage from distant into a more recent, imagined, and personal history (*GW* 120). We see evidence of Jones's imaginative example for this journey in the section of this poem entitled "The making of the Rivers and the Prairies." Here Matthias creates for an American sensibility a celebration of the history of the land that echoes Jones's account of *oreogenesis,* of the geological history of the Welsh hills and the landscape in "Rite and Foretime." In explicit textual echoes of the form of Jones's poem, Matthias uses place-names that evoke the history of land and places familiar to an American midwesterner:

> Before that rhetoric, that epigraph,
> gushing of the ancient, unheard waters all along
> the terminal moraine. Before the melt,

Maumee ice flow inching toward a Wabash
where no water ran, a Saginaw
into a dry Dowagiac. Before an unbound Kankakee,

glacial borders pressing ice lobes out
to flood the valley where no valley was, to spread
the drift two hundred feet and more above

Coniferous, Devonion and Trenton rock
Before the flood, copper manitous locked up in stone
on distant islands not enisled

before the miners who could dig for them
where no mines were and build the pregnant mounds
by forest trails that were not blazed.

[. . .]

Before the Potawatamis. Before the French.
Before the Studebaker &
the Bendix and the Burger Chef . . . .

[. . .]

From a millennium of glacial drift, the prairies
now had formed: Portage, Palmer,
Sumption . . .
       Terre Coupée. . . . (34–36)

Matthias may be unique in attempting this kind of self-conscious thematic
and stylistic imitation of Jones. Indeed, as the title poem of his volume
"turns," and many other poems since then, indicate, deliberate parody and
pastiche are an important part of his own poetic technique. The Jonesian
echoes are particularly effective here because of the contrasts they expose
between Jones's sense of place and the contemporary American poet's far less
rooted search for his own history in the "deposits" of his mundane midwestern surroundings.

In Jones's "Rite and Fore-time" humankind first enters geological history in the earliest relics of a cult of the dead in Europe, and the poem celebrates the continuity between these early "proto-makers" and subsequent human artists, through the prayer for the dead in the mass. The connection between human form makers and a divine Creator is palpable throughout this geological sequence. Matthias uses Jones's technique to a different end, to contrast the vastness of the land's history before widespread human habitation to the shallowness and fragmentation of culture among contemporary inhabitants of the same place. The record of European presence and absence on the land in this section begins and ends with the brief period of French sovereignty in North America. The making of the prairies is introduced by the Anglo-American explorer Francis Parkman's exclamation about the vanity of the French pretensions to empire in North America:

> Francis Parkman writes: "What remains of sovereignty
> thus pompously proclaimed?
>
> Now and then
> the accents of some straggling boatman or
> a half-breed vagabond—
>
> this and nothing more." (34)

In this context, the geological antiquity of the land becomes an ironic commentary on the futility of human pretensions to empire, a sense of antiquity troubling to American culture's focus on progress and material success. The old place-names contrast with the names of consumer goods, the Studebaker, the Bendix, and the Burger Chef—reflecting the rise of human invention and commercialism on this same land. The sequence as a whole ends by reflecting on the relative insignificance of the marks that the French conquerors left behind on this vast and ancient landscape and its people. Within limits, the poet's text—"before him on his page" (49) makes a memorial—a kind of anamnesis, even if it lives only in imagination—of human presences in the place. It shows how the history of human presences in the place leaves its mark, persists in poetic memory. Yet in another way, its memorial is deliberately meager, like the ephemeral, fictitious pageant in honor of La Salle with which the poem ends, or like the French echoes which Parkman noticed in some American dialects. The illegitimate sovereignty proclaimed by the French extends into the contemporary empire which has displaced them, and to which the poet himself belongs—the America of Cadillacs and Burger Chefs, whose rivers are full of tin cans and tires, and from which the Potawotamies, the Miamis, and the Native mythmaker Tisha have been driven out forever.

In both "East Anglian Diptych" and "Facts from an Apocryphal Midwest" the words and thoughts of human artists and chroniclers help connect the contemporary poet, in his effort to make a shape out of place and human history, to a tradition of other human makers. "Ley Lines, Rivers" features Edward Thomas, walking the countryside to write his book about the Icknield Way, just before the Great War, and John Constable, painting the countryside of East Anglia, and both artists are presented as men driven by the love of the land and a commitment to the demands of art to write or paint, despite other demands of personal life. Significantly, both pursue their art against a background of war. Reflecting on Thomas as the struggling artist, writing a book he doesn't like because he needs the money, the poem looks forward to a conversation between Thomas and "a friend who'll ask / *And what are you fighting for over there?*"

> he'll pick a pinch of earth up off the path
> they're walking and say: *This!*
> *For this,* he'll say.
> *This This This*
> *For*
>
> > *this*
>
> ("An East Anglian Diptych," *GW* 6)

And Constable, asked why he is drawing landscapes, gives the same answer—affirming the rooted connection between the artist and the land he walks on and the place where he works, whether he works in words or paint (13). Parallel to Thomas and Constable in "Facts for an Apocryphal Midwest" are the chroniclers, LaSalle and Francis Parkman, whose personal histories are blended with their reflections on the history of the land. Both of these sequences implicitly show the artist as a pilgrim—walking paths, following trails, exploring the land to find its beauty, its history, its human past. In the third sequence of *A Gathering of Ways,* the poet's role as pilgrim moves us into a dimension that draws together the historical and the spiritual longings of humankind, following the history of medieval pilgrimage routes to Compostela, in France and Spain. The often bloody chronicle of wars, crusades, Inquisition, and sectarian strife in this sequence nonetheless affirms, however paradoxically, the persistence in human beings—and especially in human artists—of a spiritual longing that both transcends and illuminates history. For the poet, this is increasingly expressed in what he calls the "song" sung by those who have gone before him on this pilgrim way, eyes open to the cruelties surrounding them, yet still walking and singing. Like David Jones's pilgrim Aneirin Lewis in the trenches of the Great War, who "sings where he walks, yet in a low voice, because of the Disciplines of the Wars" (*In Parenthesis* 42), they proceed through time and place, singing songs which affirm the persistence of the pilgrim's longing, a longing which in some way defines and discovers a path or "way" through history.

From the beginning, "A Compostela Diptych" draws attention to the musical sounds of words from the chronicles of pilgrimages to Compostela, especially the account given in the Provençal troubadour/historian Aimery Picaud. It also draws on chronicles and gestes from the twelfth century through the *Song of Roland,* the poema del Cid, and stories of Muslim poets and warriors in Spain and the leaders of the Spanish Inquisition, to the twentieth-century Spanish Civil War. The poem keeps returning to the music that is in the names of the roads: "Via Tolosona, Via Podiensis," and to the refrain of a story of the conquest of Spain by King Charlemagne: "From Mont Saint-Michel to Sens / from Bensancon to Finisterre, a darkness fell at noon, the walls of houses cracked, down / from all the belltowers tumbled bells." The same refrain frames other accounts of conquest in the history of Spain, so that the cracked walls, the tumbling belltowers become themselves a repeated "song" or geste recounting the brutalities that have determined the history of this land.

Yet behind the stories of conquest, Inquisition, and oppression, from the twelfth to the twentieth century, the "song" becomes increasingly a kind of redemptive thread running through them, reflecting a higher and deeper level of human longing: even when it is echoed ironically in the "Hoc Carmen Audite" of Torquemada (106). It is the making of the geste, the song, more than the acts recorded, that ties the twentieth-century poet to those who have gone before him on this pilgrimage. Thus in the first section of "A Compostela Diptych," the poem presents pilgrims and heretics walking together and singing, and the names of the roads they walked become a part of the song as they are a part of the contemporary poet's text:

Whichever way

they came they sang.
Whatever song they sang they came.
Whichever way they came, whatever song they sang,

> they sang and walked together on the
> common roads: Via Lemosina,
> Via Turonensis; Via Tolosona, Via Podiensis. (57)

The singing pilgrims here recall not only Jones's soldiers in the trenches of the Great War in *Parenthesis,* but also, more subtly, the repeated gestures toward a transcendent dimension of human historical experience which Jones achieves in his use of the Eucharistic celebration in *The Anathemata.*

Matthias's poem finds solidarity among human beings as pilgrims and singers of songs, and connects his own enterprise with theirs. A critical passage in the "France" section of "A Compostela Diptych" seems to parody in its questioning, in its very choice of words, the exploring voice that we hear in Jones's later work—especially in "The Anathemata" and at the beginning of "The Tutelar of the Place" (*Sleeping Lord* 59–60)—a voice which seems to speak of all of history at once, and to see in it the fundamental acts of sign-making which make us human. This echo of a Jonesian voice also announces the poetic procedure of questioning and seeking that is at the heart of Matthias's poem:

> But was it this that found the floriations
> in the columns, found in capitals
> the dance that found the music of the cloister & the choir,
>
> the song that found the south for Eleanor of Aquitaine?
> *Trobar,* they said: to find.
> To find one's way, one's path, to find the song (75)

Like Jones, Matthias seems to know that "there is one tale to tell even though the telling is patient of endless development and ingenuity and can take on a million variant forms," though he might rather have said "there is but one song to sing" and his enjoyment of the meaning of *trobar* reflects a shared appreciation, with Jones, of Picasso's aphorism, "I do not seek, I find" (*A* 35).

"A Compostela Diptych" is replete with verbal echoes of Jones, both in its voice and in its multilingual verbal texture. Matthias acknowledges in his afterword to the poem that David Jones has been throughout this sequence "a welcome and benevolent presence" (*GW* 122). Even more striking is the way in which Matthias has carried forward in his own highly personalized way the Jonesian imaginative legacy that discerns connections by celebrating human artworks from era to era, throughout history. Jones focuses on visual art and material craftsmanship and connects these to the verbal artifacture of the poet and the sacramental mystery celebrated by the priest at mass. Matthias, for his part, hears songs and sees dances more often than he focuses on the visual arts, and where Jones connected artifacture and liturgy, Matthias connects the song to prayer, in the pilgrims' song along the Compostela way, and in the troubadours, for whom there was an equivalence in "to sing, to pray." Their enterprise is connected to that of the modern poet through the figure of Ezra Pound, who ponders the temerity of the Provençal poet Arnaut Daniel, at the end of the "France" section (*GW* 78) and, most significantly, through the figure of John Matthias himself, the man who has written this geste, and who ends the poem by placing himself in it, as the latest in a series of witnesses to the process of pilgrimage which finds its shape, throughout history, in the song of the poet.

This personal dimension, introduced explicitly at the end of the sequence, typifies the originality of Matthias's work seen in the context of a Jones "legacy." In the end, we find the historic journey to Compostela, the effort to "find the song" are carried out most fully in the contemporary poet's personal response to the heritage of past pilgrims, and to the charged and transcendent "silence" that lies over the paths that they traveled:

> Towards Pamplona long long after all Navarre
> was Spain, and after the end
> of the Kingdom of Aragón, & after the end of the end,
>
> I, John, walked with my wife Diana
> down from the Somport Pass following the silence
> that invited and received my song (*GW* 115)

This poet's song speaks into the "silence" that follows all the human adventure, suffering, conquest, and oppression evoked by the pilgrimage route. What is left beyond the chronicle is an inviting, hospitable silence, and, surviving and singing into that silence, the poet's song, which comes, ultimately, out of the very personal experience of one person confronting personal and corporate history.

In the afterword to "A Compostela Diptych" Matthias acknowledges that he never reaches Santiago in life, or in the poem, but that the experience of pilgrimage reflected in the poem "became a pilgrimage in earnest when, without warning, I had first to help another person struggle toward physical and spiritual health, and then, unwell myself, begin a similar journey of my own" (121–22). The nature of this journey is illuminated in a lyric poem which appears in *Swimming at Midnight* under the title "Dedication to a Cycle of Poems on the Pilgrim Routes to Santiago de Compostela." In a poignant, heartbroken account of his daughter's struggle with suffering and illness, the poet here compares her difficult journey of recovery to the struggle of the ancient pilgrims. "She did nothing wrong," he writes, "And yet she walks in chains / along a Lemosina or a Tolosona Dolorosa" (*SM* 153). Conveying with devastating poignancy the grief of a parent who must watch a child struggle to heal herself, the poem closes by connecting the pilgrimage to Compostela with the personal pilgrimage to healing, and offers the journey as a prayer for wholeness:

> The journey's so entirely strange I cannot fathom it.
> And yet this map, this prayer:
> That she will somehow get to Compostela,
>
> take that how you may, & that I will be allowed to follow.
> And that Santiago, call him what you like,
> Son of Thunder, Good Saint Jacques, The Fisherman,
>
> Or whoever really lies there—
> hermit, heretic, shaman healer with no name—
> will somehow make us whole. (*SM* 153–54)

Here the quest for the song becomes and reflects a profoundly personal journey to wholeness, experienced in companionship with those who have gone before. In this weaving together of corporate history with his own experience, Matthias makes his own Jones's account of the poet's vocation "to make a shape out of the very things of which oneself is made" (*A* 10). Jones developed an analogy between the work of the poet and the priest, both of whom offer "effective signs" made out of the things of human experience and transforming and redeeming that experience. In Matthias, the sacramental analogy is between the poet and the pilgrim, the one who sings and the one who prays, both reaching into the silence "to find the way, one's path" (*GW* 75) through life and history, to reach into the silence beyond history which "invites and receives" the poet's making. Matthias's quest "to find the song" unites *A Gathering of Ways* as the offering of Eucharist unites the diverse elements of Jones's *Anathemata.* This quest, pursued in community with those

artists, makers, pilgrims, and chroniclers who have sought, sung, and prayed **167**
it before, establishes continuity and reaches toward wholeness, across the
strata of time, place and history. It thus invites readers and poets alike to
enter into companionship with this poet's journey along the pilgrim way.

Works Cited

Jones, David. *The Anathemata.* London: Faber & Faber, 1952.
———. *In Parenthesis.* London: Faber & Faber, 1937.
———. *The Sleeping Lord and Other Fragments.* New York: Chilmark Press, 1974.
Matthias, John. *A Gathering of Ways.* Athens: Swallow, 1991.
———. *Northern Summer: New and Selected Poems.* Athens, Ohio: Swallow, 1984.
———. *Reading Old Friends: Essays, Reviews and Poems on Poetics 1975–1990.* The Margins of
    Literature Series. Albany: State University of New York Press, 1992.
———. *Swimming at Midnight: Selected Shorter Poems.* Athens, Ohio: Swallow, 1995.

❧ A Poem Is a Place Is a Walk

A Reading of Two of John Matthias's Sequences

LARS-HÅKAN SVENSSON

*N*orthern Summer, John Matthias's fourth volume of verse, published in 1984, is, as its subtitle indicates, a collection of "new and selected poems." The new poems notably include two longer sequences, "A Wind in Roussillon" and "Northern Summer," which both bear eloquent witness to the poet's concern with place, belonging, and identity. "Northern Summer," true to its title, takes us as far north as Matthias has ever strayed as a poet. In fact, the poem not only grapples with the matter of Scotland (including Matthias's own Scottish ancestry and his attempt to relocate his European home in Scotland) but includes some crucial forays into Scandinavia—clearly a result of Matthias's collaboration with the Swedish poet, translator, and essayist Göran Printz-Påhlson on a volume of *Contemporary Swedish Poetry*, published in 1980. Written shortly after "Northern Summer,"[1] "A Wind in Roussillon" was, at the time of its publication, Matthias's most extensive poetic venture into southern Europe, though its precise and haunting evocations of the Mediterranean landscape had to some extent been prefigured by similar passages in the short sequence "From a Visit to Dalmatia" (from *Crossing*).

Though "A Wind in Roussillon" and "Northern Summer" are not, strictly speaking, companion poems, there are good reasons to examine them in tandem. Having pondered, among other things, place and identity from the mid-Atlantic vantage point adopted in the "Stefan Batory" and "Mihail Lermontov" sequences a few years earlier, the poet now returns to a consideration of the same issues in two new, widely dissimilar surroundings. Both "A Wind in Roussillon" and "Northern Summer" are powerful poems of place. Each poem reports on the poet's attempt at familiarizing himself with a new milieu. However, in so doing, he does not permit the prestigious localities he is exploring to impose themselves on him; rather, it is he who imposes on them two sets of heuristic terms—chiefly consisting of snippets of poetry totally unrelated to the places before him—which he reinterprets and recombines while absorbing and identifying the peculiar character of the two landscapes he is gradually learning to know.

At the same time, both poems—and particularly "Northern Summer"—reflect the artistic choices the poet is facing and, in a sense, are as much about finding an appropriate language in which to describe a place as about the place itself. The poems, then, describe an ongoing process which is not complete until the poems are complete. The geographical and conceptual ordering that goes on in the poems is therefore necessarily eclectic and unsystematic despite the poet's consistent attempts at organizing his material. While some passages deal with well-known, perhaps even picturesque, sights, which are deliberately treated as such, in other sections of his poems the poet seeks out unremarkable, "unpoetic" places, which become invested with personal significance. This is of course not surprising in itself, nor is the procedure as such without precedent in the Matthias corpus. A number of his previous poems, most notably "Clarification," "Epilogue," "Brandon, Breckland," and "Poem to Cynouai," and of course the "Batory" and "Lermontov" cycles, deal with place in a similar way, yet no previous poem assigns such a climactic function to place or makes such subtle use of it as the two sequences at issue. More than any of his previous poems they are concerned with the experience of coming to terms with the strangeness of an unfamiliar place, an attempt which is thwarted in both cases. Significantly, both poems contain emblematic portraits of famous exiles, inserted in a kind of *mise en abyme* fashion.

In both cases, too, the discursive attitude to place is paralleled by references to the speaker's exploration of the respective settings by foot, bus, or train (just as the speaker of the "Stefan Batory" and "Mihail Lermontov" cycles travels by boat). In fact, the two poems under discussion recall the "walk poem," the particular lyrical genre which Roger Gilbert, following some suggestive hints by A. R. Ammons, has shown to be a major category in contemporary American poetry.[2] It should be added, though, that Matthias's later sequences about the ley lines of East Anglia, the pilgrimage route to Compostela, and the paths and trails of the American Midwest—unthinkable without the two precedents discussed here—are more explicit instances of "walk poems." In "Northern Summer" and "A Wind in Roussillon" a lot of

170 walking and traveling is done, but the format of the individual sections is not typically determined by that of an actual walk as it is in the most typical examples examined by Gilbert.[3]

Both "Northern Summer" and "A Wind in Roussillon" are difficult poems, packed with historical and literary references which serve structural as well as ornamental functions. A full appreciation of these subtle and humorous poems is only possible if the reader makes an effort to sort out their literary and historical references, which are now specific, now deliberately obscure; much of the following essay is an attempt to do precisely that.[4] Interestingly, Matthias's method is apparent from the very way he handles the basic poetic sources which have shaped the two poems. The starting point of "Northern Summer" is an epigraph appropriated from the Swedish poet Göran Sonnevi. This epigraph is broken down into a number of kernel phrases, which enter into a complex dialogue with each other as well as with various other phrases of Matthias's own devising and a wealth of historical data to do with the various localities described in the poem.[5] By contrast, "A Wind in Roussillon" consists of a mosaic of poetic subtexts, which, together with historical data, form an intricate thematic and structural pattern. Interestingly, both poems have a circular form, ending where they begin, a formal design which is worth pondering since in each case the image or phrase permitting the poem to come full circle is derived from a literary source. This calls for further examination; suffice it to say here that I take it as evidence that the two poems constitute a transitional stage between Matthias's early sequences and the full-blown walk cycles collected in *A Gathering of Ways* (1991), which testify to a more inclusive and celebratory sense of place.

Göran Sonnevi's "Void which falls out of void" is one of the poems Matthias and Printz-Påhlson included in *Contemporary Swedish Poetry.* Its third and final stanza reads as follows:

> The flight of sentimentality through empty space.
> Through its elliptical hole
> an heraldic blackbird's
> black wings, yellow beak, round eyes, with the yellow
> ring, which defines its inner empty
> space. (67)

The poem as a whole describes a mind occupied in exploring and familiarizing unknown areas of experience, referred to as "void" and "empty space."

The multiple, not to say infinite, nature of such voids is suggested by the first line, "Void which falls out of void." Throughout, there is a striking contrast between abstract, geometrical terms typifying such voids and intimate, concrete references to individual experience. In the second stanza, the speaker admits that his body "falls in infinity through empty space" (67) but, in the process, he experiences a mental resilience exemplified by a Charlie Parker solo from the famous 1953 Massey Hall concert. In the third stanza, the same experience is described on a more abstract level as "the flight of sentimentality through empty space" (67). The flight of sentimentality is paralleled by that of "an heraldic blackbird." The adjective may at first seem somewhat surprising, but it is of course the bird's plainness that makes it exemplary. This is brought out by the ensuing description of the bird's features; the deliberate formality imitates the language used to describe heraldic signs. The linking of the blackbird with "sentimentality" is also noticeable. To be sure, "sentimentality" is not a frequent word in Sonnevi's vocabulary, which typically oscillates between colloquial phrases, including obscene slang, and abstract, scientific terms of a sometimes highly specialized kind. In view of Sonnevi's predilection for formal and specialized language, "sentimentality" should probably not be understood exclusively—or even chiefly—in the modern negative sense but also as referring to acute sensibility as it did in the eighteenth century: the blackbird's flight through empty space, as described in Sonnevi's poem, is indeed a sentimental journey. However, this view is implicitly questioned by Matthias's speaker, who puts a different interpretation on some of the components of Sonnevi's lines.

The first section of "Northern Summer" is a case in point. Though its title is "The Castle," it soon becomes apparent that its subject matter is not the castle as such. In the first stanza, a tour book rambles on for fourteen lines about the picturesque qualities and charming position of Wemyss Castle near Fife. Crucially, however, the monologue is interrupted at the precise moment when it is about to state whom or what the sight of this romantic spot might compensate. For a eulogy this is of course a critical moment to be interrupted at and leaves the field open to speculation as to what it is that the picturesque surroundings serve to conceal; however, the matter is not gone into. Instead, the poem's speaker makes a disparaging comment on the artificial language of such descriptions: "the language of a tour book / threading aimlessly / through sentimental empty space" (*BA* 93). Next follows an entirely different linguistic specimen, introduced by the paradoxical statement that building on this kind of language is to behave like a second generation that *builds* on the *ruins* of a first. The model examined here is the

172   precise, unadorned language used by Edward I in a letter to his favorite cousin, Aymar de Valance, in which the king complains about his former liege man Sir Michael Wemyss's treason and orders the destruction of his manors and gardens.[6] However, this second stylistic sample, too, is interrupted in mid-flow; in fact, it ends on a somber note after exactly the same number of lines as the excerpt from the tour book: "and all / may thus take warning—" (94). Discreetly, the passage also introduces what will turn out to be one of the major themes of the sequence as a whole—the opposition between north and south—a point further elaborated by the reference in the final line to Bruce (fought but not defeated by Aymar de Valance), making Wemyss an early center of Scottish devolution. Of more importance here, though, is the purpose of the comparison between the tour book and Edward's letter. Both examples are characterized by phrases derived from the Sonnevi epigraph and both are adapted to a new context. Whereas the turgid journalese of the guidebook is seen as an instance of language "threading aimlessly / through sentimental *empty* space" (emphasis mine), the exact, goal-directed language exemplified by Edward's letter suggests the "Flight / of an heraldic bird / through space that is *inhabited*" (emphasis mine) (93, 94). A distinction is thus made between empty and inhabited space—a distinction which has no precedent in Sonnevi's poem. Empty space is associated with sentimentality in the pejorative sense of the word, and inhabited space with the full presence of the heraldic bird. The two kinds of language thus reflect two perceptions of the castle and hence two different attitudes to place: one romantic and passive, the other factual and possessive. Yet place is not necessarily all that is at stake here: it is tempting to see the two linguistic specimens of two opposed ways of writing and the section as a metapoetic statement. In either case, the speaker's preference seems to rest with the second alternative, embodied by a beautiful phrase which, along with the Sonnevi tag which follows it, is one of the poem's recurring thematic refrains: "Language / moving upon consequence / Consequence / upon a language: Flight / of an heraldic bird / through space that is inhabited" (94).

The second section is entirely different in tone: energetic, self-mocking, colloquial, at times even slangy. Most of it is designed to establish a sense of place in the most down-to-earth meaning of the phrase. The voice we listen to is that of someone taking stock of new surroundings. This is apparent even from the title, "Pied-à-Terre," which refers to the speaker's habitat, a newly restored folly symbolically positioned between the castle and the mine. From this dubious vantage point the speaker characterizes his nonexistent relationship to his host by means of a humorous adaptation of one of Sonnevi's key terms: Captain Wemyss is "holed up in his castle" by "this awful rain" just as the speaker is "holed up" in his folly with his pads and pens (94). However, consideration of the captain's impressive pedigree results in a humorously self-pitying quotation of Sonnevi's first line, which is found unsatisfactory and then corrected:

> *The flight of sentimentality through empty space!*
> A rhetoric, at least; (an awkward line).
> The flight of Sentiment
> is through a space that's occupied. (95)

Captain Wemyss, who can look back on twenty-seven generations of purest Scottish blood, occupies the same space he inhabits in a way the speaker, with just one-eighth of watery Kirkpatrick blood to his credit, can never do.

The jokey tone turns ruminative as the speaker ponders two anecdotes concerning James V and James VI gleaned from "the Edinburgh historian" Sir William Fraser (95). These introduce another important motif—the cave, which can be a home or a hiding place, or a mine[7]—and the second one touches on the treason theme associated with Edward's charges against Sir Michael Wemyss in section I. Both aspects are relevant here. However, the main effect of these two episodes is to make the speaker realize that he is the guest of absent hosts, representing history and tradition, rather than of Captain Wemyss. If so, it is impossible to calculate "the cost of lodging" (96). Once more the "corrected" version of the Sonnevi adage is invoked to suggest that the speaker is bound to come up against a tradition which leaves no room for him. It is in this light that we must understand his meditation on the behavior of the legendary hero, Mynyddog Mynfawr. Like the other lords of Gododdin, Mynyddog was defended by a retinue of professional soldiers, who in return for carrying out their duty loyally and well were treated to food and drink by their lord. At one time, legend has it, "Mynyddog feasted this warband for a year in the great hall of Eidyn, perhaps awaiting a favourable moment, and then sent them out to attack the enemy" (Jackson 4).[8] Matthias's speaker, who appears to be familiar with this story, makes it the basis of his query concerning Mynyddog's alleged generosity toward his men. However, he also formulates a second question, which portrays Mynyddog as a somewhat less lavish mine owner. The two alternative versions of Mynyddog's treatment of his men appear to reflect on the preceding inquiry into "the cost of lodging." Since Mynyddog's treatment of his men is not susceptible to present-day investigation and since the anachronistic vision of him as a greedy mine owner has no foundation whatsoever in legend, it is clear that the speaker is using his material figuratively (even though the lines about Mynyddog appear to imitate the meter of the Gododdin epic)[9]. This digression seems to hark back to the topic raised in the first section. Mynyddog feeding his men mead and wine before doing battle is clearly a picturesque and generous character, whereas Mynyddog sending his men sober down his mine partakes of Edward's austerity and efficiency. In thus revising the main theme of the first section, the speaker seems less certain about his preference. This is true also if the passage is interpreted metapoetically, which seems perfectly possible in view of its abstract and figurative character.

The dialogue with Sonnevi about space and sentimentality continues in the next section, whose first line, "The flight through empty space of Sentiment" (96) is immediately corrected by the speaker's addition of the suffix "mentality" in line two. Sentimentality, however, is not the reigning mood of this section. The abandoned mine, even when observed from the likewise deserted beach, rouses the speaker to indignation and compassion. At the same time, these emotions are expressed in a curiously formal and indirect way. Thus, the disused lift, at first not identified as such, is said to resemble a gallows, erected by the legates of "the dead god Coal," equating mining with a primitive, sacrificial religion. The motif of hanging, which recurs throughout the sequence, is associated with some gigantic injustice, all the more terrifying for not being fully stated. The middle part of the poem consists of a barely controlled account of the deplorable working conditions of the miners. In fact, in describing the lives of these "virtual slaves" (97) the speaker rises to a rhetoric which recalls key passages in Gray's "Elegy Written in a Country Churchyard." In particular, the negated statements "No Free Miners from the Forest of Dean . . . No *gales,* no lease for them" parallel similar negated phrases in Gray's poem and invest them with a lofty pathos.[10] The reference to the Free Miners of the Forest of Dean also contains a social comment corresponding to the elegy's allusions to rebels such as Hampden and Cromwell.

The exploitation of the miners is expressed in very precise phrases which are rounded off by an allusion to the ballad of Sir Patrick Spence: "His child went underground at six / to earn an extra seven pence / lest he sail to Noroway with Sir Patrick Spence" (97). This is the second time a balladlike tone is heard in "Northern Summer." Like the jesting line in the second section, the deliberately archaic third line also has a jinglelike quality, emphasized in this case by the rhyme "pence" / "Spence." This line also serves to introduce the motif of the northern voyage, expanding the idea of a north/south conflict implied in section I. In Sir Patrick's case, sailing northward of course turned out to be a fatal enterprise, and in the version printed in Scott's *Minstrelsy* his voyage is explicitly connected with Norway:

> To Noroway, to Noroway
>> To Noroway o'er the faem
>> The king's daughter of Noroway
>>> 'Tis thou maun bring her hame. (see also Percy 98–100)

The *Oxford Anthology of English Literature* has the following comment on the ballad:

> Possibly, a historical event lies somewhere in the background: either the drowning of many Scots nobles in 1281, on their return voyage from escorting the Scottish king's daughter, Margaret, and her new husband, Eric of Norway, to their new house; or the death at sea of Margaret's daughter, the Maid of Norway, when she was being fetched home . . . a few years later. But no Sir Patrick Spence is connected with either voyage. (443 n. 1)

The reference to "Noroway" also contains an allusion to the Wemyss family. Andrew of Wyntoun, the chronicler mentioned earlier, records that Sir David Wemyss sailed to Norway in 1290 as Edward I's ambassador to escort the Maid of Norway back to Scotland ("Withe al hast in til Norowaye," Amours 5:161). In Matthias's poem, the line thus has a double function: it suggests escape from inhuman working conditions but also certain death while performing an act of loyalty.

The final part of the poem looks back to section II. The description of the fire leaping down the tunnel in the final two stanzas of section III (97) has an obvious symbolic dimension, which is clear from the notion that the fire could burn a hundred years, possibly as far as London. The final line ("Everyone . . . got out") may link this passage to the description of Mynyddog's men escaping or not escaping, as the case may be, from battle. There is of course also an echo of James VI's panic in the cave.

The uncanny stillness of the once-pulsating mining area is conveyed by a laconic one-liner, repeated three times: "The tower's erect upon the hill, but nothing moves" (96, 97). When the line is repeated for the third time, the order of its components is reversed so as to explain and contradict the present lack of movement:

A tanker streams across the bleak horizon.
The tower's erect upon the hill. (97)

After section III's immersion in place follow two more discursive sections which are intimately linked with each other. Their affinity appears not only from the similarity of their respective titles but from some passages of striking verbal resemblance. Thus, for example, Mary is seen as looking out of a window in IV just as Elcho gazes out of "casement windows" in V; both sections focus "The empty space / between the window and / the place he stood beside his horse . . . was filled at once / with Feeling" (IV, 98) and "The empty space between the window / framing Elcho and the place the clansmen camped / filled up in time with sentimental tales" (V, 100). The smoldering coal first encountered in III recurs both in IV ("Every fireplace here at Wemyss was blazing / full of fine Wemyss coal," 98), where it serves to intimate the incipient attraction between Mary and Darnley, and in V ("history smoldered with surprises / older than the coal fields / on the Wemyss estate," 99), where it carries political associations. At the same time, it is obvious that the themes treated in the two sections differ. Section IV views the abortive love affair between Mary and Darnley against a background of cynical comments, culminating in Bothwell's observation that Darnley suffered from syphilis, not smallpox. Thus, in a roundabout way, it revises the notion of romance associated with the castle in the first part of section I, examining Darnley's courtship of Mary *in situ* and comically contrasting the speaker's ambitions with Darnley's ("I had come / to get a pan . . . He had come to woo a queen," 98). Since the previous section decries the notion of empty space being traversed by sentiment, the assertion that the empty space between the window and the place he stood beside his horse "was filled with Feeling" must be read as criticism, much as the final line ("At Wemyss it was a sentimental morning") implies that Mary's and Darnley's infatuation was ill-omened (99).

If section IV, then, explores sentimental matter against a decidedly unsentimental background, section V casts an equally cold eye on the uneasy relations of Bonnie Prince Charlie and David Wemyss, Lord Elcho. Whereas the beginning of the poem, with its enumeration of Charles's full name and presentation of him as "the grand Chevalier," focuses on the flamboyant and charming aspects of his personality, Elcho is portrayed as a "brooding and attainted" observer of the glamour and excitement at Holyrood House (99). Though a Jacobite, Elcho had been opposed to the rising in 1745 but joined it just as Prince Charlie was nearing Edinburgh and was chosen one of his council. He later accompanied Charles in his flight abroad, which led to his not succeeding either to his estates or titles (*Dictionary of National Biography*, 60:247). Elcho's loyalty to Prince Charlie (which did not exclude severe criticism, as one of Matthias's acknowledged sources, John Pringle's *Culloden*, makes clear) thus resulted in the loss of lands (making him "attainted") just as his ancestor, Sir Michael Wemyss, suffered the loss of his manors and lands because of his treason against Edward. These later events are only implied in the poem, which reflects on Elcho's fate by means of two emblematic fantasies. The first one concerns the deceptive nature of political hopes: history's smoldering surprises turn out to be "older than the coal fields / on the Wemyss estate"—a clear parallel to "the fine Wemyss coal" egging on Mary and Darnley (99). The second shows us Elcho framed once more by a Holyrood window, disclosing that "the empty space" between it and "the place the clansmen camped" fills up with sentimental tales—a clear warning signal— and, ironically, "the progeny / of all those partridges" of which that old cynic Knox had talked (100). Elcho is not envisaged as preoccupied with these futile or cynical visions; on the contrary, he is entranced by the "flight of an heraldic bird / whose spiral into time / was on a furious northern wind—" (100). In other words, the forces making havoc with his life are connected with a northern wind—perhaps anticipating Charles Edward's abortive campaign into England—driving before it Elcho's hopes, symbolized by the heraldic bird.

In a general sense, section IV reviews the sentimental and romantic problematic introduced in the first half of section I. Two competing discourses are set against each other: the cynical realism of men like Knox and the sentimental love seemingly embodied by Darnley (and revived by Peggy, the cook, who—in lieu of a tour book—points out the place where Darnley had dismounted). Section V, in its turn, reviews the theme first surveyed in the second half of section I: not only does its first line—"Or talk about Charles Edward then"—imitate that section's "Or build on, say, an Edward's language," but it reexamines the issues of loyalty and treason in an abstract, half-metaphorical manner, which seems at once to involve real issues and metapoetic ones (99, 93). The poem recognizes this dualism by stating that "Language moved upon inconsequence / and consequence / at once," linking the alternatives resulting from it to two voices whispering behind the "you" staring down Royal Mile (99–100).

The motif of the whispering voices provides a transition to the next section, where the speaker recalls being read to as a boy by his mother. The actual loyalty is once more Fife ("I am awake in Fife"), as in section V, but

178 just as the preceding section is full of imagined scenes from Charles Edward's sojourn at Holyrood, most of section VI consists of the speaker's memories of key situations in *Kidnapped* and *Waverley* plus comments on the function and nature of fiction by their respective authors. The first half of the section is pervaded by a strong sense of nostalgia and fear which results from the intermingling of two linked memories: that of listening to the puzzling and exciting events described in the two books (alluded to by means of questions in typical Matthias fashion) and that of the boy's childish desire to cling to his mother (who shields him from the dangers of the plot by her very voice). Interestingly, the reminiscing adult speaker remembers his reluctance to read himself in terms borrowed from Sonnevi and exploited in the previous section: "There is a *space* / I have not learned to *fill* / somewhere *between* printed marks and sounds . . . when all I want to do is drift on lang / uage into dream. . . . " (100, italics mine). The first part of the quotation transforms the erotic desire and existential anguish expressed by similar phrases in sections IV and V into childish fear of separation while the reference to dreams in the last lines anticipates the extract from Stevenson's dedication of *Kidnapped* to his friend Charles Baxter, which occurs at a singularly effective moment. The recapitulation of the mixed plots of *Kidnapped* and *Waverley* has just reached a point where the speaker meets an "ancient crone" (reminiscent of old Janet in chapter 37 of *Waverley*) who "offers me a boiled hand" (100). At the point of maximum tension the amalgamated account of the plots yields to Stevenson's ironic reference to *Kidnapped* as a work merely intended to offer the gentleman reader temporary relief from some more serious pursuit such as the study of Ovid and pack him "off to bed / with images to mingle / with his dreams" (101). Stevenson's self-disparaging view of his novel as mere escape from pressing reality contrasts with Scott's contention, illustrated by means of an heraldic metaphor, that the basic human passions described in literature remain identical throughout the ages. The speaker's response is commensurate with the emotional reaction that the memory of his mother reading Scott and Stevenson to him has produced. Whereas in the first section the matter at issue is whether picturesque or factual language is better as a means of expression, here it is the same conflict raised to a higher power—that of literary language—that is examined as the variation on the Sonnevi tag would seem to indicate: here we are concerned with the "flight of an heraldic bird through *language*" (101, italics mine). The two alternatives, of course, in a sense revise the basic options of the opening section, and the rest of section VI considers them in an attempt to reach a conclusion and understand his identity, his sense of place. Briefly, he favors the notion that romantic characters such as Charles Edward or Alan Breck and Cluny Macpherson carry the day but then has to concede that "time has gone to live with / Waverleys and Balfours, with townies / like Rankeillor and his lowland lawyer ilk" (102). However, as the final lines suggest, the two temperaments complement each other in a dialectical process: sentiment is transfigured into history and history into sentiment.

The seventh section, set in Kirkcaldy, begins as a walk poem proper, the bulk of the text taking the form of a neatly structured monologue which the poet delivers while moving around town. As I shall argue, the entire sequence adopts a compositional pattern sometimes known as "recessed symmetry" (see Fowler 99ff), and section VII offers a miniature version of it: an evocation of "loyal old Kirkcaldy" is followed by a brief reference to "descendants of those Covenanters Cromwell shot" (102) treating their jute with linseed oil; this leads on to a consideration of Robert Adam and Adam Smith, mention of whose reticence about the forty-five and bonded miners surrounds a number of quotations from *The Wealth of Nations;* the next stanza provides indignant comments on these very quotations, leading on to ambivalent criticism of Adam and his sons, whereupon the deprivation exuded by the smell of jute on linseed conjures up faces thirsting for "darker oils / sucked up Shell, BP, and Exxon rigs"; and finally we are back where we started: Kirkcaldy's execution and his vision of "a crazy German / sitting firmly on a Stuart throne" (103, 104). Kirkcaldy's privileged position in this section calls to mind the theme of disloyalty and punishment, but the main issue dealt with here is of course the financial basis of society and the lack of social justice, a theme already dwelt on in section III. Its conclusion is a pessimistic one: not only does Kirkcaldy die while experiencing a vision of a crazy German on the Stuart throne, but "History [gives] William Pitt *The Wealth of Nations,* / the brothers Adam peel-towers & Fort George" (104). The end of section VII thus looks back to the end of section VI: the dialectical struggle recorded there is temporarily resolved in that history emerges victorious while beggared sentiment flies straight into the hills.

Section VIII, devoted to "Ossian, etc.," makes more extensive use of the Sonnevi stanza than any previous section, amalgamating it with tags and phrases introduced earlier in the poem and revising them in humorous and ingenious ways. In focusing on Macpherson, it offers a climactic treatment of the sentimental and picturesque subject matter first touched on in connection with the tour book's description of Wemyss Castle; and like several earlier sections, it develops its theme by pitting two contrasting characters and attitudes against each other. The career of James Macpherson, the arch-faker, is scrutinized in a manner which adapts his achievement to the language established in earlier parts of the poem. Thus, for example, Macpherson's initial inspiration is associated with "the howling of a northern wind" (104), which of course primarily alludes to the Highlands but perhaps also to a number of passages involving northern winds in the earliest fragments translated by Macpherson (see, for example, the fragment quoted in Saunders 80–81). Selma "filled . . . with names & deeds" cannot but recall the earlier use of space filling with various metaphorical matter (104). The same expression is used about those of Macpherson's readers who willingly let themselves be duped by his Gaelic epic:

> Staring at Macpherson's book,
> they filled the emptiness before their eyes
> with what they were. (104)

Macpherson's contrast is the Earl of Wemyss, who buys a phony Venus signed Van Dyck from a London dealer:

> Staring at the canvas on his castle wall,
> the Earl filled the emptiness before his eyes
> with what he thought he saw. (105)

The portrait of Macpherson is curiously ambivalent. On the one hand, the speaker is sympathetic to the anxiety and suffering which accompanied his early years and the mysterious nature of his first inspiration. On the other, once he makes his appearance and Ossianic melancholy becomes the fashion of the day, the pejorative phrases introduced earlier in the poem describe his achievement: "language threaded aimlessly through empty space" and the tour book's conventional rhetoric is invoked to suggest Macpherson's depiction of nature (104). The reader is even offered a belated continuation of the phrase which was broken off in mid-flow in the first section:

> *the sight of which*
> *could not but amply compensate*
> admirers of the sentimental and the picturesque. (104)

While this passage leaves us in no doubt about the weakness of Macpherson's forgery, the last stanza but one where the speaker symbolically leaves his folly and walks out on the shingle offers a more complex perception of his fraud. Macpherson is viewed as an editor trying to smooth over minor imperfections in the original by "what came to hand" (106). In the process, magic briefly descends on names like Fingal, Oscar, Gaul. The ensuing reference to "a field of slaughter" (106) evokes Macpherson's childhood memories of the aftermath of the forty-five, suggesting that his artistic forgery serves a curative purpose, though it ultimately results in unacceptable manipulation of its emotional matter:

> Seeking to fill emptiness, Macpherson
> marked its boundaries,
> surveyed & gerrymandered sentimental space (106)

The political metaphors in these dense lines of course anticipate Macpherson's later career in London. His journey to the south tellingly contrasts with the northbound movement of the heraldic bird. And yet the implication is that the Earl of Wemyss's importation of a fake Van Dyck from London is an even worse fault.

Unlike the other sections of "Northern Summer," the ninth and final one has no title and thus offers no indication either as to where it might take place or what its real or ostensible subject matter might be. In fact, the only suggestion of a locality is that contained in the first new lines which relegate the poems' sense of place explicitly to an affair between the words on the paper and the mind that observes them, at once their origin and puzzled audience:

> And I stare quizzically at what I've written here,
> at language that has used me one more time
> for consequential or inconsequential ends that
> are not mine. (107)

Clearly, we are back where we started. Just as section I began the sequence's investigation of place with a review of possible ways of expressing it, section IX ends with a retrospective survey of their relevance. From the very beginning, we are discouraged from believing that any stable positions have been reached. If anything, the speaker's uncertainty has grown: the two alternatives which were set against each other in section I are now inspected a final time but, significantly, in the form of questions, one after the other, and in language which, though appropriating the Edward/Aymar de Valance analogy, has been slightly changed to emphasize its metaphorical value. Speaking Edward's language is now the equivalent of "a second generation *speak[ing]* / the ruins of a first" (107, my emphasis) suggesting that the political implications of the phrase are now subservient to literary ones.

Trying to evolve a language which will give a genuine and clear expression of place is ultimately to find one's own identity. In returning to a review of this purpose the speaker has to admit that "language . . . has used [him]

182 for consequential or inconsequential ends that / are not [his]. As a result, he now also questions the "arbitrary boundaries / *castle,* queen, and *mine*" (107), which refer us both to previous sections of his poem and to landmarks in the actual area with which he has been trying to familiarize himself. Though these boundaries are created to delimit "a space by no means empty" (107), it is becoming increasingly clear that the speaker is alienated from it, a condition that the act of composing a poem cannot hope to cure. In fact, the authenticity of the project is jeopardized in a crucial sense: those acts which in previous sections seemed to guarantee the poet's sense of place are now not only questioned but in fact dismissed as imaginary and downright mendacious: "I never closed the book. I never left the room / to walk along the beach." The speaker's soul searching reaches its nadir in the next few lines where, brushing aside the term *tourist,* he defines himself as paying guest "of language of / the place" (107). The distinction emphasizes that the relationship between the speaker and the environment out of which his art grows is one which can be gauged in terms of the toll it takes, a fact already touched on a few lines above, where the poet realizes that "the cost of lodging / is exacted by a pile of books" and by the components of his poem (107). It is also worth pointing out that the phrase blurs the distinction between "language" and "place," thus offering further evidence of the ongoing dismantling of the speaker's sense of place.

At various points in the sequence hints of northbound travel have presented themselves as a means of escape from suffering and pressures of various kinds. Such thoughts now once more occur to the speaker himself, coalescing with memories of two notable instances of the futility of academic source-hunting. Ironically, one of these concerns plagiarism of the work of the arch-plagiarist himself, Macpherson, whereas the other introduces the famous casket letters possibly linking the lives of Mary Queen of Scots, Bothwell, and Bothwell's longtime paramour, Anna Throndsen. As against these two examples of how one might fill empty space with vacuity, the speaker considers the alternative of the active life, represented by Bothwell, whose voyage across the North Sea to Norway in 1567 was undertaken to avoid capture by his old enemy, Kirkcaldy. Though Bothwell's voyage eventually led to his capture by Danish authorities and to long-term imprisonment and death, the speaker seems revived by his example, and the passage beginning "Or you"—incidentally a collage of phrases culled from Robert Gore-Browne's book on Bothwell—signals a new mood and views Bothwell's Scandinavian odyssey in a sympathetic and fascinated mood (108). In typical Matthias fashion, Bothwell's progress from the Orkneys via Karmoi and

Bergen to Copenhagen, Malmö, and Dragsholm Castle, where he eventually died, is not depicted in a straightforward way but charted by two indirect devices: questions, not affirmative statements inform us about what happened; evocative details come to the fore while vital information (such as the identity or names of the people involved) is suppressed. The version of events followed here contains some bitter irony, for by the time Bothwell came to Bergen he was already a prisoner in fact if not entirely in name. Under such circumstances the appearance of the "black heraldic bird" is probably to be seen as emblematic of disaster; but in light of the symbolic use of the bird earlier in the poem, it might perhaps also be seen as a metaphor for Bothwell's exploration of experiential empty space of a kind tellingly suggested by "silence deep as Dragsholm" (the speaker earlier talked of "heading further north / and pledging silence," behavior recalling Bothwell's; reticence about his identity was of course one of Bothwell's tactics when interrogated in Bergen) (108). As the sketch of Bothwell's life approaches his demise, circumstances pertaining to earlier periods in his life but playing a real if enigmatic role in his downfall come to the surface. The speaker seems to conflate Gore-Brown's and Antonia Fraser's discussions of the Casket Letters and the twelve love sonnets used as evidence at the trial of Mary Queen of Scots for he quotes Fraser's reference to Brantôme and Ronsard (whose negative views apply to the French of the sonnets, however) while at the same time appropriating Gore-Browne's view that Anna Thronsden was the author of the sonnets and possibly of the so-called "Medea letter" (see Gore-Brown 100–10 and Fraser 385–420).

The mysterious phrase *"l'oiseau sortira de sa cage"* (108) derives from this letter. In it, a lady issues what would seem to amount to a warning to the recipient of the letter: "Faites bon guet si l'oiseau sortira de sa cage ou sens son per comme la tourtre demeurera seulle a se lamenter de l'absence pour court quelle soit" [Beware lest the bird fly out of its cage, or without its mate like the turtle-dove live alone to lament the absence however short it may be; Fraser's translation.]. Whatever situation this phrase originally referred to, its application to the situation at hand in Matthias's poem is highly ambiguous. If, at one time, it suggested that Anna—assuming that it is she who is its author—might flee from her lover, it might now reflect on Bothwell's attempt to escape his pursuers: Kirkcaldy, Hanseates, Danes. If so, it must be added that he escaped his enemies at home only to end up as a prisoner in another country. In fact, he spent several years at Malmöhus Castle, which is only some twenty-five kilometers from the city of Lund, where Göran Sonnevi lived when he wrote the poem that yielded "Northern Summer's"

184 epigraph—an ironic circumstance that must have held some significance for Matthias.

The trajectory envisaged in the confident statement "Bothwells' route is mine" is thus not exactly a safe one, a fact perhaps implicitly recognized by the speaker as he vows to "think of Anna Throndsen" (whose unexpected presence in Bergen when Bothwell was being interrogated there added to his difficulties) (108). However, fascinated as he may be by Bothwell's experiences in the north, the speaker disengages himself from any Scottish affiliations by also vowing not to return with the Maid of Norway, as Sir David Wemyss did in 1290, or the Duke of Orkney's head, a macabre if subtly ambiguous promise, which refers both to Kirkcaldy's attempt to capture Bothwell and, more specifically, to the head of the so-called mummy of Bothwell inspected by Gore-Browne in Denmark while preparing his book (in which a photo of it is reproduced). The speaker declares himself devoid of both piety and revenge, then. In view of this it is not surprising that he amuses himself by entertaining thoughts of having his bird of Sentiment stuffed by a Hanseatic taxidermist at an advantageous rate. This last image of course also hints that the speaker's quest is nearly over. As if to clinch the matter, another exile—far more successful than Bothwell—is introduced. Always a step ahead of the Gestapo, Brecht, as is well known, worked his way through Denmark, Sweden, and Finland before finally "making for L.A." by way of Vladivostok (See, for example, Hayman 173–251). The "smallish hidden door" high up in Lapland that he talks about in a poem written at about this time[11] is treated by Matthias's speaker as a real option, one through which the emblematic bird—reduced to *"black wings, yellow beak, round eyes"*—passes a final time before disappearing for good.

The ninth section thus not only ends with the very image with which the first began: it also emphatically closes the discussion about place, writing, and identity, which I take to be the poem's main concern. It remains to summarize the nature and form of that discussion. In the "Afterword and Notes" appended to *Beltane at Aphelion,* Matthias makes the following comment on "Northern Summer:"

> The attempt to integrate myself with this particular landscape and history was not, it seems to me, successful; and the poem deals with an ultimately alienating experience. Perhaps for this reason, the most important section is the seventh [*sic*], "A Voice," where in fact I hear not only my mother's voice reading from Stevenson and Scott, but also my wife's reading the same texts to our daughters. (*BA* 195)

It is easy to agree with the poet that section VI occupies a pivotal position in the sequence—and in fact represents its point of maximum emotional intensity—as will also appear from the following schematic analysis of the experience it anatomizes. Very briefly, this experience is described in the following way: section I serves as a proem introducing the reader to the setting and the task the author has set himself; section II, set in the folly, explores the speaker's reservations, chiefly of a political and social nature, about the environment described; section IV, focusing on Mary and Darnley, examines the picturesque setting as a milieu for romance, whereas section V, contrasting Charles Edward and Elcho, takes a close look at political allegiance and its price; section VI reviews the speaker's Scottish connections at a much more personal level, taking as its starting point his memories of listening to his mother reading classic Scottish novels to him as a boy; section VII, harking back to section III, reviews social and political issues; section VIII, again set in the folly, studies the case of a famous Scot, Macpherson, the arch-dissembler; while section IX, finally, provides an elaborated finale, resulting in the speaker's decision to opt for a northbound escape which will take him to Scandinavia and ultimately to his country of origin. The nine sections thus record so many phases in a complex emotional and intellectual drama consisting in the speaker's attempt to make himself at home in surroundings that ultimately prove uncongenial. The "recessed symmetry" perceptible in the sequence is based on a variety of structural components thematic as well as positional, and can be indicated in the following way:

I introduction; metapoetic examination of place

II folly

III mine; discourse about social and political matters

IV Wemyss as setting for romance

V Holyrood as setting for political romance

VI Scotland as setting for literary romance

VII Kirkcaldy: discourse on financial matters

VIII folly; picturesque versus realistic approach

IX summary; metapoetic approach to place

What the poem describes, then, is simply an attempt to search out genealogical and emotional roots by means of a thorough exploration of place, an attempt which is abandoned as the poem's speaker realizes that his true allegiance lies elsewhere.

———

"A Wind in Roussillon" describes an itinerary that takes the speaker of the sequence through some of the historic sights of southwestern France. Equally important as a structuring principle, however, is the symbolic, parallel journey undertaken by the Tramontane (the region's version of the *mistral*) and whose effects the poem painstakingly traces:

> The Tramontane that's blowing pages
> of an unbound book through Roussillon
> departs on schedules
> of its own. . . . (*SM* 122)

These lines, which trigger a number of associations, are answered by the last section's very last lines, where the object of veneration surprisingly turns out to be the Tramontane:

> Lady binding the book in leather & iron,
> Mother of scattered pages,
> Work of secret patience, Tramontane. (127)

Although Matthias has confessed to a certain lack of interest in Romantic poetry in his essay "Places and Poems" (*Reading Old Friends* 39), a wind blowing pages through a landscape cannot but recall the gentle breeze invoked at the beginning of *The Prelude* or the destructive elemental force ripping loose leaves of varying descriptions in the "Ode to the West Wind." It is true of course that Matthias's wind is manhandling not leaves but "pages / of an unbound book" (122) and that in the concluding lines of section X it is described as binding "the book in leather & iron" and addressed as "Mother of scattered pages" (127), but the reference is unmistakable. While "pages / of an unbound book" need not necessarily refer to paper as a medium of literary creativity, the final emphasis on "binding the book in leather & iron" does suggest producing a weighty tome. The Tramontane is thus simultaneously involved in scattering and collecting just as Shelley's west wind is both a destroyer and a preserver, and though this activity should be understood primarily in a general sense, it also carries a more specific, artistic submeaning which is paralleled in the fifth and final section of Shel-

ley's ode, which makes a clear connection between poetic creativity and the
wind's destructive transformation of the speaker ("Make me thy lyre, even as
the forest is: / What if my leaves are falling like its own!").

Powerful though the Romantic connotations evoked by the Tramontane
may be, two other poetic texts, both of them identified by Matthias in the
notes appended to *Northern Summer,* are explicitly alluded to in the poem.
Both help clarify the meaning of the wind (though they have nothing to do
with each other, or with Roussillon, or the south of France, as such). The
first, and more important, of them is François Villon's famous epitaph in the
form of a ballad, supposedly written while the poet was waiting to be executed. Expecting to be left hanging after death as a warning example,
together with some other prisoners also condemned to death, the poet—or
rather his skeleton—addresses posterity:

> Quant de la chair que trop avons nourrie,
> Elle est pieça devoree et pourrie,
> Et nous, les os, devenons cendre et poudre. (Villon 152)

> [As regards our bodies which we have nourished too generously,
> they were devoured long ago and have been left rotting, and we,
> the bones, are turning into ashes and dust.]

In the third stanza, Villon specifies the degree of decomposition that the
bodies of the executed criminals have suffered:

> La pluie nous a bués et lavés,
> Et le soleil dessechés et noircis;
> [. . .]
> Puis ça, puis la, comme le vent varie,
> A son plaisir sans cesser nous charrie (152)

> [The rain has soaked us in lye and washed us and the sun has
> dried and darkened us; . . . At will, the wind ceaselessly pulls us
> in this or that direction according as it blows]

The Villon epitaph thus constitutes a powerful matrix investing the beginning of Matthias's sequence with dark hints of transience which are curiously
at odds with the seeming vitality of the wayward Tramontane. The Romantic connotations of the wind as an inspiring as well as destructive force are
set off against the monosyllables of the Villon quotation which, given first in

188 French, then in English, provides a chilling reminder of the human condition. The implicit meaning of the French quotation is extended into the second section of Matthias's poem. Though the description of the train leaving the Gare d'Austerlitz on time and taking the speaker through a carefully and lovingly rendered French countryside appears to provide an effective contrast to the pessimistic scenario of the first section, certain expression in lines 3–5 carry faint echoes of the Villon poem, lending a dark undertone to the splendor described in Matthias's poem: "wheat and barley *dry up* in the *sun* / & trees appear *hung* heavily / with cherries, lemons, oranges" (122, emphases mine.) This imagery keeps recurring throughout the poem: it appears in section VI, where it refers to the fierce battles going on during the Crusades ("blood ran all the way from Montségur to the Quéribus Château before it finally dried," 124), and again, significantly, toward the end of section VII, where the poet notes, apropos of Antonio Machado's death in Collioure, that "The sun that parched the bones / dried up the town, dries up the southern sea" (125). The method of repeating a key image is one that the reader recognizes from "Northern Summer."

Though Villon's poem of course in itself has nothing to do with Roussillon, it haunts Matthias's vision of this particular part of France. A similar function is fulfilled by another poem, seemingly also chosen at random but worked into the poem's texture with great care by Matthias: Stéphane Mallarmé's "Prose pour des Esseintes." The opening stanza of this difficult poem has furnished the idea of a bound book, which is suggested both in the opening and the closing lines of Matthias's poem and recurs in section IX, where the speaker describes a visit to Tour Madeloc, an old signal tower which, together with the Tour de la Massane (also mentioned in IX), was part of a network of lookout posts. The final lines of Matthias's poem seem to be based on a direct adaptation of Mallarmé's poem, whose first two stanzas read as follows:

> Hyperbole! de ma mémoire
> Triomphalement ne sais-tu
> Te lever, aujourd'hui grimoire
> Dans un livre de fer vêtu:
>
>
> Car j'installe, par la science,
> L'yhmne des cœrs spirituels
> En l'œvre de ma patience,
> Atlas, herbiers et rituels.

Anthony Hartley's prose translation of these lines in his 1965 Penguin edition of Mallarmé runs as follows:

> Hyperbole! from my memory can you not triumphantly arise, today like an occult language copied into a book bound into iron: for by my science I install the hymn of spiritual hearts in the work of my patience, atlases, herbals, rituals. (62)

In "A Wind in Roussillon" Mallarmé's two stanzas recur in the following form:

> Communication is a subtle thing through our electric sepulchre. In the Punic wars, Valerius could only talk in hyperbolic terms with smoke and fire. . . . Power hymns instalments to its spirit now in all works of impatience: wars, towers, rituals, TV. In memory, Valerius, you arise. Like an occult language found in an iron-bound book. (126)

Clearly, Hartley's rendition of "aujourd'hui grimoire" as "like an occult language" corresponds to "Like an occult language" in Matthias's section IX. In fact, nearly all the other phrases found in Mallarmé/Hartley have a counterpart in Matthias's poem. The similarities are so striking that one suspects that Matthias used this very edition. If so, he will also have read what Hartley has to say about the obscurity of the poem:

> it would seem to deal with an attempt to contemplate directly the eternal Ideas and with the poet's inevitable failure to do so. M. Richard has described the theme of the poem as that of an opposition "between the two essential movements of inspiration," a passage towards the ideal and the "science" of its conscious definition. (62)[12]

In other words, the two stanzas describe the contrast between the perfection of artistic vision ("Hyperbole") and its necessarily inferior physical manifestation or expression ("grimoire," "hymne," "œuvre de patience") through the artist's expertise ("science"). This original problematic is by no means irrelevant to Matthias's poem, but it has been integrated into a wider thematic context involving human communication at large (even communication across the centuries), and so the original emphasis has been changed at the same time as some of the components have been transposed (and others added). Matthias's imitation of Mallarmé's poem is heuristic, and it is not surprising that the links between the two poems are fairly tenuous. One involves an inscription[13] commemorating the monument erected "while he was still alive" (*vivus*) by the Roman commandant at Madeloc, Valerius Flaccus, which, being composed in Latin, in itself constitutes an instance of "grimoire," "occult language" (the French word *grimoire* is a perversion of *grammaire* and often associated with Latin) (*Le Grand Robert*, s.v. *grimoire*—the two major meanings listed by *Robert* are *"livre de magie"* and *"ouvrage ou discours obscur"*). The other is the "martial music," which the speaker "drinks in" a few lines above and which provides an associative link with the "prose" of Mallarmé's poem, *prose* being "another term for a sequence in the medieval meaning of that word: an ornamental interpolation into the plainsong of a mass" (*Le Grand Robert*, s.v. *prose*—see also Gill 232 n. 50). Mallarmé's poem of course also refers to "hymn," a notion which in a more concrete sense is seized on and continued in the final section of Matthias's poem, whose form imitates that of a prayer. (Section X, too, in a sense constitutes "martial music.") The one word which does not occur in Mallarmé's poem—*power*—is the key word in Matthias's adaptation of it. Matthias's section IX is about the varying forms of the hyperbolic language of power and about the *Nachleben* of power. In Rome, Valerius was put on a coin; in Roussillon, he left his bones and his inscription, which, miraculously, competes with the news transmitted via "the electric sepulchre" for the poet's attention. In Matthias's version, the actual expressions which the hyperbole may take—symbolized by atlases, herbals, rituals—are reduced to "works of impatience" (wars, towers, rituals, TV), whereas Valerius arises in memory in a way that artistic expression is incapable of in Mallarmé's scheme of things. Thus, whereas in "Prose pour des Esseintes" the fact that hyperbole has been reduced to "grimoire" bears witness to the inferior value of such manifestations, Matthias's poem seems to take a sympathetic view of "occult language," and the iron-bound book in which it is recorded is not a symbol of obscurity and imperfection but a repository of forgotten wisdom and cultural treasures.

The "iron-bound book" of section IX harks back to the "unbound book" mentioned in the opening lines of section I, a passage which section IX, with its Mallarmé echoes, serves to revise. Whereas the Tramontane is perceived as a destroyer at the poem's outset, its activities in section X either complement or cancel each other out since the wind is invoked simultaneously as "Lady binding the book in leather & iron" and "Mother of scattered pages" (127).

If the Tramontane is thus truly a preserver as well as a destroyer, it certainly does "work of secret patience" and can be viewed as a corrective to the "works of impatience" listed in section IX (127).

The Mallarmé echo is not the only case of intertextuality in section X. Its pseudo-pious invocations of the Holy Virgin are evocative of the lauritanian litany, whose catalog form and devotional content it gently parodies. While the beginning seems genuine enough, charity and consolation being among the benefits the Virgin is asked to bestow on her followers in the most commonly spread form of this litany, line 2 refers us to the thematic concerns of the rest of the sequence, establishing a pattern which is observed throughout the section. Thus, the middle lines of the ensuing stanzas are clearly related to the localities described in the poem or to its thematic pattern (compare with "The village cries out for rain," "The pilgrim is flaying the Jew," and "Mother of scattered pages"). At the same time, the formal patterning of this section is very marked: thus, for example, assonance is an important structural principle ("landfall"—"languors," "noon"—"nightshades," etc.). The most striking examples are found in the last two stanzas, which have a climactic function. The addressee is both "Mother of Jesus" and "Mother of jackals," and the subverted morality of the society described appears from the next line, where "The pilgrim is flaying the Jew." I have already dwelt on the paradoxical content of the last stanza, but in this particular context it is worth pointing out that there is further symmetry through the double assonance of "scattered pages" / "secret patience" (127).

Despite the litany-like qualities of section X, its immediate source, however, is a poem by the thirteenth-century Provençal troubadour Guiraut Riquier, "Be m degra de chantar tener," from which Matthias quotes at the end of section VIII after introducing him as "some / pitiful last troubadour" who "sang out to Templars / gazing down at him beside the sea" (126). Despite the impression of authenticity that these lines convey, the dramatic scene that they depict is, as far as I am aware, wholly imagined by Matthias, who thus manages to link together three historical moments in a cunning pattern: the troubadour (who is well known as the last troubadour—see, for example, Anglaide, who devotes his final chapter, "Le dernier troubadour," to Riquier) has already performed his song before "the smoking bones," which the famous revolutionary general Dugommier won back after Dufour, the commandant at Fort Saint-Elme, had turned over the fort to the Spanish. Matthias's comment—"No one sang the cruel cannonade they loosed / on the Château"(126)—seems to suggest that such a song would have been appropriate; now, no one is gazing down from Fort Saint-Elme, nor does the

192   poet sing out a complaint similar to Riquier's, which he nevertheless quotes, thus willy-nilly conditioning the reader's appreciation of this section's closing mood:

> No one gazes
> down from Fort Saint-Elme. Nor do I sing out
> *Dona, maries de caritat . . .*
> *Lady, mother of charity . . .*
> *I was born too late . . .* (126)

Though rejected here, the two Provençal lines recur as the basis for section X's pseudo-litany; the poet thus goes back on the declaration made in section VIII by providing a fantasy inspired by a poem whose content is only suggested.

By disclosing the identity of the poem in the author's notes appended at the end of *Northern Summer*, Matthias would seem to endorse the possibility that Riquier's poem is thematically relevant to his own sequence, and to a certain extent this is so. In the six stanzas of "Be m degra de chantar tener," Riquier ponders the decline of troubadour poetry which, in his view, is brought about by the decadence prevalent in his country. Poetry springs from joy, he claims; there is no joy in his life, yet he has been endowed with the gift of transforming any experience, painful or pleasurable, into memorable poetry. However, this is of no consequence, for poetry is held in low esteem, and pride and malice are rampant. A "double death"—the Saracens and godlessness—is threatening the poet's country, and those in power seem indifferent. In the final stanza, the poet asks God and the Virgin Mother to have mercy on him and his countrymen:

> Dona, Maires de caritat,
> Acapta nos per pietat
> De ton filh, nostre redemtor,
> Gracia, perdon et amor. (Berry 78–79)

> [Lady, mother of charity,
> obtain for us, through pity,
> of your son, our Redeemer,
> grace, pardon, and love.]

Thus, in a general sense, Riquier's lament for what he perceives as the end of a glorious epoch constitutes one of the hyperbolic discourses evoked in

Matthias's poem. However, only two aspects of Riquier's poem are highlighted: the plea for mercy (which has been transformed into the litany of section X) and the wistful afterthought, voicing the poet's pervasive sense of belatedness. Interestingly, in Matthias's poem this rueful insight comes last, whereas the corresponding line in Riquier's poem ("Mas trop suy vengutz als derriers") appears at the end of the second stanza, well before the invocation of the Virgin Mother. This transposition of the two lines is Matthias's own invention but may owe something to his immediate source: the English composer John Buller's *Provença,* "a remarkable piece for large orchestra, mezzo-soprano, and electric guitar" (John Matthias, letter, 23 January 1997; the three stanzas quoted below in English from the liner notes for Buller's *Provença* are "all of the text I ever saw").

The liner notes for the LP album containing Buller's piece include the following condensed translation of Riquier's poem:

> I should refrain from singing
> for songs must spring from joy,
> and I am so besieged by sorrow
> that pain assails me on every side.

> Thus my songs can have for me
> no flavour, for they are joyless;
> . . . I was born too late.

> Lady, mother of charity,
> obtain for us, through pity
> of your son, our Redeemer,
> grace, pardon and love.

The sense of belatedness highlighted by this version of Riquier's poem is further emphasized by Buller's own liner notes, which state that his work concludes "with lines from Guiraud Riquier, the 'last of the troubadours,' singing only that he was born too late." Acutely alive to the political and social complexities associated with the particular place where he is standing, the speaker reviews some of the different scenes which have been enacted here. Starting out in the present, he moves backward in time, gradually becoming more and more involved, until at the moment of total identification he checks himself, paradoxically stating that he does not cry out of the very words and sentiments which in fact reverberate in the reader's mind as

194   he turns to the next section. "I was born too late"—though technically repudiated, Guiraud's complaint nevertheless adds a new dimension to the theme of transience introduced right from the beginning of Matthias's sequence.

Thus, the Villon, Mallarmé, and Riquier echoes, though different in kind and function, are related to each other in intricate ways and constitute an important intertextual nexus, which, in its turn, is linked with a large number of linguistic and thematic motifs. To keep track of all these is beyond the scope of this essay, but conveying some idea of the ways in which they are layered and contribute to the poem's meaning and sense of unity is essential. Some of this structure emerges on a first reading, but since some of the later sections review and expand images and ideas which seem fully functional when they first appear, it is probably more true of Matthias's sequence than of many other poems of this kind that it requires rereading and reinterpretation.

As I have already suggested, the major thematic opposition of "A Wind in Roussillon" introduced in the first short section, where movement and stasis are imitated by the contrast between the full sentence describing the Tramontane blowing through Roussillon and the verbless statement "Et nous, les os" (which is repeated twice for good measure) (122). Out of this initial opposition between wind and bones grows much of the symbolism of the ensuing sections. The wind playing with the scattered book leaves and departing "on schedules of its own" becomes a real train departing "on time" in section II (122). Whereas the closely observed beauty of the landscape seen from the passenger car window leads on to a similar instance of intense natural beauty in section IV, three details look ahead to sinister collocations in later sections. The wheat and barley drying up in the sun lead on to the vision of blood running all the way from Montségur to the Quéribus Château before it finally dried (VI, 124), the sun "that parched the bones" drying up the town and the southern sea (VII, 125), and the village imploring the "Lady of drought" for rain (X, 127). Similarly, the gray slate left behind in section I is evoked by the "graying faces" of the low, ruined house called John and Jeanne in section V. Finally, the vineyard "circled by a wall of heavy stones" in section I links up with the cemetery visited in section VII. Significantly, the cemetery is seen as a "silent town within a town," and some of its as-yet unoccupied space is marked *"reservée"* (124). This ironic intimation of the privacy of the grave reflects uncomfortably on the next section's description of similar signs protecting Fort Saint-Elme: *"Privée, Bien Gardée."*

The poem's preoccupation with suffering and mortality is reinforced by a number of associative links on a more abstract level as well. The speaker of the poem is conscious of being a visitor to foreign parts (see, for example, section VII, where, after mentioning naked bathers and tourists, he "intrude[s] upon the silent tenants searching / for Antonio Machado" [124], or the beginning of section IX, whose descriptive language suggests a tour guide or an entry in a traveler's diary). Most of the other characters appearing in the poem are strangers to Roussillon, and so the theme of exile is a natural one. The poem portrays two exiles: Mme Danjou, the Irish political idealist described in section VI, who helped Spanish Republicans cross the border and a few years later helped Jewish refugees across the border in the opposite direction; and the famous Spanish poet Antonio Machado, who fled from Franco's Spain and died in Collioure in 1939. Section VII quotes, in fragmentary form, two lines from one of Machado's early poems ("El sol es un globo de fuego, / la luna es disco morado," Machado 38). The contrast between the sun and the moon, which this quotation introduces, is pursued in the last few lines of the poem, where the furious heat of the sun is set off against the suggestion of death and the moon in the line "Savilla is distant and alone." This phrase recalls a line in "Canción de jinete," one of Lorca's early poems ("Córdoba. / Lejana y sola"), whose explicit subject matter is the poet's premonition of death. Thus, the parching sun invoked at the end of section VII is accompanied by a line which seemingly only refers to Machado's birthplace, but in point of fact also subtly evokes his death.

As the example of Machado shows, the theme of death is closely related to that of exile in "A Wind in Roussillon," and, since Machado was a victim of political persecution and war, with that of war, too. The poem is in fact permeated not only by intimations of mortality but by references to war and oppressive violence, though the latter seem to feed the general sense of transience rather than produce it. The Falklands war, which would have been uppermost in Matthias' mind at the time of composition, since he spent the summer of 1982 in Britain, is only hinted at in passing in section III and again in section IX, though one of the phrases employed by Mrs. Thatcher in the rousing speech reported in *Le Monde* ("nous étions vraiment une seule famille") (123) is repeated to ironic advantage in the final line of section III: linking it with the Villon line effectively deflates Mrs. Thatcher's Napoleonic rhetoric, adding a chilling dimension to the family values espoused by her. However, though the Falklands war certainly casts a shadow in the poem, it is by no means the only war referred to, and the poem is not primarily concerned with topical issues. Mme Danjou's library in section VI is full of books on the politico-religious divisions of southern France, but she herself is an example of instinctive antifactional humanitarianism. No particular

196   judgment is passed on Dugommier's retrieval of "the smoking bones"; if anything, Dugommier sets things right again after Dufour's treason.[14] Valerius Flaccus finally is viewed almost as a victim of the imperialism that he serves. At any rate, his type of warfare would seem to compare favorably with present-day behavior, which is as cruel in Las Malvinas (that is, The Falklands) as in The Lebanon.

Perhaps discussing the poems' representations of different examples of warfare is slightly beside the point, though. Its dramatization of various kinds of discourses or, to use the term suggested by the Mallarmé allusion, *hyperbolical languages,* seems a more fruitful approach to a poet who has always been alert to different registers, and who, after all, begins this sequence by opposing the pages of an unbound book with the silent eloquence of bones. In so far as this contrast is to be seen as a representation of the battle between art and all-devouring time, it is worth noting that Machado, the poem's chief literary representative, is praised for singing "these dead his mortal words forever" (125). However, the major and most powerful discourses of the sequence are not poetic ones. Section III contrasts two types of rhetoric, both of them discredited on the grounds of the bizarre impression their unhappy marriage between content and form makes. In the case of the "see-through plastic model of the Virgin," which can be filled up "with holy water from a tap," it is the matter-of-fact language used to describe the toylike plastic Virgin and the businesslike suggestion that holy water can be had from a tap that is most striking (12–123). Perhaps also the "see-through" quality of the Virgin colors one's appreciation of Mrs. Thatcher's surge of patriotic rhetoric which, somewhat surprisingly, is compared to that of a Bonaparte.[15] Here, an intriguing play with perspectives can be observed, too. Not only are we invited to savor the defamiliarizing effect of reading Mrs. Thatcher's speech in French, but we are invited to do so by an American poet (who, on the whole, does not emphasize his American identity and who comes wryly on Mrs. Thatcher's rhetoric not explicitly but by joining her corporate tag about the British nation being one single family with a sobering Villon phrase).

A competing discourse of an entirely different kind is exemplified in section VI, where Mme Danjou, after her impressive wartime record has been given, merely says, "One felt . . . that one had work to do" (124), a comment whose simplicity is undercut by her alleged lack of practice. The low-key nature of this remark, occurring in a section itself noticeable for its stark language, is clearly in keeping with the aesthetics of this sequence, which rarely indulges in metaphors and rhetoric. Its descriptions of natural beauty consist, as I have remarked apropos of sections II and IV, to a large extent simply of showing, not telling. Section V, which is based on a poem by Yves Bonnefoy, is similarly simple in tone. Bonnefoy's original (Bonnefoy 189), which in itself is not a rhetorical showpiece, has been made even simpler by Matthias, who has given it a local, personal touch by adding "in Perpignan" and rendering the "Jean" of the French original as "John." By the same token, he has added one line ("Your name is Yves Bonnefoy"), which has no counterpart in French, and left out the last line of the original ("Nous le laisserons vivre pour les morts"). The overall effect of these changes is to further emphasize the everyday, real character of the house without suppressing altogether those elements which gave it a symbolic force in the original. Thus the fire, suggesting the transmission of life and human experience to future generations, has been retained, and the "great winds" which "pass the threshold" are two other such symbols; while the threshold is a cherished Bonnefoyan symbol,[16] the wind is particularly appropriate to Matthias's poem. Read in the context of "A Wind in Roussillon," section V, with its semisymbolical, semirealist character, seems to celebrate the same ordinary, solid humanity that is explored in section VI, while at the same time celebrating art and a particular poet by giving Bonnefoy's name to the person who builds the fire and then withdraws.

From this survey of the individual sections of Matthias's sequence it should be clear that many of them are designed to suggest a real place endowed with a particular mood and often too with a particular symbolical force. The speaker's exploration of these different places typically takes the form of a walk. The sequence as a whole, then, as I have argued, forms a journey between different stops or stations, most of which are described in close enough detail to give the reader a sense of a guided tour. Matthias's poem could, in other words, be read as a set of poems collectively and (often) individually reminiscent of the form which Roger Gilbert has called a "walk poem." The ultimate purpose of such a poem is "the externalization of an interior seeking," as A. R. Ammons has it. In the case of "A Wind in Roussillon" that seeking is circular in form, beginning where it ends in the manner of "the greater Romantic lyric" examined by M. H. Abrams. Both beginning and end are rather abstract in character and without a clear sense of place, although the flight of the Tramontane in section I might in a sense be construed as a metaphorical counterpart to the train journey described in section II (and possibly including the newspaper-reading reported in section III). All the other sections convey a sense of physical movement, and two of them (VI and VII) might be claimed as clear-cut walk poems, whereas V

198 involves inspection of a house and eventual withdrawal and IX relates a walk and subsequent meditation on its content (much as "I wandered lonely as a cloud"). "A Wind in Roussillon," then (which incidentally also has the journalistic or diarylike language which Gilbert associates with the walk poem), can be seen as an interesting variation on a major contemporary American genre, interesting not least because it externalizes its seeking in an ancient European setting.

Notes

1. In reply to a query of mine, Matthias writes: "As closely as I can remember, 'A Wind in Roussillon' was written in the summer of 1982 . . . after Diana [the poet's wife] and I returned to Trumpington and Cambridge from the south of France. I see that I have said [in *Northern Summer* and *Beltane at Aphelion*] . . . that the title poem was begun in Fife in 1980, continued in America, and finished in Trumpington 'three years later.' It must, in fact, have been finished two years later because I was done with that poem before I began to work on 'Roussillon.' That also means that the other date given in *Northern Summer* must be wrong. I must have written the middle sections 'in a cabin on Lake Michigan' in the summer of 1981, because in the summer of 1982 we were in the Roussillon" (letter to the author, January 21, 1997).

2. *Walks in the World* (Princeton: Princeton University Press, 1992).

3. Willard Spiegelman, in his review of *A Gathering of Ways* ("The poem as Quest," *Parnassus* 17.2/18.1 [1992–93]: 423–41), compares the techniques employed in the three sequences collected in this volume with those examined by Gilbert.

4. I find it difficult to accept at face value Matthias's comment in the "Notes" appended to *Northern Summer* that "it all depends on where you went to school. American readers may not recognize one set of references, British readers may not recognize another" (220). Matthias's extremely eclectic poems seem to me to require more annotation than their author claims for them.

5. *Northern Summer* contains bibliographical information which gives a good idea of the "odd assortment of books and authors" to which the poet is indebted "for facts, fancies, passages of verse or of prose, translations, information, scholarship and scandal" used in the course of composition (217–21). The same bibliographical information is also provided in *Swimming at Midnight* and *Beltane at Aphelion*.

6. The letter is found in Sir William Fraser's *Memorials of the Family of Wemyss of Wemyss* (Edinburgh: privately printed, 1888). Sir Michael Wemyss had done homage to Edward in 1290 but later took part in the Scottish uprising against Edward led by Bruce.

7. The etymological explanation of the name of Wemyss as deriving from the Gaelic *uamh* can be supplemented by the information that *weem* is a Scots word for "a cave used as an underground dwelling-place by the early inhabitants of the country" (*OED*).

8. K. H. Jackson, *The Gododdin* (Edinburgh: Edinburgh University Press, 1969), 4; cf. fragment A 21 ("The men went to Catraeth, they were famous; wine and mead vessels was their drink for a year, according to the honourable custom. . . . Of those that hastened forth

after the choice drink none escaped but three") and A 32 ("The men hastened forth, they feasted together for a year over the mead; great were their boasts. How sad to tell of them, what insatiable longing! Cruel was their resting-place; no mother's son succoured them").

9. Two lines meet the requirement of nine or two syllables to a line; the three long lines have a clearly marked caesura; and two lines have end-rhyme, while the first one has an internal rhyme. For the meter of the Gododdin epic, see Jackson 53–56.

10. Cp., in particular, stanzas five and six: "The breezy call . . . / The swallow twittering . . . / The cock's shrill clarion . . . / No more shall rouse them . . . / For them no more the blazing hearth shall burn, / Or busy housewife ply her evening care; / No children run to lisp their sire's return."

11. The phrase occurs in section VIII of "1940," *Poems 1913–1956*, ed. John Willett and Ralph Manheim, 3 vols. (London: Methuen, 1976), 3:347.

12. For a recent explication of this enigmatic text, see P. Bénichou, *Selon Mallarmé* (Paris: Gallimard, 1995), 218–42.

13. In E. Cortade, *Collioure: Guide Historique et Touristique* (Perpignan: Sceau du Baille, 1965); in the "Notes and Sources" appended to *Swimming at Midnight*, mention is made of an inscription found on a stone which may have formed part of funeral monument: "V.A.F.P.P.M.I.V.S.C.L.I.E.E.M. On a donné de cette énigmatique inscription une interprétation valable qui d'ailleurs n'a jamais été contredite." According to Cortrade, the inscription may have commemorated a member of the Flaccus family, some of whom are known to have fought successfully in southern France.

14. The story of Dufour's treason occurs in the Cortade pamphlet mentioned in note 13. "Collioure fût occupé par eux grâce à la trahision du commandant du fort Saint-Elme, un nommé Dufour, qui permit au général ennemi Navarro d'occuper la place." I owe this information to John Matthias.

15. Napoleon was a great admirer of Macpherson's Gaelic poems, on whose style he is said to have modeled some of his dispatches (Saunders 21), but that is the limit of his rhetorical interest or skills, as far as I am aware.

16. One of his collections is called *Dans le leurre du seuil* (In the lure of the threshold). For an article which discusses Bonnefoy's use of architectural space and puts the metaphors employed in "Jean et Jeanne" in context, see Martin Kanes, "Bonnefoy, Architect," *World Literature Today* 53. 3 (summer 1979): 440–46.

I wish to express my gratitude to John Matthias for patiently answering various questions concerning dates and sources.

Works Cited

Amours, F. J., ed. *The Original Chronicle of Andrew of Wyntoun.* Vol. 5. Edinburgh and London: Blackwood and Sons, 1907.

Anglaide, Joseph. *Les Troubadours.* Paris: Colin, 1929.

Berry, André. *Anthologie de la Poésie Occitane.* Paris: Stock, 1961.

Bonnefoy, Yves. *Poèmes.* Paris: Mercure de France, 1986.

Dictionary of National Biography. Vol. 60. London, 1899.

200   Fowler, Alastair. *Triumphal Forms.* Cambridge: Cambridge University Press, 1970.

Frasier, Antonia. *Mary, Queen of Scots.* London: Weidenfeld & Nicolson, 1969.

Gilbert, Roger. *Walks in the World.* Princeton: Princeton University Press, 1992.

Gill, R. *The Early Mallarmé.* Vol. 2. Oxford: Oxford University Press, 1986.

Gore-Brown, Robert. *Lord Bothwell.* Garden City, N.Y.: Doubleday Doran, 1937.

Le Grand Robert. Paris: Robert, 1985.

Hayman, Ronald. *Brecht: A Biography.* London: Weidenfeld & Nicolson, 1983.

Hartley, Anthony, ed. *Mallarmé.* Harmondsworth: Penguin, 1965.

Jackson, K. H. *The Gododdin.* Edinburgh: Edinburgh University Press, 1969.

Kermode, Frank, and John Hollander, eds. *The Oxford Anthology of English Literature.* New York, Oxford, Toronto: Oxford University Press, 1973.

Machado, Antonio. *Poesías Completas.* Novena edición. Madrid: Espasa-Calpre, 1962.

Matthias, John. *Beltane at Aphelion: Longer Poems.* Athens, Ohio: Swallow, 1995.

————. *Reading Old Friends: Essays, Reviews, and Poems on Poetics, 1975–1990.* The Margins of Literature Series. Albany: State University of New York Press, 1992.

————. *Swimming at Midnight: Selected Shorter Poems.* Athens, Ohio: Swallow, 1995.

Matthias, John, and Göran Printz-Påhlson, eds. *Contemporary Swedish Poetry.* Chicago: Swallow, 1980.

Percy, Thomas. *Reliques of Ancient English Poetry.* Vol. 1. London: Swan Sonnenschein & Co, 1891.

Saunders, Bailey. *The Life and Letters of James Macpherson.* New York: Haskell House, 1968.

Villon, François. "L'Épitaphe de Villon." In *Œuvres,* ed. André Mary. Paris: Garnier, 1962.

❧ Petitio, Repetitio, Agensay, Agengrownde, Matthias

JOHN PECK

Information has seduced *tout le monde*. The collective formation of memory, however, no longer goes *in*, having abandoned Augustine's vast camps and palaces of recollection for the microfields of the wired chip. We grow primitive. Ortega and Benjamin anticipated this turn of ours; Frances Yates and Father Ong have diagrammed the art lost. And poets since Yeats have patrolled the shifting perimeters, sending out pickets but also anticipating, strategically, some possible renaissance of memory. That renaissance, when it comes, will rely on an inner discipline, not on some precocious child of the cognitive and neurological matchmakers. An inner discipline, as the defunct arts of memory have shown, constitutes a place, locus, topos, which mimics topographies, but immaterially: the inner chip *sans* silt and *sans* silicon. Such immaterial location troubles the sleep of our empiricism, yet so it should, for even neurosurgeons, when they successfully remove an epileptic focus from gray matter, discover that it eerily resituates itself a few weeks later in a new spot. The literal places of our attachment and customary life, however, under threat everywhere, now assert their claims on our attention all the more. Just where might all this leave a poet who is alert to it? Wherever *where* is, with growing clarity through his work John Matthias is there, wherever *there* might be. Transatlantic in both sensibility and tenancy, he has of course dug carefully in actual places. As I shall argue, however, the ground which he turns over has to do with something more comprehensive than the familiar themes of American-European bridals, bridgework, and spiritual trading compacts. Placed and sited, and seen, much of it, as the inside-outsider sees it, this ground nonetheless looks forward and in rather than backward and out, when all is taken on balance. No snazzy new task, this patient alchemy, but it has become newly needful. And very old stands one of its tools, the linked parallelism and repetition of those

forms we call early but which reiterate their elements freshly, now, in coun-
terpoint to the mesmerizing cybernetic tapdance of zero-one, zero-one. Or
so I believe that Matthias's work can show us.

Geoffrey Harpham writes, "Late capital has made its way in the world
through an apparently pliant responsiveness to local concerns, local values,
local practices, local prejudices: it sells its totalities without insisting on totality as an abstraction . . . . Late capitalism's totalizing strategies are, in short,
effective to the extent to which they can pass themselves off as a resistance to
totality itself" (230–31). George Orwell anticipated this point, but so too did
David Jones in his Roman poetry, particularly in *The Sleeping Lord*. The
Roman cliché stays true, acquiring subtlety and acceleration. Even without
the Roman comparison, forces remain much the same in their effects on the
coherence of place and custom. For that reason, I take two features of the
final section of John Matthias's "East Anglian Poem," its echoes of Jones and
its symmetrical repetitions of phrase around symmetrical question and
answer, to offer good metal. The acknowledgment of Jones itself sounds a
repetition, implying that the way he saw what he saw remains valid. The
other repetitions get at an undersense of the changes we know and will continue to suffer. And they do this not chiefly through reinstating historical
pattern but through penetrative form. One function of informed repetition
vis-à-vis the deforming pressures of global capital is repeatedly to sound the
tuning fork across textures of bland cacophony.

After the spectral bride at the mouth of the Thames

> Did the tethered swans fly above him?
> Did the deer follow behind?
>
> And after the pounding of magic into the swords?
>
> . . . .
> From the hands of the Goddess of Death
>
> The tethered swans flew above him
> And the deer followed behind (*SM* 96–97)

However differential the language of the cultural critic such as Harpham, it
cannot clarify forms of feeling *au fond*. The poet does that. The feeling
addressed by "East Anglian Poem" is contemporary as well as minutely historical. This feeling also derives from locality, not from sources alone, for
Matthias has lived there intermittently with his family. But how does that

clarification of feeling emerge? From penetrative form, by way of radical simplification that does no injustice to complexity, and then repetition. David Jones employed litanies, apotropaic charms, and modified refrains, an arsenal that is hardly up-to-date. That was part of the point, of course. In Matthias's "The Noble Art of Fence: A Letter" we find this: "I choose, my Lord, / the short and ancient weapons of our land" (*SM* 99). While he follows Jones's suit, that choice does not prevent him from adapting these old repeaters to the experiments in defamiliarization elaborated by Language poets. The form of feeling that Matthias clarifies can submit to both treatments. Since memory rises because it has been challenged, that form of feeling lends itself to a questioning of the ground for speaking, then to progressive revisions of the answer—a sequence unfolded gradually through Matthias's work.

He has used repetition for ends remarkably gentle, as I shall argue. But nothing less than weapons have gone with him in his kit, in work both short and long. Not that this points to victory. Among the choice shorter poems I would set "Six for Michael Anania," whose fourth and fifth sections deploy subtle and then frontal varieties of repetition.

> We did not mean property.
> We did not mean money.
>
> We did not mean Pope
> Or the Place de la Grève.
>
> But no more maneuvers.
> All are vowed to death.
>
> Too late. I have done all I can.
> (Section V, "Rosencreutz to Saint-Germain," *SM* 35)

The effect in such writing is that of a lance point, or parrying sword edge, wielded precisely and rapidly, however vast the matter. The urgency of the rhetoric corresponds to need: one must repeat and vary the essential stroke, past items that would detain both manager and magus. As this passage also indicates, the urgency may come not only from prospective action and hope but also from retrospective clarity and fatigue. And that seems true to our cultural situation both as a whole and in its particulars. Quite double, then, the upshot of the exquisite sixth section, which seems pertinent to both collective destiny and metaphysics: "Qualities tend / To perfection. // We may assist" (35).

The weaponlike adaptation of phrasing from litany might of course become a regressive reaction to a destructive world-process. But Matthias makes it reductive in a firm way, or simply concentrative, in the sense that *il faut répéter pour mieux sauter*. An indirect comment on this stance comes in Matthias's "Double Sonnet on the Absence of Text: 'Symphony Matis der Maler,' Berlin, 1934:—Metamorphoses." In its short compass this poem repeats four times, all in the first sonnet, Cardinal Albricht's advice to the disheartened painter at the end of the opera (the libretto is Hindemith's own): *Geh hin und bilde.* The equation of painter and Nazi-fleeing composer is explicit: "He lies among his tools. / *Geh hin und bilde. Geh hin und bilde /* Polyptich as polyphony" (*SM* 36). One detail from the Isenheimer Altar's crucifixion panel, of John the Baptist's hand, supplies the answer to the skewering question posed to any *Gebrauchsmusik* or *Gebrauchskunst:* which use? (In the second sonnet a foxy Strauss performs for Goebbels.) "*Geh hin und bilde.* For Albricht, Luther / Or for Muntzer? *Geh hin und bilde.* / The pointing finger of an evangelic hand / Outlasts apocalypse" (36). The Peasant Wars of the Reformation, the European catastrophe of the 1940s—both are survived by an artistic *index* pointed at crucifixion, flexed backward by tension, with Saint John's words in Gruenewald's painting elided here, only tone or gesture persisting in Mat[th]i[a]s's experiment: only the reiterative, underlining form of the nonverbal act persists. A refrain is made of words, but just over its verbal horizon it forms a nonsemantic reiterative gesture. It uses words to get behind them. The second sonnet presses toward some of the implications of that fact.

> Abandoned, all the words: for what
> They cannot settle will be left alone.
> Leaving us just where, Professor?
> Contemplating cosmogonic harmonies with Kepler.
> In oblivion with courage and acoustics. (36)

Notice that if the libretto must go, then this poem's repetitions of one of its bits stand qualified. That is, the semantic aspect of the poem's refrain from Hindemith yields to the musical ones. Reduction turns minimalist in the interests of enduring effect. The final line speaks for a poetry that turns to face a culture's falsifying complexities and reductions of integrity with penetrative reductions. Their acoustical and wordless thrust comes from doing too late all that one can. Or it comes from the multivalent drum taps struck by prospective hope but also by retrospection in at least two modes (remember this—it will prove useful; or, remember this—it is now beyond your reach). In one mode repetitions point in order to underline or undercut; they are deictic. In another they make sounds that only forms can make, forms that are of words but not themselves a word. When verbal forms of repetition work in this second, minimal way, they refrain from naming or renaming in order to round off a movement. And perhaps we should not distinguish too hastily here between primitive and sophisticated poetics. Many are the moods at either hour (and the funny moments in Matthias's work are numerous). Courage, however, is one of these, late or soon, signed on for the duration while tapping out the rhythms of what we can reliably know or do.

One can see from a relatively spontaneous poem in Matthias's third book, *Crossing,* how elements of repetition and refrain work subtly and playfully: "59 Lines Assembled Quickly Sitting on a Wall Near the Reconstruction of the Lady Juliana's Cell." At moments the variations resemble those of Susan Howe: "to a soul *that // cowde / no letter:* cowde—// could, cloud / no cloud or cold // unknowing . . . " (*SM* 41–42). Such groping both plays at stumbling and hints at the mystical. The strands of repetition—there may be more than fifteen—occupy more of this poem's texture than comparable strands in the longer poems. I suspect that only in them, however, does repetition acquire an architectonic quality. Their proper herald is the grimly splendid poem on bloody-minded state grandeur from Matthias's second book, *Turns,* "Double Derivation, Association, and Cliché: From *The Great Tournament Roll of Westminster.*" Phrases both from the Roll and Matthias himself volley down the seven sections in cascades of refrain, clanging with understatement. One of these he lodges parenthetically in the Roll text, in section II, as if it has conjectural status there, then brings it forth into his own voicing. First, then, the end of that section:

> (Who breaks a spear is worth the prize)
> Who breaks a schylld on shields
> a saylle on sails
> a sclev upon his lady's sleeves;
> who can do skilfully the spleter werke,
> whose spyndylles turn
>
> Power out of parsimony, feasting
> Out of famine, revels out of revelation:—
> Out of slaughter, ceremony.
> When the mist lifts over Bosworth.
> When the mist settles on Flodden.
>
> Who breaks a spear is worth the prize. (*SM* 72–73)

206 Thus the line's emergence. At the end of section VI, following a casual reference to Henry VII's murder of a rival, the "Power" passage from section II is reversed chiastically, to end on the same flat refrain:

> Slaughter out of ceremony, famine
> out of feasting, out of power
> parsimony, out of revels
> revelation . . .

> As an axe in the spine can reveal,
> as an arrow in the eye.

> Who breaks a spear is worth the prize. (75)

The refrain itself had folded out of a source text into the poem; then the dizzying reversibility of values in the world of power, in section VI, folds both into and out of the refrain. The very form of sounding here—reiteration together with chiastic or mirror reversal—says a great deal, compactly and wordlessly, about the ways of such a world. Probably it says this more movingly than statement might, for reasons that are neither romantic nor surreal. They are as old as the ballads and as close at hand as the same pattern in the massively compact fourth section of the poem for Michael Anania, also from *Turns,* on Nostradamus and Henry II (*SM* 34–35). There, tense-changes flicker around the mirror armature which disposes otherwise unaltered elements in chiastic refrains. Prophecy gets repeated simply, or I should say weirdly, by fact, across the transformer of grammar, in a hall of mirrors. These two poems, longish and very short, establish a limit-case in Matthias's work. At that limit structure and event both get absorbed by refrain and mirrored replication, as if approaching some region of hyperdensity. Splendid, laconic, unsurprisable by This Worlde, this architectonic refrain principle anticipates different moods in later, longer poems—that is to say, it is the compact version of more elaborate architectonic soundings, and it arrives at that tapping of the floorboards which a poet carries out, when he is finally underway, quite instinctively, to draw echoes from his possible future totality.

II

For my purposes, that totality emerges in two poems from Matthias's fifth book, *Northern Summer* of 1984, "A Wind in Rousillon" and the title poem, and finally in "A Compostela Diptych" from *A Gathering of Ways* in 1991. Each in its fashion weighty, these three poems compel me to treat them in less detail than I would like. But I shall use my observations as supports for broader reflections nonetheless, for I find the stakes wagered in these poems high indeed.

Though the troubadour Riquièr is present in "A Wind in Rousillon," this poem is not distilled from the roads of France à la Pound. It sits tight, as Matthias the tourist sits tight, to study wind patterns as they transit one Mediterranean place: the terrible wind of history from Rome through Catholic Christianity through anti-Semitic Vichy and World War II, and the breath of poetry from Riquièr through exiled Machado, who died there, to Bonnefoy. But the most embracing wind is feminine—the parching African Tramontane to which Matthias assimilates contrary attributes of the ageless Mater Magna in the tenth section's litany. This section would resemble the Litany of Loreto were it not so compact and so anchored in the history which it swiftly condenses. The Lady, who indeed is the wind, comprehends the sybilline ("scattered pages"), the memorious (binding them), the soothing, the poisonous, the seductive, the redeeming—spirit in all its oppositions. This power represents Matthias's valiant Irish-born hostess, who risked her life to protect Jews, but also stands as "Mother of ostentation, Mother of ordure, // . . . Mother of Jesus, Mother of jackals" (*SM* 127). I feel no real pressure from David Jones's comparable figures behind Matthias's Lady, for each of the six stanzas in his litany invokes a complex feminine aspect only to have it pass through this place, not abiding there (your house is not the tower, your shrine has grown black, the sea god lounges in your chapel . . .). No prayer, this, although it begins by repeating most of Riquièr's line at the end of section VIII ("Mother of charity").

Dare I ask just what this litany is, then? The poem collects and arranges atrocities, cannonades, persecutions, massacres, the gentle and ecstatic breaths of poetry, news flashes, intimacy, piety mawkish and true, whiffs of atmosphere. It attempts the ancient bardic task, on non-native ground, of anamnesis or full recollection. Of course, the pages scatter even as they are bound. The litany which Matthias writes is the only adequate focus, and closure, of all this. How so? The several distinct poetries quoted in the poem are paralleled by even broader constatations in the litany, and by tones abrupt, biting, ironic, gentle, pleading, and sybilline. What this litany performs is so simple that we do not perceive it. Whereas poetry's action is to register both cruelty and love, both coherences and dispersions, goods and evils, in registering these opposites what is its own ethos? The litany presents this ethos as

208　care, vast but neutral, the care that wind has for the ground: embracing but sliding, both binding and loosing. The contradictions that must be felt if the real is to be loved are in its care. No illusions!—but also the whole of the feminine power, and with it the minimally violating rhetoric of litany. This, then, the poem distills for us when so much of the language for care has been worn out (the Lourdes flotsam in section III) or reduced to bones *("Nous, les os")*.

Since much of what this caring power must embrace stems from our cruelty, this litany suggests to me that Matthias's repetitions often aim at the ethos of neutral but penetrative care, the care that is not charity, the feminine comprehensiveness that goes far beyond maternal protection—it may even be quite pitiless—and so aiming at an illusionless beauty. This is classical.

But short of that, too, this litany is Matthias's way of not being cruel. For since he responds assiduously to the stories and words of others, the choral dead, he knows what it is to feel not only his own moral and intellectual passions turning sharp edged but also those of others, and perhaps to amplify them, including their sharpnesses. Or to judge passion in others and not in himself. The clear-eyed magnanimity of the poem for Sir Thomas Browne, and the damning but quiet choral voice in the plague ditty, "Spokesman to Bailiff," bracket the vast terrain across which Matthias's eye ranges with both heart and piercing judgment. These extremely fine poems emerge from the moral tussle, I should think. And litany resolves that tussle on an embracing plane.

To resume, then: the large step taken by "A Wind in Rousillon" has Matthias pouring the whole of anamnesis, with literal considerations of place, through the vast, dialectical sieve of neutral care, and that sieve is litany. Which is to say, anamnesis and literal place pass through the other place or topos of feminine breath, a dry but preserving wind. The implications of this step, for the perception of what grounding might be internally for this topos, which is not a place but an impersonal voice, come up for me in the somewhat tentative "Northern Summer" and the decisive "Compostela Diptych."

III

This tentative aspect is of particular interest because biographical frustration, the feeling of ill fit while relocating in Scotland after fifteen Suffolk summers, accompanies an advance in the terms for inner grounding within the topos of poetic speech. Matthias's note on "Northern Summer" acknowledges only his dissatisfaction. Literal and psychological habitation, and the discomfort that comes from not finding it at a new site, occupy the poem's foreground. Matthias rummages through the history of the place—Scotland's romantic courtiers, political exiles, miners and entrepreneurs, Pretender-backing lairds, radical theologians, radical economists, and hoaxing bard Macpherson in full array—in order to get a navigational fix for his perching place. What he experienced as an empirical unsuccess, however, has good consequences—one of the poem's main terms—for the non-place of poetry.

Were I to follow the threads of repetition and variation through this poem, an intricate pattern would emerge. Readers will do this in their own way; it is enough to point to some main lines, and before that to observe that only in poems of this scale does the subtly differentiating yet driving power of these motivic refrains show itself. The centripetal limit I found earlier in "Double Derivation" has in these poems its expansive and architectonic counterpart. While the refrain elements in these long poems resemble motifs in Pound's *Cantos,* they are more through-composed than Pound's are, *pace* Ezra. And I have the sense that they address one of the perceptual furrows opened by the *Cantos:* how to see and feel ground within one's own making while it is fed by the grounds of histories and places.

These two long poems, "Northern Summer" and "A Compostela Diptych," span the decade from 1980 to 1990. In one, Matthias's English roots through marriage undergo a transplanting that he calls "alienating"; in the second he explores the French and Spanish pilgrimage roads to Santiago, ground at first "totally unfamiliar" but which he came to know in part firsthand as he wrote. This direct acquaintance takes on unanticipated depth of feeling due to illnesses suffered by both Matthias's daughter and himself before the poem was completed. (The "Dedication" poem in *Swimming at Midnight* is properly part of the whole, where Compostela and its pilgrimage roads become hyperplaces.)

That synchronistic convergence of life and writing is not without prefiguration in "Northern Summer," where Matthias's concern already was curative, but in a less resolved way. There his effort, in ways that personal involvement opened rather than summarized, was to reground poetry as well as potential residence in a realm cleared of winds. "A Wind in Rousillon" arranged or composed the winds of poetry and history. "Northern Summer" becomes a clearinghouse for this process, with personal relocation as its motive. The zone which he clears has already been cleared, of course, by native and imperial doings, leaving an emptiness at which the would-be part-time settler probes. In that emptiness both history and Ossianic pseudo-history move somewhat placelessly. The poem's presiding genius is a bird of passage borrowed from Göran Sonnevi in the epigraph, guiding the mind's

210 probes. The winds that it flies, and which Matthias clears away one by one as he examines castle, mine, Mary Queen of Scots and Bothwell, the Bonnie Prince, Stevenson, Scott, Kirkcaldy, Lord Elcho, Knox, the brothers Adam, Adam Smith, and Macpherson's Ossian, are varieties of either "consequence" or "inconsequence" upon which language may "move," consequently to some point or achievement, often questionable ("Those workmen died / in nailers' dargs to earn a casual footnote" *BA* 103), or fantastically into some emptiness. Stripped away, then, are the sentiment compensatory to the Scottish defeat tradition, compensatory projections of grandeur and grandiosity in the eighteenth and nineteenth centuries, and even the unsentimental abstract theology and social thought which compensate Scottish romance (Knox and Smith). To leave what basis? Even the tender recollection of hearing Stevenson being read aloud to him as a child, triggered by his wife's voice reading R.L.S. to their children, has language sliding without purchase: "Sentiment's transfigured into history, / and history to sentiment" (*BA* 102). The basis or the ground is something beyond the movement of that chiasmus. Getting there, however, takes some doing, because it is not enough to replace emptiness with habitation and occupation by others, by their own literal groundings. Matthias of course tries; Sonnevi's blackbird, carrying its "inner empty / space" in a "flight of sentimentality through empty space," prompts Matthias, chiastically again, to hope for some way of improving on the situation; and the sober comedy of it all is present from the outset. Setting King Edward's harsh orders for the destruction of the Wemyss seat against tourist-guide vapidities about Wemyss castle, he writes of Edward's passage:

> Language
> moving upon consequence
> Consequence
> upon a language: Flight
> of an heraldic bird
> through space that is inhabited. (*BA* 94)

Aristocratic action as beachhead for a landing? One of poetry's incorrigible dreams, its backroom longings for its own bardic and courtly youth. Yet the heraldry here also offers something else: pattern, system, a secular mandala for unmoored contemporaries on their flight-paths. Again, how so? Let me offer a few specifics.

Matthias repeats and varies phrases from section to section along several lines at once. In section I, tour-book language "threading aimlessly / through sentimental empty space" provokes his wish to "build on" heraldic languages of power and muscled habitation (*BA* 93). When one reaches the chiastic "Language / moving upon inconsequence . . . / through space that is inhabited," that phrasing is built on the twin model of Sonnevi's passage and Matthias's first adaptation of it. Sonnevi's lines are indeed heraldic, generating variants which Matthias moves around like quarterings in a shield-space as he seeks the right combination. In section II, Matthias tries to wrench free of the heraldic pattern ("the flight of Sentiment / is through a space that's occupied" and "the flight of Sentiment / is not / through empty space," *BA* 95–96), but the quarterings will not let him. In section I's chiasmus, "moving upon consequence" stands as one line, while in section III's description of the abandoned mine, a twice-repeated paragraph-line—"The tower's erect upon the hill, but nothing moves" (*BA* 96, 97)—nicely develops that crucial plain verb out of Matthias's variant on Sonnevi's bird. Section III ends by reiterating the line, but truncatedly—"The tower's erect upon the hill"—just after a dash of up-to-date, North-Sea-oil movement: "A tanker steams across the bleak horizon" (97). The blackbird's heraldic quarterings remain, as the empty space gets filled with its requisite dark smudge.

The filling of empty spaces, by this or that ruling passion, frenzy, avaricious grab, or spiritual impulse, occupies Matthias's survey of his new turf. The catalog both shivers and amuses him. It also swells out beyond the horizon of the many local Pretenders; Hume, Napoleon, Johnson, Goethe "filled the emptiness before their eyes / with what they were" (*BA* 104, repeated on 105). Such projective energies come to possess our humble verb *move;* Knox, Adam, and Kirkcaldy "moving through mental spaces" (102), and Macpherson as he "moved along / the circles of the powerful and into space / occupied by . . . " (104, 105). Such projectors are driven, of course; collective defeat calls on them to invent some "feeling" with which to invest "emptied" space (Macpherson's calling at age nine, at the '45 Rising: 105). The heraldic fit remains exact, for Sonnevi's hole of empty space and the blackbird's iris or "yellow / ring" around its "inner empty space" pattern Macpherson's paradigmatic achievement of the impossible, as he "squared the widening empty circles" (106). For our purposes, the apparent question might be, "Is not the empty space of that bird's eye this poem's poetic ground?" Our poetic theorists would answer, "Yes," but I shall return to this to propose something less creased by the void. For now, let us enjoy the fact that Matthias's wit becomes all-inclusive, for in section IX he confesses himself a forger, Macphersonly

212 describing what he has not seen. He too takes the infection. Immediately, however, he jokingly cures it by aligning himself with Sonnevi's heraldic bird—but I shall return to this as well.

In section VI, up against memories of hearing Stevenson or Scott being read to him as a child, Matthias recognizes his own calling—to differentiate his vocation as a poet, a maker, from its dreamy close cousins. All of these, including his own, are intriguingly interstitial, bird-beckoned through a gap that calls for projected feeling: "There is a space / I have not learned to fill / somewhere between printed marks and sounds / and I am lost in some way too / among the heather, frightened of the distances / when all I want to do is drift on lang / uage into dream. . . . " (100). This variant on one of his refrains ends by breaking *language* into a Scottish dialect form of *long* and a beheaded piece of French cloud: linguistic quarterings on the word-shield, marking the backcountry of this poem's disquiet and longing. Later in the section he cites Scott to the effect

> that "laws & manners
> cast a necessary colouring;
> but the bearings, to use heraldic language,
> will remain the same,
> though the tincture may be different
> or opposed. . . ."
>
> *Bearings . . . tincture . . .*
> Theft and Dream,
> flight of an heraldic bird through language
> and my mother's voice. (*BA* 101)

This panel quarters fantasy and delirium with lineage, that most solid heraldic matter: Stevenson with his Indiana wife hearing, while sick in Samoa, bell sounds in Scotland, and Matthias of Indiana hearing his English wife in Scotland, and remembering his Ohio mother, reading R.L.S. and Scott—that is, spliced lineages and the actual, stable generations, quartered on the fields of symbolic continuity, yet dreamily, feverishly.

More than that, however, the patterns of heraldry *move* into the field of language through Scott's puns on bearings and tincture, which distinguish solid, unchanging factors from the shifting ones (on a blazon, orientations and design versus color and number). And that move into language seems inevitable, since Mary, Charles the Pretender, Macpherson, Stevenson, the ambitious Bothwell, and Matthias, too, the guest with his hosts, all come ungrounded. The guest's anxiety, his disorientation, only accentuate what proves to be a native condition on the adopted ground. Eliot said through his Sweeney, "I gotta use words when I talk to you." Northern Matthias is saying that we gotta space out when we come ungrounded (as more and more of us are doing)—that is, fill it with a pattern of feeling. And that this pattern, alternatively empty and heraldic in the chiastic flip-flop which this poem enacts repeatedly, will suffice. In my own terms, this filled emptiness is the inner ground of poetic speech, the nature of its coherence as a field, topos, or "place." The emptiness which it quarters and colors, or renders stably generative, is not the negative hollow that haunts this poem and initiates its unsettledness.

Nor, therefore, is the emptiness of the moving bird's eye the only field for ground in this poem. If it were, Matthias's poetics, at least here, would neatly converge with an extrapolation made by both Continental and American literary theorists from Walter Benjamin's Baudelaire. While the bird's eye in Sonnevi's poem is not the blank eye of the camera and the dead eye of the crowd in Benjamin's essays, its central void nearly assimilates it to Benjamin's perspective, which, in Ranier Nägele's words, registers the pervasive modern impact of "an eye without a glance and as such terrifying . . . . One might add that in this motif of Baudelaire the ground of his poetry is laid bare. At the core of modernity, something happens to the eye" (131–32). That may well be, but such ground is not wholly Matthias's here. His ground shifts between the eye's void and heraldic experiments in resituation. While those experiments afford him no outcome secure from his irony, they do engage him in attempting a step beyond the Baudelairean impasse.

The attempt at that step is a form or structure of feeling, short of an achieved and settled form as convention; I borrow Raymond Williams's indispensable term here. And Matthias's attempted re-siting of ground for himself, literally but also poetically, brings him up against an uncomfortably similar structure of feeling, that of the Pretenders, sentimental and self-ungrounding. Against them, Matthias distinguishes himself as a would-be inhabitant. The Pretenders' structure of feeling stems, however, from their status as internal and actual exiles, and so their structure of feeling shades easily into the major structure of feeling in a great deal of major twentieth-century literature. Also, the more earnest structure of feeling aimed at by Matthias is actually a special case of the exile's. So where does one come out? Both structures of feeling aim at regrounding, of course, but only the one attempted by Matthias may be conscious of the enterprise and therefore alert to the elusiveness of any potential regrounding. Matthias's reflectiveness and ironic probings distinguish his structure of feeling from that of the Adapters, Adopters, Inventors, and Projectors, thoroughly enough to render the otherwise uncomfortable similarity to them less than crippling. And that margin of difference is crucial, given certain heroic ventures in modern American poetry at regrounding. The juries are not in on *The Cantos* and *The Maximus Poems* in this regard, and may not be for some time. "Northern Summer" hardly sets itself up for comparison with those poems, yet I find it heartening to hold it in mind with them, because it tries on a limited scale to do what Pound left undone and Olson left monumentally revised but incomplete: the disentangling of a reflective movement from a projective one. The heraldic symbolism, and structure, of storied ground or lived field, disengages from most of the projector's impulses; and because it can recombine its elements stably, it is pledged not to feeling but to the possibilities of feeling. Matthias's chiastic flip-flops between projected or empty feeling and heraldic structures of feeling constitutes his poetic ground in the poem. That alternation, as it were within the eighth type of ambiguity, is consciously chosen and comedically suffered, both. Neither Olson nor Pound got us to that kind of ground.

Taking up section IX again, where Matthias catches the Pretender's emptiness-filling infection and then attempts a cure. "Tourist? Paying guest—/ of language of / the place, but heading further north and pledging silence" (107). The poetic act after all is to fly and to flee, as bird, Bothwell, and Brecht. Disgraced Bothwell's route into exile, movingly speculated, is followed by a glimpse of Brecht's to Finland—with Brecht's impish glimpse of "a smallish hidden door" in Lapland, and Matthias's impish pledge of his bird-similar to a Hanseatic taxidermist, which in the dissolving last lines takes its Sonnevian attributes through Brecht's Lapland aperture (109). (Probably we saw it lift off on stubby chiastic wings: "/ of language of /".) Bothwell, like Cumberland in putting down the '45 Rising, was one "through whom the language of the place / spoke itself to consequence" (108). A real and flagrant actor, a liar, killer, ravisher, and cheat, but no sentimentalist. Brecht the sly poet—"No, Senator, I never wrote that poem"—scuttles off to make the space he has to make to carry his word. Topos with sufficient inner ground to stand on, and a smallish hidden door. The double identity for Matthias here underwrites both heraldic space (in Sonnevi's blackbird, in Bothwell's arrogant successes then flight, in "bearings" for navigation and "tincture" for ethos) and movement upon language into exile (bearings taken anew because of taint or stain, "Theft and Dream" perhaps including the notorious thiever Bothwell, in any case due to the poem's survey of dishonored connections between language and ground). Flier, flee-er, spanner of the other kind of place or topos.

Matthias has this happen through subtle reiteration of refrain elements and their variants. He makes petition for one kind of place (not to be had), but through repetition advances on a cure for that loss of literal footing, that cure being chiastic inner ground. The recapitulatory aspects of poetics, hoary and taken for granted, actually stand closer to the educated layer in culture than we admit, and break through that layer in moments of disequilibrium and need. The long prayer of anamnesis by the candle-bearer in Jones's "The Sleeping Lord," exfoliated from a microsecond of loving awareness of the dead, stands at one edge of this opening. Matthias's "Northern Summer" stands at another, folding a long, humorous, unsettled inventory around the refrains squared off Sonnevi's blackbird and then refolding it into that bird's passage across the poem, in-out-whisht-whisht, over vanishing ground.

Other poems by Matthias could serve for this comparison, but only this one lays out a phenomenology and symbolism, both, for the topos which can abide that disappearing ground. The phenomenology: dislocation, search, research, continuing disorientation, involuntary memory of feeling, demystification of claims put forward by the new ground, anxiety, mimicry of the con artists, and self-mocking exit from the tension—yet with a hint that integrity has been slyly found. The symbolism in its largest sense I take to be exile, displacement, and flight; movement into and out of language, and into and out of (compromised) action and ground; and then emptiness and habitation. The demystifying impulse within the poem's phenomenology is self-curative, for it sees through the mystiques of both place and action in order to ground the mind more adequately. Matthias's position as an inside-outsider makes that cure no less valuable or necessary.

"Exile plainly *is*," writes Nathaniel Tarn, arguing that it best symbolizes the site of poetic voicing as well as many major cross-cultural mythemes (326). His argument would seem to me invalid only if Augustine's land of unlikeness were also invalid, or the Hebraic poetic tradition all the way through Jabès were invalid. And Tarn has carefully elaborated a view of both poetics and aesthetics based on the metaphor of heraldry. Without entering into his far-reaching proposals, I simply note the harmony of his thinking with part of Matthias's symbolism in "Northern Summer," and earmark it for further reflection.

Augustine was perhaps the first to go over this vanishing ground and rise from it with wings. His inquest into memory in the *Confessions,* conducted in his love song to the silent God, progresses to this crucial inference:

> Why do I ask in which area of my memory you dwell, as if there really are places there?

> Where then did I find you to be able to learn of you . . . if not
> in the fact that you transcend me? There is no place, whether we
> go backwards or forwards; there can be no question of place.
> (200–201)

The remarkable outcome of this inference is a release from anxiety and search. Inner ground comes to hand in the immediacy of the transcendent. (The passage to which Augustine alludes in Plotinus, on time—IV.4.10.5— insists on that immediacy: "we must leave out all notions of stage and progress, and recognize one unchanging and timeless life.") Tarn's poststructuralist affirmations are attuned to this string in their own way (with mythical origin and end zoned off from process by the functional transcendence of art), even while they reinstate anxiety over the "place" of poetic speech, "on the loose, at the surface, hanging out on a highly problematic film over an equally problematic abyss" (328). Thus too, perhaps, the blackbird's song by way of outrageous Bothwell and sly Brecht. But were the anxiety not to emerge—as it does throughout "Northern Summer"—false grounding would not be seen through or demystified, and displacement to an inner grounding, heraldic and comedic/dishonorable in the poem, could not take place. (*Take place:* our usage will not release this handrail.)

Even the oral transmissions of the written—the readings aloud in section VI—call into question just where the poet might be. Their flyways are not inhabited, and the ground shifts across oceans. The rubbery mutuality of "Theft and Dream" rides with the "heraldic blackbird through language" along with one's mother's voice. The shift to the oral, and presumably therefore to primary poetic ground, momentarily enlarges personal disorientation, and cannot reassure the mind writing. Just where does the mind go once it is propelled from previous imaginative groundings by the winds?

IV

Here I must digress doubly, first on the cultural matter of grounding, and then on the Romantic opening of the furrow that I assigned to Pound earlier, in which one sees one's inner ground coming into view. I must do so in order to generalize the significance of Matthias's themes.

Hölderlin argued at the beginning of our epoch that to engage deeply with one's art one must find one's own cultural matter, *das Eigene;* but, he maintained, one's own in this regard is something foreign, *das Fremde,* to be won and shaped, such as Greek Olympian transcendence has been for Europe. The ramifications of this view extend far and deep. In its light the foreign is no mere tourist's haul of tasty, strange morsels; it is part of a chiastic reversal (as Andrzej Warminski shows, 23–45) wherein their own nativeness becomes our own foreignness, and vice versa. It is not an episteme concerned with the relation of consciousness to object; it is a patterning of terms with torqued diagonals instead of quarterings, much like the reversals and variants that emerge in "Northern Summer," sometimes set out chiastically there. Hölderlin's advice is not easily taken by our contemporaries, for the civilization we inhabit has turned omnivorous of other cultures, like a momentarily dominant biophage, leaving most of us unable to see in the foreign anything other than ourselves. Baudrillard's witty and outrageous books on the United States have no counterparts among us. About all of this the anthropologist James Redfield draws a sage inference.

> A society of such power [modernist and ubiquitous] must inspire anxiety in its members . . . . We are not sure that modernism coheres as a culture should cohere . . . . Our interest in cultural systems may then be interpreted as a search for the sources of cultural coherence, of control . . . . Ethnography, from this point of view, is an effort intellectually to rescue ourselves from our own history. (101)

Before I ask about the effort poetically to rescue something comparable, I would point out that Redfield's view accounts for the red-shift along which Hölderlin's advice has receded from view. This ethnographic standpoint, achieved satirically already at several points by Swift's Gulliver, emerges from the fact that what is native to us is the monstrous and expanding cabbage of modernization, with its attendant unease. Such now are the walls of thy habitations, O Zion! In the foreign culture we do not seek our own in Hölderlin's sense, then, but rather *an entire system of cultural coherence,* the reading of a whole culture, as if to prevent a collapse within our native realm.

Fashionable interests in tribal cultures of course buffer this unease. But those who really deal with that unease do much more. If I interpret Redfield fairly in my own terms, the sense of coherence which he attributes to an entire cultural system I would see as part of the inner ground which any person with relatively high cultural morale normally carries. What psychologists call grounding in the individual depends on this *collective* coherence. Notable among recent work by American ethnographers in respect to inner grounding as it is tied to actual places is that of Keith Basso, among the Western

Apache. There, "wisdom" matches instilled familiarity with sites, the stories tied to them, and the myths amplifying those stories. Basso registered profound respect for this sense of place as the source for moral coherence and flexibility—"an absorbing cultural form of large and subtle dimensions" (138)—and from the depth of his reaction one can sense the cultural and moral coherence that we ourselves have lost. The "aimless" threading of event and language over place in Matthias's poem, even the outcast, wanderer status for Matthias in his bird-Bothwell-Brecht fantasy, mirrors the cultural morale so widely lost among us. That fantasy ends his poem well, for with it he invites us at least to notice the wind-blown, disreputable facts.

For it usually takes a shock or displacement to instill such notice. And here I turn to Hölderlin's contemporary Wordsworth, who registers the loss of inner ground paradigmatically, with no abysses scanted, yet his morale largely intact. In mind for me are the dream of the Arab in Book V of *The Prelude* and the memory of crossing the Simplon Pass in Book VI. In the first, the literal setting of seaside cave and book is transformed by the apocalyptic dream which uses them. Culture as vessel for the immortal soul? Stone and shell, the mind's unaging monuments—all are to be destroyed, shows the dream; the quiet seaside scene to which the dreamer returns is charged with that tension. In Book VI, the memory of an anticlimactic alpine crossing suddenly, ten years later, cracks open over a vaporous abyss, over imaginative power itself, which transforms the remembered landscape into figures of the eternal. As for France, whose great breakout turned to a crack-up . . . and as for England, in turmoil but unbudgeable . . . these deep frustrations recede before the opening of old ground onto a permanent basis, through a shock that proves to be stabilizing. These two episodes go beyond the cultural coherence which, in Redfield's terms, had begun to send fissures up through the cultural morale of the elite. Beyond, into a grounding that is inner—in Book V beyond culture's power to last and in Book VI beyond nature's power to outlast it. Tremendous anxieties get wrapped into both episodes, but as in Augustine's realization about placelessness before transcendence, anxiety turns to something else: calmly charged acceptance, and steady elation before the operation of creative power's abyssal "unfathered vapors." Both episodes are secular articulations, varyingly apocalyptic or revelatory, of the structure of consciousness. And they are prototypical: their imaginal phenomenology supplies new inner ground, abyssal and decreative, to the topos or place of poetic speech in a culture that has begun moving toward modernization. Or for the great poets in that culture.

Structure of consciousness: Book V's episode ruptures actual earth and recharges it through dream-vision, whereas in Book VI voluntary memory is opened primally during the waking state. For our purposes, coming as we do after Proust, Baudelaire, and Benjamin as students of involuntary memory, it is remarkable that these two episodes taken together step around Wordsworth's own preoccupation with the storehouse of personal memory, and our own as well. These two episodes transvalue actual ground and then voluntary memory through dreamed and then waking visions. The visions, and not memory, are involuntary, inherently so. The Romantic and modernist ground of involuntary personal memory drops away; these episodes reground topos through Great Memory and the cosmogonic breath of the Platonic Receptacle. From Wordsworth, therefore, I extract a premonitory intuition of the wisdom in stepping around Proustian and Baudelairean sensibility (which Wordsworth knew also) even before it had to perform its great labors. Those labors, reparative and compensatory, in Benjamin's terms make of consciousness a zone narrowed to shock, or repeated traumas large and small. Wordsworth knew such shocks well, but did not narrow consciousness in that way. His kind of intuition offers inner regrounding to poetic speech, and to attenuated cultural coherences, more integrally than does the *mémoire involuntaire* which fuels the parallel and later process.

Involuntary memory, *pace* Benjamin, and Proust, gives a mild taste of the possessional state. And as exiles driven forth from a naive installation in cultural coherence, we can appreciate rhetorical forms that can stand up to that state. Grounding and regrounding require a form that will let the mind be possessed by formerly grounded experience, yet also at the same time move with a cleared, demystified imagination toward some unforeseeable next phase. That rhetoric is compactly represented by the variable refrain. It can face backward toward possessional imagery and involuntary memory, while through variations it can turn to untangle personal from historical feeling and face forward. Apparently recursive, repetitions can also be, in this situation, eminently progressive. The past which tap-taps within them, sometimes gripping them, they also take apart and demystify. The next phase of grounding which they have not reached they tap-tap a way toward, a way that is more musical than propositional. The position which the mind can hold with their help is paradoxical, simultaneously possessed and wide awake. As such, it may condense Romantic and modernist forms of feeling in deceptively simple ways.

The possessional state haunts "Northern Summer." Matthias's varying refrains move him through it (they are language moving upon the consequence of ungrounding) and serve in part to free him from it. The root of these repetitions in oral poetics Matthias shifts explicitly to the written—an attempt at regrounding the topos of speech—without quite allaying the underlying paradigmatic anxiety. For this poem offers only the protrepsis to a long movement of reconstruction. Let me turn now to the poem which undertakes that movement decisively.

V

"A Compostela Diptych" commences with a quiet catalog of the tributary roads to the great pilgrimage center at Santiago. There was a time, it begins, when people could imaginally cohere around themselves and around the ragged, slashed, yet still bold idea of Christendom by actually covering the ground on foot—there was a living time, not *Es war einmal,* when cultural morale and inner grounding could be paced out wearily and joyously. And everything Western Europe has made and unmade of itself, on that inner grounding, is suggested by this whole poem's progression, which gently and persistently moves again by way of parallel constructions that nestle within themselves phrases and words variably repeated. As I am one of its two dedicatees I hesitate to praise it lavishly, but I must. This essay already suggests enough about how I would read this poem for me to leave things safely to a reader's discovery. I will observe only that the gathering place for an inner regrounding, which as a reader I may try to detach for very good reasons from actual ground, to entrust it to the place of poetic speech—to which Matthias indeed entrusts it—cannot be emotionally detached, for most readers, from the actual ground there covered, especially if some parts of it be known to them. This speaks well of the poem's fundamental tension, which is at once vast and tightly knit. By a nice chance Matthias in section VI of part I, where Eliot and Pound traipse the domains of Ventadorn and Arnaut Daniel, encounters a venerable fellow conjurer with winds, although in another spirit: *"I am Arnaut who gathers the wind . . . . / I am Arnaut who swims against the tide"* (*BA* 168). The "Diptych" gathers winds past Rousillon, past Scotland, for a great yet modestly performed sifting of shared cultural elementals, which are ineluctably and also unforeseeably European—for it is Europe that maintains a link with the East that we have not matched, and a knowledge of the Near East and Africa, however filtered through brutal domination, that antedates our experiment. Pilgrimage has faded as a vital institution. But as symbol of a dedication to inner regrounding perhaps it cannot be bettered.

Let me sketch this poem's way with regrounding by attending to its climax. The final section of the poem's second part begins with the enormous blast from detonated magazines near Coruña and Santiago. The preceding section had ended with Franco's rise; the auditory illusion is a nice one, making an episode from the Carlist Wars seem to shatter the uneasy quiet of the 1930s. But the imaginative power of this stroke is such that it sends a cymbal crash out over the whole poem, which tallies goods and evils from chorused sources and winds from the dead, so as to mound up, disentangle, clarify, see lovingly, see through, hear again, hear for the first time, the ground of poetic speech in the West. As in: "a strange boat arrived off Finisterre . . . . // (Or so they say. Or so they said / who made the book)" (*BA* 156). Or as in,

> So it began. So they said it had begun.
> A phase (a phrase (a moment in
> the spin of some ephemeride (a change
>
> not even in the modes of music
> from the Greek
> to the Gregorian. . . . (*BA* 157)

Those nesting unclosed parentheses open onto the *Abgrund* in the regrounding of speech. Strains old and older, qualification on qualification? Well, of course. But play it again, Sam, play it again. The repeated gesture here—a modern historian's scrupulous notations on oral tradition—does not wed itself to contemporary hermeneutic skepticism. Our evidence is the final section's structure, which pours comprehensive sound, that would include oral legends across the generations, into inclusive and peaceful silence, in the subtly constructive spirit that one can trace right through Matthias's various strands of subversiveness. The munitions blast in the poem's final section, through cascading stanzas, rocks bells in Santiago, ships at sea, houses, and Basque shepherds. "Then in the high & highest places everything was still. // As it was in the beginning" (190). These lines, repeating and varying so as to include the companion doxological phrase about the end, proceed to embrace—with the silence of the ground of grounds—St. Francis's sermons and songs, the Logos and the Deunde, Ignatian propositions, the Grail legend ("where they say, they *say* / the Grail came to rest," 191), Mithraic oaths, the bellow of dying bulls, the silence of abbeys, abbots, monks in the fields, sacristy, stores, garden, and copy room, the language of Castillian *juglares,* and then Matthias's own powerful hymn to primordial silence—"aphonia // before a whisper or a breath, aphasia / before injury, / aphelion of outcry without sun . . . // Long before *it is / and ever shall be*" (192)—and finally the writer's homage to his host Delgado-Gomez at Pamplona, and to the ground they walked, ending with the refrain line. Actual ground, with actual song, sermon, and silence, and also with actual legend, history, theology, and prayer, have been taken up into silence after deafening sound. The deaths of Machado and Vallejo in the preceding section barely precede the noise of that blast; great voicing is dying, and then? However venerable the prototype for the refrains in the final section, their work is to freshen and renew: to make the past resonant, blown into tight compass by all that damned powder, and then to open toward a new basis from the highest places, *loci altissimi,* those places with a total survey of the ground.

This coda arrives at a time when voice has been stringently questioned by the third Objectivism, Language poetry. Aspects of voice had been elevated by Williams and Olson and O'Hara, but the recent Objectivist ascesis dovetails with the stifling of voice, orality, and other ego vagaries by the deconstructive turn to writing/text. Matthias's particular value as a writer is his consistent scrupulosity about texts, about both acknowledging them and wittily reworking them, but along with that his steady exploration of a voice. No fence-straddler, he simply makes the fence unnecessary. The coda to "A Compostela Diptych" shows his use of refrain tap-tapping its way not toward his voice alone but a collective possibility for the regrounding of voice. Functional, not decorative; refrains as a compact model or seed for reconstellated forms, of which in the end there are not terribly many; refrain not as closural only but also processural; refrain anticipating retotalization, or renewed return, or neo-Platonic epistrophe; refrain as the compositional impulse in Mandelshtam's "Octets," with its eyes screwed tight while it floats in space— all of these I can imagine folding out of Matthias's post-blast quiet, just when they are needed, now, in the beginning.

VI

More than a sketch of the coda's path to regrounding must come into view, however, if one is to assess the stakes which it meets and then raises. I may seem to burden the conclusion of this poem with baggage from other trains in what follows, but my interest is simply in having them arrive at the same terminal so that their passengers may greet each other.

First, the coda consolidates the poem's firmly quiet, that is to say, private religious attitude. Whisper it not in Gath, where the usual literary perceptions of what constitutes religion hold sway, but Matthias's poem is no enlargement of Arnold's "Stanzas from the Grand Chartreuse," no bittersweet adieu to Christianity, though surely some will take it in that way. Yet these canned notions look past the ways in which religious attitudes, whether held to within an institution or outside it, on the roads, work as therapeutic systems, as givers of ground in the sea of the collective psyche. "A Compostela Diptych" negotiates a path toward top-to-bottom healing, prospectively collective and synchronistically personal; and the negotiation of that path is itself the structure of feeling which offers good ground. The "Diptych" attaches itself to that structure, not to doctrinal faith, because it trudges out those irrevocable increments of consciousness (the historian's "they say") which have come to travelers while they have in fact earnestly traveled the appointed roads. For precisely in those days when the roads crumble, there one must walk. And precisely those who give testimony about this may be misheard, by both those who take the roads as still given and those who disdain them completely. Neither kind of mishearer gets it. And they may be superb readers otherwise: witness Paul Fussell's irritated deafness to the complex invocation of chivalric materials in David Jones's *In Parenthesis,* a poem in some ways easier to get because its author has declared faith. But then no one ever told us that writing, especially on the road, *ob via,* would be an obvious matter.

Secondly, the coda's structure of feeling integrates several aspects of form in a remarkably unobtrusive manner. Let me set these forth in stages.

One aspect of the coda's structure of feeling has to do with scope. The whole poem inventories the Western European cacophony, slowly enough so that one hears each part distinctly, and then moves across the bridge of a destructive explosion first to touch symphonically on a landscape which compactly harmonizes the earlier cacophony and then to pass into high silence. A subtext progression transits the hope and faith of Christianity, with the sad contradictions of political Christendom, to identify only with hope rather than with any of its formularies. This silence and hope are not of the individual heart or the mystic's privacy. They are the generative *silentium* and *spes* that press from collective experience—the quiet of the communal heart, a quiet rarely invoked and in our day scarcely conceivable. A poetic regrounding that skirts it, however, may be found wanting. The destructive explosion prior to this silence sets tragic limits, of course. Yet even as that limit clamps shudderingly down, with Pindaric force ("savior and saved alike speared by the lightning flash—/ from the gods we must expect / things that suit our mortal minds,/ aware of the here and now, aware of our allotment," Pindar, "Pythian 3"), a communal, sharable, and inventoriable ground for the silence that brings peace spreads out through the poem's closing movement, even unto high places. This structure of feeling compensates the Western European ones in Pound's *Cantos,* which reach behind commercial decline and tragedy to the erotic interlude and the Eleusinian mysteries for a silence concordant with justice. "A Compostela Diptych" does not reach behind, but through.

Another aspect of the coda, deriving also from the whole poem, has to do with the slow pace I have just mentioned. With respect to "Northern Summer," Matthias has decelerated the anxiety-ridden flight through the empty space of a language losing its ground. This shows in the style of the "Diptych" as a whole, in ways that I may leave the reader to discover. More than that, although along the same lines, Matthias has achieved, through a therapeutic retracing of ground at walking pace, a deceleration of structures of feeling typical of modernist and contemporary work, whether through the eye's jump-cuts or the ear's subject rhymes. Tony Pinkney writes, "When Deleuze and Guattari declare in *Anti-Oedipus* that 'a schizophrenic out for a walk is a better model than a neurotic lying on the analyst's couch,' they clearly remain within the modernist problematic of Baudelaire's *flâneur* or Woolf's Mrs. Dalloway ambling decentredly through central London" (Pinkney 4). We should add that this kind of walking is not the pilgrim's way of beading the thread of his aim with linked episodes but the urban wanderer's courting of collisions. Pinkney notes that this kind of mental speed, wandering, and deracination make cousins of Wordsworth and Marinetti or Mayakovsky. The speed with which Pound moves in *The Cantos* (an early essay of Pound's isolated Cocteau's "hurrying ideation") is not David Jones's way, notwithstanding his breathtaking moments of scoping, for Jones lingers to polish the spolia and scrape at the deposits. In "A Compostela Diptych" Matthias has moved to recover ground, without Jones's cadenced retards, while not losing altitude in the end, and to reduce modernist speed without sacrificing the ability to get somewhere that genuinely alters mental space. Again, in this regard his structure of feeling is compensatory. Yet with respect to grounding speech it is also reconstitutive, and in that respect it is not held captive by any relations to modernist structures of feeling.

A walk that courts caroming impacts is a disguised run, or perhaps it is a flight disguised as an exploration. What such a walk-as-run knows, dreads, and yet also excitedly seeks is shock. The aspect of Matthias's coda that tallies with this typical modernist rupture, that is, with the cut and jolting slide of film, poetry, and urban experience (many critics besides Benjamin now elaborate this), is the munitions blast. The whole of "Diptych" moves up to this jolt, then enters cadence across it. The blast splices two eras, Carlist and Fascist; it both troubles perception with a disconcerting, half-concealed rhyme, and clears away the poem's patient inventory without disaffirming what it clears away. In fact, the aftershock spreads a loving inventory of Europe in its mysterious coherence. The position and function of the blast show a modernist structure of feeling working also as classical climax and the door into classical closure-in-stillness. Matthias has fashioned here a double figure, balancing the two compositional impulses against each other in a dynamic, not static, equilibrium. Within that equilibrium vibrates a repetition—concretely as two periods of war, artistically as climax and rupture—which then spreads out into the rest of the coda toward the finding of further grounding for poetic speech. The older poetics of climax and catharsis balances against the modernist rupture of it, across a point whose interior doubling and *trompe l'oreille* (just *when* did that explode?) prevent it from getting absorbed by either formal impulse, classical or modernist. Thus the ground traveled by the sound wave that follows this moment is indeed potentially new, although it is old Spain that one hears described; that tension builds quietly behind the description. I know of no other episode in contemporary poetry that manages so much so deftly, with great shock and greater quiet, to ends so generously sharable, if indeed we prove able to share them in the common life.

The blast inaugurating the coda points to another important matter in the regrounding of speech: a shift from one sensory mode to the other, from eye to ear. Only Pound anticipates this clearly, with the triangulation among Troubadour song, Greek epic, and acoustic intuition verging on the mystical in his *Canto XX*. As I shall contend, the shift from eye to ear involves poetics, at least now, in a rapprochement with hermeneutics, though in a nonskeptical key, along the lines of prolonged duration and its myths, the "always already" of the theorists and the "sound slender" that Pound hears stretching from Homer's *ligur' aoide* through Arnaut Daniel's *noigandres* or *d'enoi ganres* to something a contemporary might hear as "too far off to be heard" yet piercingly present. The strong and lovely alternative, Anglo-Saxon in Bunting's "flutes flicker in the draft and flare" (section V of *Briggflatts*), stretches far, but does not hang there like a hummingbird. Both Pound and the theorists are after one of the mind's interior waterfalls, always falling.

In his essay on Roy Fisher, apropos "The Cut Pages," Matthias draws on analogies to Fisher's jazz experience, wherein for any member of a band taking the lead the music has already begun. Matthias touches back to Fisher's line in "If I didn't"—" the poem has always / already started"—and adds a comparison to "Heidegger's notion of language speaking through our listening when, as Gerald Bruns has said, 'nothing gets signified . . . but things make their appearance in the sense of coming into their own'" (46–47). This

226 mode of appearing is not Matthias's own, but his phrase about Heidegger's notion of language "speaking through our listening" cues us to retrieve, from the coda to "A Compostela Diptych," our major matter. Earlier I dealt with Benjamin's Baudelaire, through Rainer Nägele's contention that at the core of modern experience something jarring and decisive happens to the eye. Nägele's accent is not startling, since it caps an emphasis that begins at least with Blake. What Matthias notices in Fisher's "The Cut Pages," in spite of Fisher's visual sensibility, he notices by way of the ear, not the eye. Between jazz analogies to ongoing, already-begun material, and Heidegger's attention to the listening that receives material prior to significations, Matthias moves from the now-classic modern emphasis on the eye in poetics to hearing. What do we hear, between the fading blast and the description, in the coda to the "Diptych"? We listen for more than we hear, I have argued; we may find ourselves catching strains of a new grounding for speech, "too far off to be heard" but on their way; that is, in the terms of Matthias's own phrase about Heidegger, our listening goes past the language that is present to become a quiet speaking of its own. And when did that begin, that listening? The double figure of the blast, its *trompe l'oreille,* is there to keep our answer nimble. The theoretical phrase "always already," from Fisher, stems from Continental hermeneutics; Nathaniel Tarn nicely parallels this usage with the more intuitive practice of Eluard *(poésie ininterrompue)* and the necessary illusion of ongoing thrust (Tarn 339, 346). This aside on the phrase is to the main point, however, for the classic shock experience of modernity which renders the eye a template for jarred, stilled, narrowed consciousness, alert but reactive, enjoys full compensation when one can move to the ear's steadier, potentially seamless and continuous poetic. And that is what Matthias has done, first in a tentative, dialectical fashion in "Northern Summer," where the void of the moving eye vies with the suspensions of the half-dreaming ear to frame a possible regrounding, and then decisively in the coda to "A Compostela Diptych," where a climactic hearing opens the poem's closure out into the territory of its regrounding. A generative listening, parallel to a generative silence, has always already been at work; a regrounded speaking may come out of it.

Anyone at all familiar with modern philosophy will know that the stakes in the always-already game have mounted high indeed. Early in the game Paul Ricoeur tried to wedge open the intrinsically closed hermeneutical circle where it "proceeds from a prior understanding of the very thing that it tries to understand by interpreting it," by contending that this closure also blesses one with an opening.

I can still communicate with the sacred by making explicit the prior understanding that gives life to the interpretation. Thus hermeneutics, an acquisition of "modernity," is one of the modes by which that "modernity" transcends itself, insofar as it is forgetfulness of the sacred. I believe that being can still speak to me—no longer, of course, under the precritical form of immediate belief, but as the second immediacy aimed at by hermeneutics. (352)

What this increment of consciousness practices forgetting is of course another circle, that enclosure or zoning-off (thus *locus sacer*) for the purposes not of interpretation but encounter and special handling. Poetry converges with hermeneutics in Ricoeur's spirit whenever it lets its hunger for primary immediacy and *locus* be consistently haunted by unavoidable second immediacies—when it remembers reality and justice in a single thought, in Yeats's terms. Poetry also begins to do this when it listens for an elusive sound that repeats or sustains itself at the margins of audibility, for such listening moves beyond heard demarcations toward a grounding that no single *locus* for sound provides. It is Homer's *ligur' aoide;* no, it is Arnaut's *d'enoi ganres;* no, it is distant birdsong; or, it is my wife reading Scott to my children; no, it is my mother reading Scott to me as a child; no, it is the sound of an heraldic bird winging through language. The coda to "A Compostela Diptych" brings this listening to the degree of consciousness where memory quickens even while sound fades, where forgetting and remembering get conflated with each other in both a disconcertingly bifocal blast and in a pregnant silence, and where what can emerge from listening is the perhaps-sound of a possible yet out-of-range ground.

VII

Since ground in reflective speech is metaphor, and metaphor is the ground of modern poetics, the ethereal half of the figure demands some care.

Like Greek truth, *aletheia, Abgrund* contains what it opposes. That is, disclosure encompasses closure or forgetting, and the abyss swallows, or opens into, its ground. Both Greek and German here, in their parallel ways with the humble negative prefix, perform an inclusive and dialectical way of thinking about reality. A tyro may of course get fascinated with the toy itself and excitedly cry, "Where is the ground? Why, it is in the abyss!" neatly reversing the usual commonplace perception. Thinkers actually imitate this tyro, of course. What I propose to do in closing is something else: to listen

228 to the overtones of ground in selected usages adopted in the West, so as to carry out Matthias's hint in his coda, to see what might come of listening after a loud note has been struck. The note is *chora* in Greek, *locus* in Latin, *land, country,* and *ground* in English, all with parallel overtones that point to high grounding which has no coordinates on any map. Poetic questions not yet touched on will come in en route.

Psalm 116, verse 9, in the New Jerusalem Bible reads, "I shall pass my life in the presence of Yahweh, / in the land of the living." The Vulgate: "*Placebo Domino / In regione vivorum*" (revised, 1945: "*Ambulabo coram Domino / In regione viventium*"). The range for *regione* here, from place to land to zone of meaning, parallels that for the Greek *chora*, which even in Homer is both spot or site and wider region. The range in English for *land* is similar. What the psalmist counts on is our keeping both limits of that range alive in our hearing; never are we to retreat to primitivizing *chora*, *regione*, or *land* to some piece of gritty dirt alone, thus erasing the tension. Indeed the English version of the verse's final lobe has passed into common higher usage; it favors feeling for life, not real estate. Now all of this may be amusing; but should one touch on the life of *chora* in Christian thinking, many of our contemporaries would not be amused, simply because it goes christened. What they risk overlooking is the key linking step in the idea's development toward a nonlocatable grounding. A notable example is the pair of inscriptions in the Church of the Chora's mosaics of Christ and the Virgin Mother, from fourteenth-century Constantinople. The inscription near Christ alludes to our verse from Psalm 116: IS XS HE CHORA TO ZOONTON [Jesus Christ the land of the living]. The parallel inscription for his mother reads, METER THEOU HE CHORA ACHORETOU [The Mother of God, (dwelling-) place of the placeless (uncontainable)]. A window opens in Mary's heart-space to show the infant Christ; this image typifies the icon in Orthodoxy which symbolizes patient human suffering. The instrument of incarnation, and the embodiment of full life: the two choras, both paradoxical. Land or ground in its greater sense is the unifying mystical term here, which lets us see the abyssal ground that comes into existence in living persons; or see that the ground of living is the Christ, and the ground that paradoxically contains that ground is the open soul, the God-bearer. With incarnational perception one feels ground within ground, not abyss within ground; or so theology's long passacaglia on Psalm 116 would have it. What incarnational perception would never do is reduce flesh to merest ground, ground as dust alone, for flesh is also *locus sacer*, in tension with the greater *chora*. My point is simply that one can hear this fruitful tension within the language around *chora*, ground, and land, but that now such hearing commonly requires a set of Matthias headphones, post-blast model, type Second Immediacy.

To illustrate my point I invoke the contemporary philosopher John Sallis, who weaves impressive reflections around Platonic chorology in "The Politics of the Chora." His interest is also contemporary, turning to forms of the state untrammeled by oligarchy and tyranny. Yet his thinking leaps from the Greeks to Nietzsche, Heidegger, and Arendt, as if the Christian West had been naught but a bubble. The *chora* for Sallis is not at all concrete in its higher reaches; tension has been smoothed from it, and any ghost of a notion of incarnation has been set aside. What amazes is his blithe assumption that the *theatrum populi* which remains in his *chora* would stay spectral and not turn nasty.

> Now that the intelligible paradigms have drifted away and become mere stories [Nietzsche's "fable"]—one cannot but wonder whether our time is perhaps preeminently the time of a politics of the *chora*. Assuming that one can still think the outside of being after being has proved a vapor and a fallacy. Now there would be only: images taking place—indeed in a place in which all the markers of certainty would have dissolved. (70)

So much for Ricoeur's ability to hear being. And, welcome aboard, all you flitting simulacra from the pages of Baudrillard! Sallis almost makes me wish for a primitive concretization of *chora* as native turf, with fences. Does Dr. Sallis not hear the sophistic "perhaps" and "would have" diluting his acid? His Platonic *chora* is a skeptical one, more in line with Gorgias than Plato. The missing link, between Plato and the Nietzschean sophist in Dr. Sallis, is that Christian thinking about ground, person, and polity which he consigns to vapor. It would make a difference, could he listen for its reverberations, but he has stopped doing that long since. The end of Matthias's poem speaks to just such stoppings of the ears among a large portion of our educated class. There are grounds for such listening when listening itself may apprehend part of the ground.

My second and final context for ground comes from the past 150 years in Western medicine. Near the beginning of this essay I briefly screened the mobile site of the epileptic focus. It can move house. Only temporarily does it lease a piece of our temporal lobes. And so, like the aura which anticipates a seizure, the focus, too, defies a plain answer to the question, "Where is it?"

To go farther, however, the rheumatic specialist Dr. Paul Plotz calls into question the regular medical assumption that a core-site, however elusive, can be found for a given disease. That assumption is not only common, but also well funded: witness the hopes currently pinned on the human genome project. Dr. Plotz points to a disease in his own field which has been tied to flaws in a gene for membrane protein. Several patients with normal genes of this type also display the symptoms of Emery-Dreifuss syndrome; so "where is this disease?" Motor neuron and mitochondrial illnesses challenge location in the same way, as well as several slithery zones "at the solid core" of molecular genetics itself. About diabetes Dr. Plotz asks: is it in the urine, blood, pancreas, islet cell, the end organ insulin receptor, thymus, cytotoxic lymphocyte, the gene for glutamic acid decarboxylase, or HLA molecules? Or several of these? "Or under the slippery rug?" (161).

This sage question has consequences for both the Enlightenment medicine behind current practice and the molecular biology that is revolutionizing it. The rational and taxonomic structures animating them both break up on the beachhead of "Where?" For the humanist and poet, that Socratic "Where?" becomes indispensable. Those of us who follow Czeslaw Milosz's survey of biology's challenges to humane values across the board would welcome it, I should think. The tool has reach, for "Where?" touches back to Plato's distinction of "there" in *chora* as grounding from the concrete "there" in the unreflective usages of *chora* as land and native ground. The reach within that distinction has consequences not only for biology and medicine, of course—witness Sallis's smoothing away of the term's tensions in our political context—but biology's status as queen among the disciplines places it first.

Dr. Plotz foresees for medicine a double task: the fragmentation of inadequate, too-inclusive disease descriptions upon findings that refuse to stand in one place, but also the unification of inquiry around the lived destinies of sufferers. The first task corresponds to the sacrifice of a hypostatized, solid *chora* to the subtler *chora* of ongoing regrounding. The second task respects subjective testimony, and individual anamnesis and epichrisis, in all their variety, as parts of the grounding for illness—illnesses as lived matters, not only as entities fixable by the nails of causality to the putatively concrete ground of a condition. I find in this once-and-future medical attitude a compensation to, perhaps even a remedy for, the acidic pressure of biological thinking on the rest of our mentality. For this attitude detaches itself from neither the regrounding of diagnosis nor the narratives that also presume regrounding of another sort. The grounds can neither be hypostatized nor ignored, with this attitude, and with it regrounding is taken in stride.

The clarifying reach of that interrogative "Where?" extends into poetics and interpretation, too. At the risk of oversimplifying, for none of it is simple, I wish to trace a few contours which that question throws into relief, questions that Matthias's poetry navigates without concretizing.

Some of the Language poets, notably Charles Bernstein, lend trust to no language that is not self-contained in its operations, chiefly out of the conviction that a commercial culture sucks any rhetoric whatsoever parasitically dry. Therefore, Bernstein's

> insistence that poetry be understood as epistemological
> inquiry; to cede meaning would be to undercut
> the power of poetry to reconnect us
> with modes of meaning given in language
> but precluded by the hegemony of restricted
> epistemological economies . . . .
> [in "formally active" poems] the meaning is not absent or
> deferred but self-embodied as the poem
> in a way that is not transferrable to another code
> or rhetoric (17–18)

The reader may recall Archibald Macleish's more genteel version of this: "A poem should not mean but be." Bernstein resists "institutionalization of interpretation," yet his affinity with Macleish is an affinity with the institutionalization of one kind of interpretation at mid-century, a kind familiar from the Romantic and nominalist positions of early modern, English Romantic, and Emersonian poetics. The Third Objectivism, in Bernstein's figure, adds to this the Gertrude-Steinian swing toward the medium itself as guarantor of liberal freedom. In this way the old nominalist redoubt, the inveterate entrenchment in things as guarantor of individual expression in a mass culture, gets taken into *la langue lui-même*. But not all of language: linguistic universals are held in suspicion, because the enemy, too, exploits them. The Third Objectivism, then, converges with skeptical hermeneutics in divesting authorial agency of higher grounding. Both relocate authority in impersonal reservoirs of potential within linguistic operations, not linguistic universals. This convergence may seem to ensure against the more insidious effects of commercial and political decadence—may *seem* to. Yet this same convergence, poetic and interpretive, returns *chora* to literal ground, the land of language and its operations: another, informational and systems-alert, materialism when taken to a certain limit. In Provence even to this day, the lost homeland is *le langage,* but the homeland honored and yearned for in

232   that equation is, precisely, higher grounding for the straitened spirit of a submerged people, a meeting place. By contrast with this, what Bernstein practices is both literal and bloodless. However necessary his attitude, from Blake's Dissenter's perspective to your friend's down the street, there is something humorless in its construal of poetic speech as a reservoir of recombinant differentials that resist convergence and convention (con-venere, meet together) and concession (con-cedere, give over together). Universals are not concession to someone else's power move in a test of Nietzschean wills. One does not cede meaning (or ground) but enters into various uses of it; nor does one's politics emerge from the facts of the medium itself. Close by the new Objectivists stand the skeptical interpreters, safeguarding indeterminacy for their own reasons (in part to keep language safe from the messy, naive crowd of authors). Here indeterminacy turns into an abyss factory; the abyssdiver and his back-flips become familiar, even reassuring; the abyss takes on the attributes of ground, an unbudgeable ground of unknowing. It affords negative transcendence to those standing/plunging on/in it; and it harmonizes with an ego psychology capable of indeterminacies but wary of any greater alternatives. Defensive or skeptical self-containment within the medium's horizon courts transcendence negatively because that, in the end, is safer in one's relations with both the Commons and the unknowable. One's "code," however intricate and paradoxical, returns homing to the blessed functions of *the* place, *the* site. A gesture is constantly made toward regrounding, but the *chora* of any regrounding constantly incorporates dualisms and stabilizes them. The abysses opening in it are something it has already bred.

From the *chora* as image theater in Sallis, politically neutral, to the *chora* as paradoxically literal ground in Third Objectivism and skeptical hermeneutics, is not a far fetch along the line of exacerbated liberal disillusionment and fear of abused authority. I for one cannot make sense of such harmonics of attitude within the frame of a few decades only, nor within an exclusively American context. The ground that has shifted and broken, and with it the corresponding impulse to regrounding that has thrust forward in endeavor after endeavor, are not neighborhood affairs in the parishes of poetry, the other arts, hermeneutics, and political philosophy in the modern university. Rather, they stem from the still-reverberating internal collapse, at their point of apogee, of the institutions we know as European and Western (and before that, for a much longer period, as Christendom's) in the First and Second World Wars. Regardless of the religious or secular coloring of their identity, these *institutions*—neither exclusively linguistic nor speculative, and arrayed across the board—have gone missing, even within their reconstructed and refurbished facades. That fact is what everyone somehow knows or half-knows; even children sense it. And that fact furnishes every move toward regrounding with its motive energy, whether it is acknowledged or not. Such energy sustains "A Compostela Diptych," where its motive is felt and implicitly acknowledged throughout. It is no spontaneous jamboree I am organizing by having that poem rub shoulders with Sallis, Bernstein, and certain recent biological and medical thinking. The poem clarifies an awareness that we can turn toward various grounding probes underway at least since Paeschendale and the Somme, probes that are seldom aware of each other but that should be, and that should feel their *European* ground or groundlessness. Matthias's coda in particular holds that awareness open to the whole potential of further grounding without defensively retrenching language and a feeling for institutions within some bastion or other of the older "code." Its crashing sound, an enigmatic *rappel à l'ordre,* and its quietly open stance, hopeful while blinking at nothing, therefore are exemplary.

My quarry in its narrowest sense is the poet's behavior and attitude when a turn inward on the topos of language's own life and functioning becomes necessary. Ever since the fragmentation of Aristotelian poetics, grounded in genres and affects, this turn has been a permanent tendency. The medical rethinking of *topos* and *chora* that I find in Dr. Plotz can stimulate a poet's thinking here, because medical rethinking can afford to abandon neither the elusive phenomena nor those who variously suffer them, neither the sliding uncontainable facts nor the slippery pathos of experience. And that means holding in a single *complexio oppositorum* both the detachment of the thinker and observer, the vocational noticer, with the care of the bearer-and-feeler-with, the care that crosses those boundaries and distinctions which the noticer must establish in order to function at all. And here I turn again to my somewhat rough yet worthy parallel form Late Antiquity, at the beginning of a recognizably modern consciousness about time, identity, and rhetorical address to imponderables and uncontainables. The Augustinian regrounding in a nonmaterial, nonspecific topos anticipates most subsequent reflective turns in that direction. The anticipation holds in several respects. First, a flip-flop occurs across categories, between place and nonplace, whose tension remains part of the revised experience. Also, in that tension, care is experienced as the reply to anxiety and disorientation, although this care, or love, may be as paradoxical as the tension, just as Augustine's address to God goes unanswered. (Should the witness of a powerful modern thinker to the paradox of this love be required, there is Simone Weil.) And finally, subjective

234 experience and specific destiny (the sufferer's anamnesis is but a special case of these) become the focus for the entire symbol of grounding in its unfolding, as distinct from naively stipulated *chora* and place.

That unfolding takes time. In Matthias's work, one can see the turn from eye to ear already in the double sonnet on Gruenewald and Hindemith's opera. There, however, the handmaiden of acoustics is a courage capable of free fall. Across the span of his writing, Matthias has come in the "Diptych" to a different pairing, of acoustics with illusionless love. That may be the best way of summarizing the thrust of his poem's long coda. And en route to that coda blows the dry but containing, paradoxically mothering wind of Rousillon. It removes inessentials, the moisture of passing thought and feeling, and preserves only what oddly abides. So, too, does the munitions blast in its radiating way remove any cobwebs in the ear for illusionless love. What I sketch here is a phenomenology, old indeed, for regrounding. And to this sketch Matthias's poems conform. First comes the experience of ground as care in "A Wind in Rousillon," then the experience of attempted regrounding in "Northern Summer," where chiastic flip-flops between eye-void and heraldic combinations-in-field move Matthias to separate reflective movement from rooted moves. Only in "A Compostela Diptych" does the movement toward regrounding reach full amplitude.

In closing, a differentiation. My own reflections on the hyperspace in which regrounding occurs for poetic speech might be taken, by those who study Heidegger, as a minimal version of his concept of the Earth. Earth antedates or outdistances being, opening a chasm in it, but is also the closure or hiddenness or silence in anything which opens itself. Nonhistorical, secretly consistent, nourishing but forgotten, the mysterious basis of "dwelling," and the secure, internal dimension of great art whose culture has passed away . . . . To the extent that the inner ground of poetic speech is silent about this or that cultural force or achievement, while the poetry may be preoccupied with it, my notion parallels Heidegger's vast conception. But it goes no farther than that, which is quite enough. Poetic speech is a very great mystery, one of whose radiant darknesses is the ongoing power it may derive from the dead while facing into the future (if indeed it can manage to do so). Nostalgia and the higher museum instincts are irrelevant. If writing is awake and not dreaming some blackbird flight through language, it tends toward inner ground within the silence that is polarized by the dead and the unconceived. That grounding is prospective. Heidegger's Opening to Being and Derrida's termination of Western history and metaphysics ("We believe this literally") are of course radically prospective. More than that I hesitate to say, being both ignorant and suspicious, an unwholesome combination. Meanwhile, however, Matthias's parallel and repeated progressions and phrases make good sonar in that vasty cave where the poet actually conducts business. Oh blessed nonplace of our meeting! No need to construct or deconstruct its foundations, for there is no place. And memory is alive, not fixed—it persists yet changes, and it creates while remaining vulnerable. In these modes, memory is about as nostalgic as a trumpet or a munitions blast. Once we have conceived of memory in these ways, we do not expect it to sit there like a bump on an analog. The end of paradigms does not mean that paradigmatics has ended as a living form of thought. The little Nietzsches, whether literary or speculative, are sometimes surprisingly literalistic, though seldom down-to-earth in their chorologies. Supreme values have continued to go to hell, from Malraux's articulate youth to the present, in ways to which Derrida's announced literalism does not do justice. Not that Matthias's poems populate their space and hyperspace with candidates for such supremacy. They cannot, for their ambition is to retain contact with what stays *in* the ground of the topos, not simply on the beloved and wind-torn ground underfoot, and beloved it surely is—an ambition that may seem modest until one places it in its time.

Works Cited

Augustinus, Aurelius. *Confessions.* Trans. Henry Chadwick. New York: Oxford University Press, 1992.

Basso, Keith. *Wisdom Sits in Places: Landscape and Language among the Western Apache.* Albuquerque: University of New Mexico Press, 1996.

Bernstein, Charles. *A Poetics.* Cambridge: Harvard University Press, 1992.

Bunting, Basil. *Collected Poems.* London: Fulcrum Press, 1970.

Harpham, Geoffrey. "Late Jameson." *Salmagundi* 111 (1996): 213–32.

Jones, David. *The Sleeping Lord and Other Fragments.* London: Faber & Faber, 1974.

Matthias, John. *Beltane at Aphelion: Longer Poems.* Athens, Ohio: Swallow, 1995.

———. *Swimming at Midnight: Selected Shorter Poems.* Athens, Ohio: Swallow, 1995.

———. "The Poetry of Roy Fisher." In *Contemporary British Poetry: Essays in Theory and Criticism,* ed. James Acheson and Romana Huk. Albany: State University of New York Press, 1996.

Nägele, Rainer. "The Poetic Ground Laid Bare (Benjamin Reading Baudelaire)." In *Walter Benjamin: Theoretical Questions,* ed. David Ferris. Stanford: Stanford University Press, 1996

Pindar. *Pindar's Victory Songs.* Trans. Frank J. Nisetch. Baltimore: Johns Hopkins University Press, 1980.

236   Pinkney, Tony. "Modernism and Cultural Theory." In *The Politics of Modernism.* London: Verson, 1989.

Plotz, Paul, M.D. "Deconstructing Disease: An Anatomy of Illness in the Age of Molecular Biology." *Perspectives in Biology and Medicine* 40.20 (winter 1997).

Pound, Ezra. *The Cantos.* London: Faber & Faber, 1975.

Redfield, James. "Herodotus the Tourist." *Classical Philology* 80 (April 1985): 97–118.

Ricoeur, Paul. *The Symbolism of Evil.* Trans. Emerson Buchanan. New York: Harper and Row, 1967.

Sallis, John. "The Politics of the Chora." In *The Ancients and the Moderns,* ed. Reginald Lilly. Bloomington: Indiana University Press, 1996.

Tarn, Nathaniel. *Views from the Weaving Mountain: Selected Essays in Poetics and Anthropology.* Albuquerque: College of Arts and Sciences, University of New Mexico, 1991.

Warminski, Andrzej. *Readings in Interpretation: Hegel, Hölderlin, Heidegger.* Minneapolis: University of Minnesota Press, 1987.

Bibliography
1971–1997

I. Books

Bucyrus. Chicago: Swallow, 1970.

TriQuarterly 21: Contemporary British Poetry. Ed. Evanston: Northwestern University Press, 1971.

23 Modern British Poets. Ed. Chicago: Swallow, 1971.

Turns. Chicago: Swallow; London: Anvil Press, 1975.

Crossing. Chicago: Swallow; London: Anvil Press, 1979.

Five American Poets. Ed. Manchester: Carcanet Press, 1979.

Bathory & Lermontov. Ahus: Kalejdoskop Forlag, 1980.

Contemporary Swedish Poetry. Trans. with Göran Printz-Påhlson. London: Anvil Press, 1979; Chicago: Swallow, 1980.

Introducing David Jones. Ed. London: Faber and Faber, 1980.

Rainmaker, by Jan Ostergren. Trans. with Göran Printz-Påhlson. Athens, Ohio: Swallow, 1983.

Northern Summer: New and Selected Poems, 1963–1983. Athens, Ohio: Swallow; London: Anvil Press, 1984.

The Battle of Kosovo. Trans. with Vladeta Vučković. Athens, Ohio: Swallow; Leek, Staffordshire: Aquila Press, 1987.

David Jones: Man and Poet. Ed. Orono, Maine: National Poetry Foundation, 1989.

Tva Diker. Lund, Sweden: Ellerstrom Publications, 1989.

A Gathering of Ways. Athens, Ohio: Swallow, 1991.

Reading Old Friends: Essays, Reviews, and Poems on Poetics, 1975–1990. The Margins of Literature Series. Albany: State University of New York Press, 1992.

Selected Works of David Jones. Ed. Orono, Maine: National Poetry Foundation, 1993.

Beltane at Aphelion: Longer Poems. Athens, Ohio: Swallow, 1995.

Swimming at Midnight: Selected Shorter Poems. Athens, Ohio: Swallow, 1995.

II. Pamphlets

Herman's Poems. Knotting, Bedfordshire: Sceptre Press, 1973.

Double Derivation, Association, and Cliché: From The Great Tournament Roll of Westminster. Chicago: The Wine Press, 1975.

238 *Two Poems.* Knotting, Bedfordshire: Sceptre Press, 1976.

Rostropovich at Aldeburgh. Knotting, Bedfordshire: Sceptre Press, 1979.

III. MAGAZINES AND ANTHOLOGIES (SINCE 1971)

"And Then He Spoke of the Language Itself." *The Nation* 15 (November 1971): 503.

"The Noble Art of Fence: A Letter." *Antioch Review* 33.3 (1972): 354–61.

"Kama Sutra." *New York Quarterly* 14 (spring 1973): 122–23.

"Turns." *Juggler* 28.2 (spring 1973): 95–97.

"If Not a Technical Song American: Statement, Harangue, and Narrative." *The Chicago Express* 30 (May 30, 1973): 6.

"Epilogue for Toby Barkan: From a New Home." *Poetry* 123.4 (January 1974): 223–36.

"For John Garvick After His Visit: Suffolk, Fall." *Poetry* 124.1 (April 1974): 18–21.

"Travellers." *Poetry* 124.1 (April 1974): 45–55.

"A Painter." *Encounter* 42.5 (May 1974): 90.

"Variations on a Theme of Horace" and "East Anglian Poem." *Poetry Review* 64.4 (1974): 330–39.

"May 4, 1970" and "For Discussion." *Second Aeon* 19–21 (1974, combined issue): 70–72.

"In Memory of the American Fifties." *Encounter* 43.3 (September 1974): 51.

"Free Translation and Recombination: Fragments From Octavio Paz." *Partisan Review* 41.2 (1974): 247–49.

"Alexander Kerensky at Stanford." *Times Literary Supplement,* September 13, 1974: 976.

"Spokesman to Bailiff: 1349: Plague." *Encounter* 43.4 (October 1974): 42.

"Sleeper." *Poetry* 125.4 (January 1975): 233–41.

"Clarifications for Robert Jacoby." *Poetry* 125.5 (February 1975): 276–79.

"A Reply." *Encounter* 43.5 (November 1975): 23.

"Songs and Conversations." *Poetry* 127.2 (November 1975): 98–111.

"On Lake Michigan." In *Heartland II,* ed. Lucian Stryk, 157. De Kalb: Northern Illinois University Press, 1975.

"Seven Around a Revolution." *Poetry Nation* 3 (winter 1975): 29–32.

"The Stefan Batory Poems." *TriQuarterly* 35 (winter 1975): 53–63.

"Gael Turnbull." In *Contemporary Poets.* London: St. James Press, 1975.

"Having Heard How Great the Fame That Elfrida . . . " In *Madeira & Toasts for Basil Bunting's 75th Birthday,* ed. Jonathan Williams. Highlands: Jargon Society, 1975.

"A Reply." In *A Tumult for John Berryman,* ed. Marguerite Harris. San Francisco: Dryad Press, 1976.

"Also Luogo Ayasuluk." *TriQuarterly* 36 (spring 1976): 88–93.

"In Columbus, Ohio," "On Lake Michigan I," "On Lake Michigan II," "Deer Crossing." *Poetry Wales* 11.4 (summer 1976): 54–57.

"Such a Kingdom." *Poetry* 128.4 (July 1976): 232–42.

"Elizabeth Daryush" and "R. S. Thomas." In *Contemporary Literary Criticism*. Vol. 6. Detroit: Gale Research Company, 1976.

"Michael Hamburger." In *Contemporary Literary Criticism*. Vol. 5. Detroit: Gale Research Company, 1976.

"From The Mihail Lermontov Poems." *The New Review* 3.36 (March 1977): 28–30.

"Pointless and Poignant." *Poetry* 129.6 (March 1977): 340–55.

"Berryman the Critic." *The New Review* 4.38 (May 1977): 51–55.

"Lars Norén" and "Jan Ostergren." Versions from the Swedish made with Göran Printz-Påhlson. *Poetry and Audience* (spring 1977): 29–35.

"Friendship." *Times Literary Supplement,* July 15 1977, 804.

"After the Death of Chekov." *Perfect Bound* (winter 1977): 44.

"David Jones" and "Anne Stevenson." In *Contemporary Literary Criticism*. Vol. 7. Detroit: Gale Research Company, 1977.

"Swimming in the Quarry at Midnight." In *The Indiana Experience,* ed. A. L. Lazarus, 29. Bloomington and London: Indiana University Press, 1977.

"26 June 1381/1977" and "59 Lines Assembled Quickly Sitting on a Wall Near the Reconstruction of the Lady Juliana's Cell." *PN Review* 5.2 (1977): 13–14.

"From an East Anglian Miscellany." *PN Review* 5.3 (1977): 49–50.

"Mid-Atlantic: Night." *The New Review* 47 (February 1978): 26.

"From a Visit to Dalmatia" and "Brandon, Breckland: The Flint Knappers." *Bennington Review* 3 (December 1978): 11–13.

"Contemporary Swedish Poetry." Trans. with Göran Printz-Påhlson. *Modern Poetry in Translation* 36 (spring 1979): 1–16.

"Evening Song" and "The Fen Birds' Cry." *The Greenfield Review* 7.3–4 (spring/ summer 1979): 118–19.

"Six Swedish Poets." *The Greenfield Review* 7.3–4 (spring/summer 1979): 120–33.

"Poems by Jan Ostergren." *Swedish Books* (December 1979): 16–18.

"U.S.I.S. Lecturer," "In Columbus, Ohio," and "On the Death of Benjamin Britten." *Salmagundi* 43 (winter 1979): 43–46.

"Poem for Cynouai." *PN Review* 16.1 (1979): 12–14.

"Four Swedish Poets." Trans. with Göran Printz-Påhlson. *PN Review* 16.2 (1979): 45–47.

"For Karl Wallenda." *Argo* 2.1 (spring 1980): 42–45.

"D. M. Thomas." In *Contemporary Literary Criticism*. Vol. 13. Detroit: Gale Research Company, 1979.

"Elizabeth Jennings." In *Contemporary Literary Criticism*. Vol. 14. Detroit: Gale Research Company, 1980.

"In Columbus, Ohio." In *Anthology of Magazine Verse and Yearbook of American Poetry,* 204. Beverly Hills: Moniter Book Company, 1980.

"Ingemar Leckius' 'The Stranger' and Jan Ostergren's 'Indian Summer, part 4.'" Trans. with Göran Printz-Påhlson. *Stonechat* 1.1 (1980): 3, 19.

"From *Northern Summer*." *Salmagundi* 50/51 (fall 1980/winter 1981): 43–48.

240   "David Jones: A Self-Portrait." *Occident* 2 (winter 1981): 8–13.

"David Jones's Letters to H. S. Ede." *PN Review* 22 (1981): 10–16.

"Speak That I May See Thee." *PN Review* 22 (1981): 17–21.

"Jan Ostergren's 'Indian Summer' and 'Contemporary.'" Trans. with Göran Printz-Påhlson. *Chicago Review* 32.4 (1981): 41–47.

"The English Poetry of Göran Printz-Påhlson." *Tarningskastet* 9 (1981): 65–75.

"Halfdream after Mandelstam: Who Spoke of the Language Itself." In *Homage to Mandelstam,* 63. Cambridge: Los Press, 1981.

"From *Small Chimes; One Voice,*" by Göran Sonnevi. Trans. with Göran Printz-Påhlson. *Swedish Books* (1981/82): 44–55.

"Unpleasant Letter." *Poetry Review* 72.1 (1981): 28–29.

"David Jones's Letters to H. S. Ede." *Notre Dame English Journal* 14.2 (spring 1982): 129–44.

"From the Kosovo Fragments: 'The Mother of the Jugovići.'" Trans. with Vladeta Vučković. *The Kenyon Review* 4.3 (summer 1982): 51–55.

"To V. V. on Our Translation of the Kossovo Fragments." *The Kenyon Review* 4.3 (summer 1982): 44–50.

"From *Small Chimes; One Voice,*" by Goran Sonnevi. Trans. with Göran Printz-Påhlson. *Translation* 9 (fall 1982): 127–28.

"Lines for Sir Thomas Browne." *PN Review* 29.3 (1982): 45–46.

"W. H. Auden and Benjamin Britten." *The Southern Review* 19.1 (January 1983): 184–202.

"Northern Summer." *Boundary 2* 10.3 (1983): 303–17.

"Stalin as Wolf," by Jesper Svenbro. Trans. with Göran Printz-Påhlson. *The Kenyon Review* 5.1 (winter 1983): 25–26.

"Unpleasant Letter" and "E.P. at Crawfordsville." *Chicago Review* 33.3 (1983): 95–99.

"Poem for Cynouai." *Cafe Existens* 20 (1983): 46–49.

"Dry Point," by Jan Ostergren. Trans. with Göran Printz-Påhlson. *Chicago Review* 33.4 (1983): 36.

"Chariots of Verse: Notes on the 1983 Biennial Cambridge Poetry Festival." *Rolling Stock* 5 (1983): 11–22.

"Robert Duncan and David Jones: Some Affinities." *Ironwood* 22 (1983): 140–57.

"Edward" and "Three Sections from Northern Summer." *Argo* 5.2 (1984): 13–20.

"Rhododendron." *PN Review* 42 (1984): 12.

"Three Poems by Ingemar Leckius." Trans. with Göran Printz-Påhlson. *Translation* 12 (1984): 235–38.

"Six Poems." *Salmagundi* 63–64 (summer 1984): 238–45.

"Ur Bathory & Lermontov." In *U.S.A. Poesi,* ed. Jan Verner-Carlesson, 685–86. Gothenburg: Cafe Existens Editions, 1984.

"Poetry of Place: From the Kentucky River to the Solent Shore." *The Southern Review* 21.1 (January 1985): 183–203.

"From a Visit to Dalmatia" and "Fathers." Trans. into Serbo-Croatian by Bogdana Bobic. *Knjizevne Novine* 681 (February 1985): 8–9.

"Four Poems by Branko Miljković." Trans. with Vladeta Vučković. *Translation* 14 (spring 1985): 304–6.

"Survivors" and "August." *Chicago Literary Review* (spring 1985): 12.

"Earth and Fire," by Branko Miljković. Trans. with Vladeta Vučković. *The Bloomsbury Review* 5.12 (October 1985): 21.

"Friendship," "Survivors," and "Words for Karl Wallenda." Trans. into Serbo-Croatian by Borislava Sasic. *Letopis Matice Srpske* 436.4 (October 1985): 360–65.

"Ley Lines." *Sagetrieb* 4.2–3 (fall/winter 1985): 9–14.

"Marobolus Makadam & Co.," by Ingemar Leckius. Trans. with Göran Printz-Påhlson. In *Dubuffet*, 34. Malmö: Konsthall, 1985.

"To the Earth Right Now" and "Inventory of a Poem," by Branko Miljković. Trans. with Vladeta Vučković. *Another Chicago Magazine* 12 (1985): 132–33.

"From *The Dimensions*," by Vladeta Vučković. Trans. with author. *Another Chicago Magazine* 12 (1985): 163–66.

"Not for Sale in U.S.A." *Another Chicago Magazine* 12 (1985): 195–208.

"Friendship," "After the Death of Chekov," "Fathers," "My Youngest Daughter: Running Toward an English Village Church," and "A Wind in Roussillon." Trans. into Serbo-Croatian by Ivan Lalić. Gradina 7/8 (1985): 90–94.

"Not for Sale in U.S.A., #2." *Another Chicago Magazine* 14 (1985): 115–31.

"An East Anglian Diptych." *Poetry Wales* 21.2 (1985): 51–67.

"The Downfall of the Kingdom of Serbia," "Musich Stefan," and "Marko Kraljević and the Eagle." Trans. with Vladeta Vučković. *Poetry World* 1 (1985): 85–99.

"An East Anglican Diptych." *Another Chicago Magazine* 15 (spring 1986): 51–67.

"Not for Sale in U.S.A., #3." *Another Chicago Magazine* 15 (spring 1986): 149–58.

"Reading Old Friends." *The Southern Review* 22.2 (spring 1986): 391–406.

Four Poems: "Epilogue from a New Home," "Halfdream in Sickness," "26 June 1381/1977," "Double Sonnet on the Absence of Text." Trans. into Dutch by Peter Nijmeijer. *Het Moment* 3 (winter 1986): 108–17.

"Facts from an Apocryphal Midwest." *Another Chicago Magazine* 17 (spring 1987): 62–80.

"Four Poems by Branko Miljković." Trans. from the Serbian with Vladeta Vučković. *Margin* 2 (spring 1987): 57–59.

"Four Poems from *The Battle of Kosovo*." *Prospice* 21 (spring 1987): 49–64.

"Not for Sale in USA, #5: The Complete Poetry of Hugh MacDiarmid." *Another Chicago Magazine* 17 (spring 1987): 169–79.

"Mozart Variations." Trans. from the Swedish of Göran Sonnevi with Göran Printz-Påhlson. *Adam* (summer 1987): 74–77.

"Not for Sale in USA, #4." *Another Chicago Magazine* 16 (winter 1987): 177–86.

"Reading Old Friends, Part 2." *The Southern Review* 22.1 (winter 1987): 206–23.

"From 'Mozart Variations.'" Trans. from the Swedish of Göran Sonnevi with Göran Printz-Påhlson. *Rolling Stock* 12 (1986): 28.

"The Future of Fire" and "The Past of Fire." Trans. from the Serbian of Branko Miljković with Vladeta Vučković. *Rolling Stock* 12 (1986): 28.

242 "Requiem." Trans. from the Serbian of Branko Miljković with Vladeta Vučković. *Poetry World* 3 (1987): 3.

"Not for Sale in USA, #6: Contemporary Scottish Poetry." *Another Chicago Magazine* 18 (spring 1988): 233–45.

"Four Songs for Four Voices." In Texts by John Matthias, Music by David Clark Isele, 1–14. Pacific, Missouri: Mel Bay Publications, 1988.

"Two Poems." In *Spiegel International,* ed. M. Asscher, 73–74. Amsterdam: Muelenhoff Publishers, 1988.

"Rhododendron." *Arts Indiana Literary Supplement,* July 1989, 43.

"From *A Compostela Diptych,*" Sections 1, 5, and 6. *TriQuarterly* 76 (fall 1989): 113–22.

"Places and Poems: A Self-Reading and a Reading of the Self in the Romantic Context from Wordsworth to Parkman." In *The Romantics and Us,* ed. Gene W. Ruoff, 36–66. New Brunswick, N.J. and London: Rutgers University Press, 1990.

"Poem for Cynouai" and "The Flintknappers." In *Fardvag,* ed. and trans. by Göran Printz-Pahlson and Jan Östergren, 130–42. Stockholm: Bonniers, 1990.

"Dedication to a Poem in Progress on the Pilgrim Routes to Santiago de Compostela." *PN Review* 75 (1990): 55.

"Academic Poem." *The New Criterion* 9.5 (January 1991): 56–57.

"Not Having Read a Single Fairy Tale." *The New Criterion* 9.6 (February 1991): 47.

"Inside History and Outside History: Seamus Heaney, Eavan Boland, and Contemporary Irish Poetry." *Another Chicago Magazine* 22 (fall 1991): 212–27.

"The Singer of Tales" and "The Silence of Stones." *PN Review* 18.2 (November–December 1991): 26.

"Requiem," by Branko Miljković. Trans. with Vladeta Vučković. *Poetry World* n.s., 1.1 (summer 1992): 120–227.

"Seven Poems." In *The Space Between,* ed. James Walton, 176–204. Notre Dame and London: University of Notre Dame Press, 1991.

"Notes on the English Poetry of Göran Printz-Påhlson." *Another Chicago Magazine* 23 (1991): 210–20.

"After Years Away." *The New Criterion* 10.5 (January 1992): 34–36.

"Three Poems: 'The Silence of Stones,' 'The Singer of Tales,' and 'Dedication.'" *Image* (summer 1992): 58–62.

"E.P. in Crawfordsville." *PN Review* 19.2 (November–December 1992): 39.

"Three Poems by Bronko Miljković: 'While You Are Singing,' 'An Orphic Legacy,' and 'Inventory of a Poem.'" Trans. from the Serbian with Vladeta Vučković. *TriQuarterly* 86 (winter 1992–93): 39–41.

"Three Poems." *Private* 6 (1993): 37–41.

"Mozart Variations," numbers 2 and 3. Trans. from the Swedish of Göran Sonnevi with Göran Printz-Påhlson. *Visions International* 43 (1993): 52.

"From *Small Chimes/One Voice.*" Trans. from the Swedish of Göran Sonnevi with

Göran Printz-Påhlson. *Visions International* 43 (1993): 52.

"An Orphic Legacy." Trans. from the Serbo-Croatian with Vladeta Vučković. *Quick Take: Selections from TriQuarterly* 1.1 (1993): 3.

"The Haunting of Benjamin Britten." *PN Review* 20.2 (November–December 1993): 21–26.

"The First Dimension." Trans. from the Serbo-Croatian of Vladeta Vučković. with the author. *North Dakota Quarterly* 61.1 (winter 1993): 209–11.

"The Singer of Tales." *North Dakota Quarterly* 61.1 (winter 1993): 110–11.

Two Poems by Branko Miljković. Trans. from the Serbo-Croatian with Vladeta Vučković. *North Dakota Quarterly* 61.1 (winter 1993): 114–15.

"Bogomil in Languedoc." In *Klonica: Poems for Bosnia,* ed. Ken Smith and Judi Benson, 40. London: Bloodaxe Books, 1993.

"Bloodaxe Books, Part I: Focus on British Women Poets." *Another Chicago Magazine* 29 (spring 1994): 215–26.

"From Mauberley to Middagh Street: Ways of Meeting the British." *Another Chicago Magazine* 25 (spring 1994): 203–10.

"Into Cyrillic." *Another Chicago Magazine* 29 (spring 1994): 84.

"The New Poetry." *The Southern Review* 30.2 (spring 1994): 409–20.

"From Mauberley to Middagh Street: Ways of Meeting the British." *PN Review* 20.5 (May–June 1994): 44–47.

"Absent Friends: Benjamin Britten's Poets and the Poetry He Set to Music." *PN Review* 21.1 (January–February 1995): 49–51.

"Everything to Be Endured" and "C.P.R." *Salmagundi* 106–7 (spring 1995): 119–21.

"Bloodaxe Books, Part II: Some of the Men." *Another Chicago Magazine* 30 (fall 1995): 238–53.

"Bloodaxe Books, Part III: Some Loose Ends and Maybe a Major Poet." *Another Chicago Magazine* 31 (spring 1996): 197–211.

"The Poetry of Roy Fisher." In *Contemporary British Poetry: Essays in Theory and Criticism,* ed. James Acheson and Romana Huk, 35–62. Albany: State University of New York Press, 1996.

"Three Poems." *PN Review* 23.3 (January–February 1997): 56–57.

"From Pages from a Book of Years," Sections I–V. *Another Chicago Magazine* 32/33 (fall 1997): 128–36, 155–63.

"Messiaen Received by Angels Singing Like the Birds," "That Music Is the Spur to All Licentiousness," "The Key of C Does Not Know My Biography." *Boston Review* 23.3 (October/November 1997).

IV. COLLABORATIONS AND SETTINGS

"Four Songs" by David Isele to texts by John Matthias. Premiere: February 23, 1975, University of Notre Dame.

"Cognition Prefix," an oratorio by David Isele to a text by John Matthias. Premiere: Sacred Heart Church, University of Notre Dame, February 15, 1976.

244 "Helix," a ballet devised by Liebe Klug for the Cambridge Ballet Theatre with spoken texts by John Matthias. Performed throughout England during 1976–77.

"Four Choral Pieces" by David Isele to texts by John Matthias. Premiere: University of Tampa, spring 1989.

V. SELECTED CRITICISM

Armstrong, Alison. "We Live Here Now." *PN Review* 32 (1983): 59–60.

Burns, Gerald. "Northern Summer: New & Selected Poems 1963–1983." *Sulfur* 19 (spring 1987): 161–63.

Corcoran, Neil. "John Matthias." In *Contemporary Poets,* ed. Tracy Chevalier, 614–15. 5th ed. London: St. James Press, 1991.

Dooley, Tim. "Faulty Visions." *Times Literary Supplement.* May 24, 1985.

Gellerfelt, Mats. "Förnämlig Poet i Modernismens Huvudfåra." *Svenska Dagbladet,* July 31, 1989.

Hessler, Ole. "Spillror ur Historien." *Dagens Nyheter* (Stockholm), July 18, 1989.

Hooker, Jeremy. "Crossings and Turns: The Poetry of John Matthias." In *The Presence of the Past: Essays on Modern British and American Poetry,* 97–105. Bridgend, Mid Glamorgan: Poetry Wales Press, 1987.

———. "To Fit a Late Time: A Reading of Five American Poets." *PN Review* 109 (1996): 37–41.

Lewis, Tess. "John Matthias, Reading Old Friends." *The New Criterion* 10.8 (April 1992): 75–76.

Lundstedt, Göran. "Sofistikerade Poetiska Övningar." *Sydsvenska Dagbladet* (Malmö) August 5, 1989.

Oberg, Arthur. "A Gathering of Poets." *Western Humanities Review* 31.2 (spring 1977): 181–92.

Printz-Påhlson, Göran. "Minotaur och labyrint." In *När Jag Var Prins Utav Arkadien: Essäer och Intervjuer om Poesi och Plats,* 230–35. Stockholm: Bonniers, 1995.

———. "Platsens poesi, satsens poesi." In *Nar Jag Var Prins Utav Arkadien: Essäer och Intervjuer om Poesi och Plats,* 63–86. Stockholm: Bonniers, 1995..

Pybus, Rodney. "Recent American and Antipodean Poetry." *Stand* (February 1986): 72–73.

Ringgren, Magnus. "Havsdikter där västerlandet möts." *Expressen,* July 8, 1981.

Sandeen, Ernest. "The Pause That Reappraises." *Notre Dame Magazine,* Autumn 1984, 69.

Sherry, Vincent. "The Poetry of John Matthias: Between the Castle and the Mine." *Salmagundi* 65 (fall 1984): 132–45.

Spiegelman, Willard. "The Poem as Quest." *Parnassus* 17.2/18.1 (1992–93): 423–41.

Svensson, Lars-Håkan. "Fran Ohio till Malmöhus: Samtal med en Amerikansk Poet." *Sydsvenska Dagbladet Snällposten,* April 4, 1982.

———. "Conversation with Jan Norling about John Matthias's *Bathory & Lermontov.*" *Swedish Radio Information,* April 1, 1981, 1–4.

Sylvester, William. "John Matthias: *Crossing*." *Credences* 1.1 (1980): 186–92.   **245**
———. "Punctured Equilibria: The Dis-Covery of Entrophy." *Boundary 2* 15.3/16.1 (spring–fall 1988): 313–29.
Thomas, D. M. "The Agony and the Entropy." *Times Literary Supplement*, June 11, 1976.
Tuma, Keith. "John Matthias, A Gathering of Ways." *Sulfur* 29 (fall 1991): 233–34.
Waterman, Andrew. "Recent North American Poetry." *PN Review* 4.4 (1977): 55–58.
Weidar, Anders "Poetisk Loggbok." *Cafe Existens,* July 15, 1981, 107–8.

Notes on Contributors

MICHAEL ANANIA has published fourteen books, including his selected essays *In Plain Sight* and his *Selected Poems* (both Moyer Bell). He has edited numerous anthologies and served as poetry editor for Swallow Press, as well as for *Partisan Review* and other journals. He teaches at the University of Illinois, Chicago.

ROBERT ARCHAMBEAU is a poet and critic who teaches at Lake Forest College, Illinois. His long poem *Citation Suite* was published by Wild Honey Press in 1997.

MICHAEL BARRETT is contributing editor of *Private Arts* magazine. He has published essays on John Ashbery, the L=A=N=G=U=A=G=E poets, and others.

BROOKE BERGAN'S publications include numerous translations and critical essays, as well as three books of poetry, most recently *Storyville: A Hidden Mirror* (Asphodel). She is Associate Director of Publications with the University of Illinois—Chicago.

JEREMY HOOKER has published nine books of poetry, including his *Selected Poems* (Carcanet), three critical books, including *Writers in a Landscape* (Wales), and some fifty articles on British and American poetry. He has taught in both England and America.

ROMANA HUK co-edited the collection *Contemporary British Poetry: Essays in Theory and Criticism* (State University of New York Press) with James Acheson. She teaches at the University of New Hampshire.

PETER MICHELSON has published six books of criticism and poetry, the most recent being *Speaking the Unspeakable* (State University of New York Press). He has received fellowships from the NEA and the Woodrow Wilson Foundation, and served in an editorial capacity with *TriQuarterly* and *The Chicago Review*. His poetry and criticism have been widely anthologized. Michelson teaches at the University of Colorado, Boulder.

248 **JERE ODELL** teaches at the University of Notre Dame and is managing editor of *The Notre Dame Review.* He has published poetry and translations in a number of journals, and organized the American Comparative Literature Society's session on the poetry of John Matthias.

JOHN PECK has taught at Princeton, Mount Holyoke, Skidmore, and the University of Zurich. He has received numerous prestigious awards, including Guggenheim and Ingram Merrill fellowships. His poetry and criticism are widely published and anthologized. *M and Other Poems* is the most recent of his six books.

VINCENT SHERRY'S six books include *The Uncommon Tongue: The Poetry and Criticism of Geoffrey Hill* (Michigan) and *Ezra Pound, Wyndham Lewis and Radical Modernism* (Oxford). He has published and spoken on the poetry of John Matthias and teaches at Villanova University.

KATHLEEN HENDERSON STAUDT is the author of *At the Turn of a Civilization: David Jones and Modern Poetics* (Michigan) as well as numerous articles on contemporary poetry. She teaches at the University of Maryland.

LARS-HÅKAN SVENSSON is a distinguished scholar and translator at Lund University, Sweden. He has written two books on English poetry and published several volumes of translations, including works by John Matthias and Paul Muldoon.

IGOR WEBB'S books include *Against Capitulation* (Quarto) and *From Custom to Capital* (Cornell), a study of the English novel. He has written extensively on contemporary prose and poetry, and his own poems have appeared in many publications, including *The New Yorker.* He teaches at Adelphi University.